# Cognitive Science and Pedagogy

N.B. Biswas
Krishna Kalita

SHIPRA

ISBN: 978-81-7541-864-6

First Published in India in 2016

*Cognitive Science and Pedagogy*



*Published by:*
**SHIPRA PUBLICATIONS**
LG 18-19, Pankaj Central Market, I.P. Ext.
Patparganj, Delhi-110092, India
Tel: 91-11-2223 5152, 2223 6152
E-mail: info@shiprapublication.com
www.shiprapublication.com

# Preface

With the fast changing face of knowledge, it has been realized every now and then that interdisciplinary endeavours have much more to contribute than compartmentalization. The field of cognitive science is one such proof which has realized that to understand the complex concepts like mind even partially, an interdisciplinary approach is inevitable. The present book attempts at presenting the field right from its ancient history to the modern developments and to relate these developments with the field of education, particularly, pedagogy.

It has been realized that both cognitive science and pedagogy are less represented in the field of education. No studies have been found on applying cognitive science principles in the field of pedagogy so far particularly in India. Moreover, the Indian perspective of cognitive science—as delve into the Indian philosophical schools in search of the roots of cognitive science—is rare to be found. The book has been prepared targeting the readers having interest in both the fields of cognitive science and pedagogy. It will cater to crave for understanding the field of cognitive science and its relation to education in general and pedagogy in particular. It is the result of an inquisitive and intensive research process. Efforts have been made to present a baseline study of cognitive science as a field of study and exclusively and elaborately discuss the pedagogical implications of five components of cognitive science.

The timely suggestions of all the well-wishers are acknowledged with gratitude. It is hoped that the book will help to put some light on the field of pedagogy and cognitive science.

**Prof. N. B. Biswas**
**Dr. Krishna Kalita**

# Preface

With the fast changing face of knowledge, it has been realized every now and then that interdisciplinary endeavours have much more to contribute than compartmentalization. The field of cognitive science is one such proof which has realized that to understand the complex concepts like mind even partially, an interdisciplinary approach is inevitable. The present book attempts at presenting the field right from its ancient history to the modern developments and to relate these developments with the field of education, particularly pedagogy.

It has been realized that both cognitive science and pedagogy are less represented in the field of education. No studies have been found on applying cognitive science principles in the field of pedagogy so far particularly in India. Moreover, the Indian perspective of cognitive sciences as delve into the Indian philosophical schools in search of the seeds of cognitive science is yet to be found. The book has been prepared targeting the readers having interest in both the fields of cognitive science and pedagogy. It will cater to crave for understanding the field of cognitive science and its relation to education in general and pedagogy in particular. It is the outcome of an enthusiastic and [illegible] research process. Efforts have been made to present a [illegible] study of cognitive science as a field of study and exhaustively and elaborately discuss the pedagogical implication of five components of cognitive science.

The timely suggestions of all the well wishers are acknowledged with gratitude. It is hoped that the book will help to put some light on the field of pedagogy and cognitive science.

Prof. N. B. Biswas
Dr. Krishna Kalita

# Contents

# 1

# Cognitive Science

Cognitive science has been regarded as a 'rich scientific' discipline in one of the most standard literature on cognitive science, 'The Encyclopedia of Cognitive Science'. It is scientific because it adopts scientific methods to study mind. It is considered rich in the sense that it has developed with contributions from various disciplines. The attempts to understand the mind by various disciplines like philosophy, psychology, neuroscience, artificial intelligence, linguistics and anthropology were already there. But their results seemed to be partial. And thus, the birth of cognitive science took place as a collaborative effort of all these disciplines to understand mind.

## Historical Review of Cognitive Science

The history of cognitive science constitutes the relevant developments within each discipline of cognitive science along with the history of birth of cognitive science as a formal discipline in the late 20th century. The developments in the field of cognitive science have been documented by various scholars.

Westbury and Wilensky (1998) have given a brief history of cognitive science in "Knowledge representation in cognitive science: Implications for education". However, they have mentioned that the foundations of cognitive science may be traced back to Aristotle or to the rise of scientific psychology (late 1800s and early 1900s) or more recently to the emergence of cybernetics. Nadel and Piattelli-Palmarini (2002), while writing the general introduction "What is Cognitive science" for '*The Encyclopedia of cognitive science*' have discussed the pre-history of cognitive science. To discuss about the cognitivism, they have presented briefly about behaviourism, against which cognitivism arose. In the modern era (after 1900), the developments in computers, cybernetics, linguistics, etc. have been discussed. Some crucial meetings, symposium, etc. have been regarded as of recent history of cognitive science, where the actual birth of cognitive science took place. Miller (2003) has presented the recent history of cognitive science and its relationship with cognitive revolution in "The cognitive revolution: a historical perspective". He also emphasised the interdisciplinary nature of cognitive science. Boden (2006) in her book, "Mind as machine: A history of cognitive science" has provided a very comprehensive history of cognitive science. She has shown how cognitive science has developed so as to help solve problems about mind, brain, and personality. It starts from 'setting the scene' to 'what next' and includes machine simulation, interdisciplinary beginning of cognitive science, computational psychology, contributions of linguistics, connectionism, developments in neuroscience and philosophical aspect of mind. Chipman (2010) reviewed 30 years of progress in U.S. cognitive science research related to education and training. It was found that cognitive science has made significant progress in important areas of education like reading comprehension, mathematics learning and physics education. The cognitive science research approach has yielded instructional methods, sometimes embodied in artificially intelligent tutoring systems, sometimes in more traditional human-implemented teaching, that have been shown to produce significant improvements in student achievement. Education proved to be an important focus of and motivator for research in cognitive science. Srinivasan (2011) has placed Dartmouth Symposium of 1956 as the official beginning of cognitive science in the paper "Cognitive science: Emerging perspectives and approaches". According to him, advances in key interfacing disciplines especially computer science, psychology, neuroscience and linguistics enabled the development of Cognitive Science as a discipline of its own studying the mind. Cognitive science is considered as a strong interdisciplinary effort to understand mind. The paper discusses the major approaches to studying the mind including the information processing approach, cognitive modelling, cognitive neuroscience, embodied and situated cognition as well as the emerging trends of increasing interdisciplinary and pluralism in cognitive science.

Thus, it is apparent that though the 'discipline cognitive science' is a product of last century only, its subject matter has developed gradually through different efforts in a wide area to understand the mind. Its origin may be rooted to as ancient times as that of the ancient Greek philosophers and its actual birth may be regarded to be as recent as the 1950s.

## Concept of Cognitive Science

The emergence of the new field called "cognitive science" is one of the most significant scientific developments in recent years. It aims at studying cognition by pooling the resources of a number of disciplines, including cognitive psychology, artificial intelligence, linguistics, philosophy, neuroscience and cognitive anthropology. Cognitive Science is the study of the processes by which the humans and other animals come to know properties of their external environment and convert that knowledge into action as well as relay that knowledge to others by means of communication. Broadly, it can be defined as the scientific study of minds and brains—natural or artificial, human or animal. Practically, it is delimited to the areas in which one can reasonably attempt at attaining real understanding. The researches in cognitive science have the prospects of serving several important areas—mental health, social engineering, education, computer technology, etc. Its growing and widespread applications has made cognitive science one of the four pillars of the 21st century, the other three being Nano, Bio and Information Technology. But cognitive science is the least represented out of these four pillars, particularly in the Indian scientific scenario.

Cognitive science as a field of study mainly aims at an integrated and concerned effort towards developing a complete theory of intelligent systems. It aims at—

(a) Developing a theory of intelligent systems.
(b) Drawing the architecture of cognition.
(c) Understanding how cognition enables an organism to interact with and adapt to its environment.

Intelligent systems have been described by different research approaches. Allen Newell and Herbert Simon's work on the physical symbol system hypothesis supports much current work in cognitive science. They hypothesised that a necessary and sufficient condition of intelligence is the system's ability to manipulate symbols. On the other hand, connectionist researchers focus on the perceptual and pattern recognition aspects of intelligence. Another aim is to draw the architecture of cognition, which means the structure of cognitive systems. And the last one is to understand how and how much cognition influences our behaviour in relation to the environment.

### Branches of Cognitive Science

Cognitive science, as an interdisciplinary study of mind and intelligence, encompasses a large network of key disciplines. These are philosophy, psychology, artificial intelligence, linguistics, anthropology, sociology, education, neuroscience, etc. These disciplines, which contribute towards understanding mind from different points of view constitutes the branches of cognitive science. A brief description of the main branches of cognitive science has been attempted here.

**Philosophy:** In ancient times, philosophy referred to higher learning or development of knowledge. As such, philosophy is still considered to be the highest and oldest knowledge of the world. The scope of philosophy is very wide and comprehensive. It forms the foundation of almost every discipline. It endeavours to understand everything that comes within the realm of human experiences. It attempts to give a comprehensive view of nature and a universal explanation of the nature of things. The main branches of philosophy include—Metaphysics, Epistemology, Ethics, Logic, Aesthetics, Philosophy of mind, Philosophy of education, Philosophy of language, Philosophy of religion and Philosophy of science.

The epistemological branch of philosophy investigates the structure and growth of human knowledge by locating it in human minds and societies and is therefore, more closely associated with cognitive science. The agenda of cognitive science is set by the two and a half millennia old tradition of Western philosophy as well as the ancient tradition of Indian logic (Gardner, 1985). In recent years, 'philosophy of mind' has been intimately associated with the field of cognitive science in several ways. One is that the results of cognitive science researches have potential applications to traditional philosophical problems in epistemology, metaphysics and ethics. Second, cognitive science can serve as an object of philosophical critique, particularly concerning the central assumption that thinking is representational and computational. More constructively, cognitive science can be taken as an object of investigation in the philosophy of science, generating reflections on the methodology and presuppositions of enterprise. Another role of cognitive science is putting new ideas and concepts in perspective, and linking them with abandoned or distorted ideas and concepts from the past.

On the other hand, philosophy plays a dual role in cognitive science. First, it provides cognitive science with both a world-view as well as ways to go beyond it in order to overcome the puzzles which arise from this world-view. In this role, philosophy functions as philosophy of science, in its proactive form. Philosophy also plays an important role in defining the basic analytic categories pertaining to thought, knowledge, perception, emotion and others.

It is important to note that the significance of philosophy is not lessened even by the two centuries of scientific psychology. Rather, its relevance has grown with the growth of various branches and programmes of cognitive science. Here philosophy functions as philosophy of mind, in a broader sense. It also includes philosophy of psychology, philosophy of language, epistemology, ontology and phenomenology. Apart from contribution to these specific issues, philosophy also helps in global issues that relate the various sub-disciplines of cognitive science. It is traditionally concerned with the general problems on both a meta-scientific and commonsense (everyday) level. Another important prospect of philosophy is that it can help in constructing as well as evaluating the global theories that are necessary for further integration of the field of cognitive science.

**Psychology:** Psychology is defined as the study of human behaviour, which was earlier considered to be the study of mind. But recently, it has confined itself to study of behaviour. It adopts various approaches to study behaviour. The field of psychology grew with the structuralist, functionalist, behaviourist and cognitivist views of behaviour subsequently. The behaviourists dominated the field for a long period. But the later part of the 20th century saw 'cognitive revolution' which was dominated by the idea that cognitive processes can be scientifically studied. The final decades of the 20th century saw the decline of behaviourism and the rise of cognitive science, an interdisciplinary approach to study cognition. In 1957, Noam Chomsky challenged radical behaviourism by reviewing Skinner's book 'Verbal Behaviour'. He argued that people could produce an infinite variety of sentences unique in structure and meaning and that these could not possibly be generated solely through experience of natural language. As an alternative, he concluded that there must be internal mental structures. Similarly, work done by Albert Bandura showed that children could learn by social observation, without any change in overt behaviour. This must be accounted for by internal representations. The rise of computer technology also promoted the metaphor of mental function as information processing. This combined with a scientific approach to study the mind, as well as a belief in internal mental states, led to the rise of cognitivism as the dominant model of mind and study of behaviour in psychology.

The theoretical focus of traditional cognitive science is the computer simulation of the mind. It asserts that animal and human psychology occurs through computational processes in organisms involving physical symbol systems. Psychological processes are realised in animals and humans by innate symbol systems in which the programmes of the mind are initially given. These systems are subsequently modified through experience. This conception offers a theory of how cognition takes place in the organism—through the interaction of symbols that are processed by internal operations. Psychological experiments that approach mental operations from diverse directions are, therefore, crucial for cognitive science to be scientific. Major branches of psychology are developmental psychology, clinical psychology, educational psychology, experimental psychology, cognitive psychology, industrial psychology and social psychology. The branch of cognitive psychology is dedicated to the study of cognition and mostly contributes in the field of cognitive science.

**Anthropology:** Anthropology is the discipline that studies races, cultures, languages, and the evolution of the human species (Baker, 2007). It has origins in the natural sciences, the humanities and the social sciences. The term 'anthropology' is derived from the Greek terms 'anthropos' meaning 'man' and 'logia' meaning study. Its basic concerns are: 'What defines Homo Sapiens?', 'Who are the ancestors of modern Homo Sapiens?', 'What are physical traits of humans?',

'How do humans behave?', 'Why are there variations and differences among different groups of humans?', 'How has the evolutionary past of Homo Sapiens influenced its social organisation and culture?' and so forth. The field of anthropology covers a vast scope which includes the human body, the human evolution, biology and genetics. Modern anthropology has been divided into four branches—Cultural anthropology, Linguistic anthropology, Biological/Physical anthropology and Archeology. By the 1950s, the subfield of cognitive anthropology emerged out of a blend of linguistic and socio-cultural anthropology (Bender, Hutchins and Medin, 2010). In parallel to the cognitive revolution, cognitive anthropology blossomed in the 1960s and 1970s. It explored the organisation of knowledge in a variety of domains in different societies. The definition of culture depends on the interest in knowledge and representation in other areas of cognitive science. Cognitive anthropology studies the relationship between culture and mind. It primarily studies knowledge and thinking in natural settings. Its main contribution has been to show that there are important cultural differences in perception, memory, and inference (Nuckolls, 1999). A collaboration between cognitive science and anthropology is productive as anthropology is interested in cultural knowledge and meaning. It has been established after a series of experimental observations that culture affects both the thoughts and thought processes of the people. These observations include researches which show that language affects thought and the cognitive consequences of collectivism versus individualism. The cultural differences range from basic perceptual processing to categorisation, reasoning, and attribution processes. These two kinds of observations build a bridge between anthropology and cognitive science. In the 1990s, some cognitive anthropologists took their inspiration from the fields of cognitive science and evolutionary psychology. They also aimed at combining the results of ethnographic studies with the findings and method of the sciences.

**Linguistics:** Linguistics is a field of study which is dedicated to understand, describe and explain the human faculty of language. It is the scientific study of human language. It can be broadly divided into three categories—the study of language form, of language meaning, and of language in context. The study of language structure or grammar focusses on the system of rules followed by the speakers of a language. The study of language meaning is concerned with how languages employ logical structures and real world references to convey process and assign meaning. Language in its broader context includes evolutionary linguistics, historical linguistics, socio-linguistics, psycho-linguistics, neuro-linguistics, language acquisition, and discourse analysis. The major branches of linguistics may be considered as—Cognitive linguistics, Comparative linguistics, Computational linguistics, Descriptive linguistics, Generative linguistics, Historical linguistics, Language acquisition, Psycho-linguistics and Socio-linguistics.

The evolution of spoken human language requires the development of two things—vocal tract and cognitive abilities. The first is used for speech production and the cognitive abilities are required to produce linguistic utterances. One of the significant abilities required for development of language is that of high level reference. It means the ability to refer to things or states of being that are not in the immediate realm of the speaker. There is a consensus that mind is necessary for language development and use. Therefore, the development of a full theory of mind in humans was necessary to understand language development in humans. Noam Chomsky (1957) argued that humans are born with a universal grammar hardwired into their brains. This universal grammar consists of a wide range of grammatical models that include all the grammatical systems of the world's languages. Among the various branches of linguistics, cognitive linguistics in particular, attempts at understanding language creation, learning, and usage in reference to human cognition.

**Artificial Intelligence:** Artificial intelligence is a very important branch of cognitive science. It is originally a branch of computer science which studies and aims at producing intelligence of machines. It is defined as the study and design of intelligent agents, where an intelligent agent is a system that perceives its environment and takes actions that maximise its chances of success. The basic claim of the field was that the intelligence of humans can be precisely described and simulated by a machine. The branches of AI are—Representation and Logical AI, Constraint satisfaction, Bayesian networks, Machine learning, Neural networks, Planning, Knowledge engineering and Search.

Artificial intelligence and cognitive science are two distinct disciplines, with overlapping methodologies, but different goals. The central idea of AI is computational modelling of intelligent behaviour. This is the main contribution of AI to cognitive science. Both artificial intelligence and cognitive science come within a framework that assumes that cognitive processes can be modelled in terms of manipulations of encoded symbols. Moreover, the recent developments of connectionism and parallel distributed processing share the basic assumption concerning the encoding nature of representation. However, the issue of manipulation is controversial. In all these approaches, representation is construed as a form of encoding correspondence.

**Neuroscience:** Neuroscience is the scientific study of brain and the nervous system. It helps to understand how we perceive and interact with the outside world. It studies the physical basis of our behaviour. It is an interdisciplinary science that collaborates with other fields such as chemistry, computer science, engineering, mathematics, medicine, philosophy, physics and psychology.

Studies of brain have become more sophisticated after the invention of the microscope. This led to the development of the neuron doctrine—the hypothesis that the functional unit of the brain is neuron. The scientific study of the nervous system increased significantly during the second half of the 20th century. It has become possible to understand the complex processes occurring inside a single neuron, and in a network that eventually produces the intellectual behaviour, cognition, emotion and physiological responses. Neurons form functional circuits, each responsible for specific tasks to the behaviours at the organism level. Thus, neuroscience can be studied at many different levels ranging from molecular level to cellular level. The major branches of neuroscience are—Molecular neuroscience, Cellular neuroscience, Behavioural neuroscience, Cognitive neuroscience, Computational neuroscience, Systems neuroscience and Developmental neuroscience.

Cognitive science is indebted to the field of neuroscience in general, and cognitive neuroscience in particular. Cognitive neuroscience addresses how mental functions are supported by the brain. The imaging studies in neuroscience have led to some generalisations about mental processes and about the human brain that supports them. These may be summarised under the headings of localisation, interaction, control, and plasticity. High density electrical or magnetic recordings from the scalp and MRI have made it possible to determine the time course of the activations and learn about the direction of information flow.

Neuroscience also attempts to understand the control signals that prioritise a particular way of doing a task. The networks underlying simple reflex activity becomes more flexible through experience. The activation of many networks is common to all people. It implies that it has genetic origins (Posner and Rao, 2009). But the working of these networks differ among individuals, which influences their performance. The individual differences among people are the results of interaction between gene and the environment.

Thus, the field of cognitive science crucially relies on an integration of the results produced by its core disciplines. This integration is very significant for the research in the separate disciplines; to have an impact on cognitive research in general; and also, for the implementation of cognitive science in various social aspects. It is true that the assimilation of knowledge from different fields is an important characteristic feature of cognitive science. But additional original work is equally important. In an interdisciplinary area like cognitive science, it is necessary to integrate diverging (apparently) data and results of the contributing disciplines. For this, new concepts should be developed that can be used within different disciplines and increase the level of understanding between the different areas. It is also necessary to develop general theories that bring together ideas from the various areas, synthesise them in a constructive way, and make it comprehensible to all parts involved. This synthesis may be done by philosophers who are trained in the philosophy of science and epistemology as they have a skill for critically assessing theories and methodologies. Thus the branches of cognitive science are intimately interrelated to each other. They contribute to the field of cognitive science as well as have the prospects of using the results of researches in cognitive science.

## Components of Cognitive Science

The field of cognitive science is a vast area and includes a large number of psychological aspects related to cognition. Such aspects constitute the components of cognitive science. It includes attention, perception, memory, imagery, language and psycholinguistics, consciousness, knowledge representation, thinking, reasoning, creativity, problem solving, decision-making and emotion. Attention is the cognitive process of selectively concentrating on one aspect of the environment while ignoring other things. Perception is the process by which an organism attains awareness or understanding of its environment by organising and interpreting sensory information. Memory can be defined as the mental storage of information and the processes involved in the acquisition, retention and retrieval of that information. A mental imagery is an internal representation that produces the experiences of perception in the absence of the appropriate sensory input. Language is a large collection of arbitrary symbols that have significance for a language using community, and that follow certain rules of combination. A central goal of cognitive science is to understand how human beings comprehend, produce and acquire natural languages. The term 'consciousness' covers a wide range of cognitive functions, including voluntary actions, decision making, attention, awareness and self-monitoring. It is the normal mental condition of the waking state of humans, characterised by the experience of perceptions, thoughts, feelings, awareness of the external world, and often in humans, self-awareness. Knowledge representation is a central concept in cognitive science. Knowledge is described as representations of facts and concepts organised for future use. Thinking is a cognitive activity. It involves mental exploration of objects, activities and experiences instead of motor exploration. Reasoning is a complex mental process that needs a well-organised brain. Reason is a means by which thinking comes from one idea to a related idea. More specifically, it is the way rational beings propose and consider explanations concerning cause and effect, true and false, and what is good or bad. Reasoning may be inductive or deductive. cognitive science have attempted to study and explain how people reason, e.g. which cognitive and neural process are engaged in reasoning and how cultural factors affect the inferences that people draw. Creativity is the ability to improve, whereby through improvement value is added. Theories of creativity have focussed on a variety of aspects. The most dominant are usually identified as the four Ps—process, product, person and place. Problem solving is an extremely complex activity that involves intellectual skills, knowledge and cognitive strategies and meta-strategies that modify attention, perception, the input and the storage of information, and the retrieval of knowledge from memory. Decision-making involves choosing among various options. It involves some problem-solving, since individuals try to make the best possible choice from a range of options. The focus in decision-making is on the factors influencing preference. Plato regarded in emotion to be one of the basic parts of the human mind along with reasoning and desiring. Emotions are related to cognition in at least three ways—as stimulants of cognition, emotions are cognitive in the sense that they involve propositional attitudes, the most literal interpretation of cognitivism about emotions would be committed to ascribing emotions a 'mind-to-world direction of fit'. All these components constitute the components of cognitive science as they are the elements which are studied in the field of cognitive science.

## Cognitive Science as a Field of Study

Mind is the most complex entity in the whole universe. It is complex in the sense that it is not easy to study mind as it cannot be observed, measured or manipulated. Disciplines like science and philosophy have been answering various questions that arise in the life of human being. Science helps in our understanding of the external observable world. And philosophy helps in finding out the answers to the questions related to our life. Nevertheless, human mind has always remained dubious and mysterious, both to science and philosophy and to human beings in general. There were still many unanswered questions about the human mind.

In the past half century, mind has been the subject-matter of research, more than in all the time that came before that. This has also resulted in an increase in the number of disciplines that study mind. With the increase in these disciplines, new technologies and methodologies for studying the mind have also been introduced. But the complexity of the mind has led the experts of these disciplines to attempt at a coordinated effort to understand it. This coordinated effort of the experts of various disciplines to understand the brain has emerged as the field of Cognitive Science. As science is famous for its acquaintance only with the external world, cognitive science as a field of study has distinguished itself from other sciences in that its full attention is on the discovery of our mental world or "inner space".

Cognitive science can be roughly summed up as the scientific interdisciplinary study of mind. It results from the efforts of researchers working in a wide array of fields—philosophy, psychology, linguistics, artificial intelligence, anthropology and neuroscience. Each field has its own unique set of tools and perspectives. Its primary methodology is the scientific method, although many other methodologies also contribute. Different methodologies are brought to bear on a common problem: the nature of cognition. The magnitude of complexity of the mind necessitates an interdisciplinary effort to study and understand it. No single perspective is adequate. Only an intercommunication and cooperation among the practitioners of these disciplines can result in an adequate study of mind. Study of cognition includes mental states and processes such as attention, perception, memory, imagery, language and psycho-linguistics, consciousness, knowledge representation, thinking, reasoning, creativity, problem solving, decision-making and emotion. These constitute the components of cognitive science.

Cognitive science does not merely means the sum of all the contributing disciplines but their intersection or converging work on specific problems. So, cognitive science is not a unified field of study like each of the disciplines themselves, but a collaborative effort among researchers working in the various fields. The bond that holds the intersecting disciplines of cognitive science together is the topic of mind or their common goal to understand the mind and another is the use of scientific methods to study the mind.

To understand the field of cognitive science, it is necessary to know its theoretical perspective on the mind. This perspective centres on the idea of computation, which is also known as information processing. Cognitive scientists view the mind as an information processor. Information processor must both represent and transform information. According to this perspective, a mind must incorporate some form of mental representation and processes that act on and manipulate that information.

Cognitive science tends to focus on a particular level analysis. It tries to understand minds as though they were computer programmes. Cognitive scientists want to understand how information is processed in minds at a very detailed level. They want to understand cognition at a level of such detail so that one could make a computer programme that would process information in the same way. Cognitive science looks for explanations not like traditional computer programmes, but explanations that are encoded at the computer-programme level of detail. Most cognitive science explanations regard cognition as a programme that is running on the networks of neurons. All these imply that cognitive scientists view the human minds as software running on neural hardware. The next level in which cognitive science has interest is the neural level. For explaining cognition, cognitive scientists are finding ways to link up the neural level to the information processing level.

## References

Westbury, C. and Wilensky, U. (1998). Knowledge Representation in Cognitive Science: Implications for Education, *Proceedings of the First International conference on the Learning sciences and the challenges of the information era,* Lima: Peru. Retrieved from http://ccl.northwestern.edu/papers/cogsci/

Nadel, L. and Piattelli-Palmarini, M. (2002). What is cognitive science? (General Introduction) In *The encyclopedia of cognitive science,* 1. London: Macmillan.

Miller, G. (2003). The cognitive revolution: A historical perspective. *Trends in Cognitive Sciences, 7* (3), pp. 141-144.

Boden, M.A. (2006). *Mind as machine: A history of cognitive science,* 1. Oxford: Clarendon Press.

Chipman, S.E.F. (2010). Applications in education and training: A force behind the development of cognitive science. *Topics in Cognitive Science,* 2 (3), pp. 386-397. doi: 10.1111/j.1756-8765.2010.01098.x

Srinivasan, N. (2011). Cognitive science: Emerging perspectives and approaches. In G. Misra (Ed.), *Handbook of Psychology in India* (pp. 46-57). New Delhi: Oxford University Press.

Gardner, H. (1985). *The mind's new science: A history of cognitive science.* New York: Basic Books.

Baker, L.D. (2007). Anthropology, History of. In *Encyclopedia of race and racism,* 1, pp. 93-97. USA: McMillan Publishers.

Bender, A., Hutchins, E. and Medin, D. (2010). Anthropology in cognitive science. *Topics in Cognitive Science,* 2 (3), pp. 374-385.

Nuckolls, C.W. (1999). Cognitive anthropology. In W. Betchel and G. Graham (Eds.), *A companion to cognitive science* (pp. 140-145). Oxford: Blackwell Publishing Limited.

Chomsky, N. (1957). *Syntactic structures.* Netherlands: Gravenhage.

Posner, M.I. and Rao, S. (2009). Cognitive neuroscience: Developments and prospects. *Current Trends in Cognitive Science,* (Platinum Jubilee Special), pp. 419-429.

# 2
# Pedagogy

## Brief History of Pedagogy

'Pedagogy' has generally remained the interest of the philosophers, psychologists and sociologists. Though, very few have dealt with it directly. Philosophers can help in learning, research and innovation by providing explanations and clarifications of some confusing or ubiquitous concepts. Since philosophy is the foundation of education in general, and particularly pedagogy, an analysis of the viewpoints of various philosophers regarding pedagogy will lay down its evolution.

### *Socrates and Plato*

Socrates and Plato were two of the founders of Western philosophy. Socrates' most important contribution to Western thought is his dialectic method of inquiry, known as the Socratic Method. It is a commonly used tool in a wide range of discussions, and is also considered as a type of pedagogy. It was first described by Plato in the Socratic Dialogues. Plato was a speculative philosopher who sought behind the changing phenomena of nature, the absolute and eternal. He talked of education for the body and education for the soul.

Most of Plato's "Dialogues" use the Socratic Method or the method of Dialectic. In this method, a question is put. The answer offered by the respondent is generally an attempted definition which is then refuted. He conceived a hierarchy of thinking and the level of understanding: each sort of thinking could achieve. Opinion could only assist in understanding of the visible world. True knowledge of the universal forms could only be achieved through the higher reasoning process of the dialectic.

The process of dialectic is an interpersonal activity between a leader and a participant. In this process, both the leader and the participant enter a higher state of consciousness, allowing psychic material to flow through them. The process of dialectic cannot be written but only experienced. At the beginning of a dialectic process, none of the participants know consciously the answer or the answers. The answer or the solution or hypothesis is a joint creation or discovery or invention of new understanding produced in the process. Thus, dialectic is a process of bringing forth realities, ideas and images which are within us and are manifested in the process.

The dialogues are often misinterpreted as mere ordinary conversations, arguments or debates. But actually every element of the dialogue has a specific meaning, purpose and importance. The dialogues must be approached as situational learning phenomena. The dialogues should have a sense of respect and anticipation. They should be carefully designed to encourage specific transformative responses in the reader or the listener.

The Socratic Method is creative in so far as it produces cognitive gain or a changed perspective. It guides us anew each time to just and right human responses. Plato's 'dialectical process of coming-to-know' seeks afresh what actions might be right for each inquiry occasion.

### Aristotle

Aristotle is another important founding figure in Western philosophy. He advocated the method of observation, that is, knowledge received through observation of things and events of nature. He found the universal observation in particular things. For him, philosophic method implies the knowledge of essences from the study of particular phenomena. He recognised the inductive method, in which the universal is arrived at from the particular, though he did not regard it as a perfect method. He thought that the deductive method, in which the particulars are deduced from the universal, provides perfect knowledge.

According to him, knowledge is about an object. It is conceptual in nature. Concepts are generalised classes of objects. True knowledge should be obtained through logical proof. Therefore, education and teaching are always about an object and should have content. The teacher instructs a learner about some knowledge, or some discipline. Teaching and learning never represent merely an interpersonal relationship or the expression of feelings. They are always about disciplined inquiry into some aspect of reality. The school should cultivate and develop each person's rationality.

### *Francis Bacon*

Bacon (1561-1626) was an empiricist. His most influential work in the field of education was "The Advancement of Learning". He attempted to provide a plan for better education system in it. He believed in a research based learning system and created methods like the scientific method. The students need to learn dynamically rather than scholastically. He wholly believed that scholasticism is not good for the educational process. He emphasised on experiment, experience, logic and reasoning for learning. It implies self-explored knowledge is more effective for the learners. He regards sense-experience as hindrance to reliable knowledge. His method is not just experiencing, but planned experiencing. Planning the experiences helps in applying logic and induction for learning. Thus knowledge is created by its own. He wants men to learn with instructors, not teachers. He urges students to question, to experience and experiment. Thus his pedagogy mostly constitute of instructions, experience and experiment.

### *John Locke*

Locke's empiricism states that all our ideas come from sense perception or reflection (introspection). Of course, it does not mean that ideas come ready made into the mind; but it is to say that every idea is ultimately reducible to elements which have been the data of sensible or introspective experience. He believed that human beings are born in total ignorance, and that even our theoretical ideas of identity, quantity and substance are derived from experience (Cranston, 1957). Sensation is the basis of Locke's argument for knowledge not being innate, but another main point in his essay is ideas and perception. This theory had profound influence on his pedagogy. Thus, the pedagogy implied in Locke's philosophy is that the learners should be given enough opportunities for perception and sensation.

According to Locke, learning is the last and least part of education. He had a great aversion of the ordinary method of teaching. He believed, the best way to get man do what he wanted is not to terrify or force them but to motivate them, to arouse and then rely on desires, while letting them think, not without justice, that they are acting for their own sakes and of their own free will (Tarcov, 1984). For the poor learners, he suggested the method of practice. This will lead to natural habit functioning beyond conscious memory. According to Locke children are curious, therefore, a good teacher should be able to seize this natural curiosity and channel it into knowledge. Moreover, he insists that teachers must instill discipline when a child's mind is elastic.

Locke advocated for self-discipline, which he meant denying oneself one's desires, crossing one's inclinations and purely follow what reason directs. But giving opportunity for self-discipline meant maintaining a perfect balance between freedom and strictness (responsibility). Education is the art of maintaining this balance—to keep up the child's spirit, easy, active and free; and yet, at the same time, to restrain him from certain things and to draw him to certain other things. Instead of reward or punishment, the incentives of esteem and disgrace should be used for this purpose. Because using reward and punishment make the child learn the content for the sake of the reward or to avoid punishment and not for the sake of the content itself.

For the development of character and reason, the teacher should not lay down many rules. Locke thinks that the teacher should make sure the child understands and can carry out the task set for him and make them repeat the task over and over.

***Rousseau***

Rousseau's approach to pedagogy is based on the philosophy that the natural world can teach us all we need to know. He stated the importance of the natural environment and that learning will take place if the provision for a learning experience is planned and acted upon, not merely left to chance. It is necessary to plan and observe so that the child has every opportunity to play its way into learning and understanding.

He argued that we are inherently good, but we become corrupted by the evils of the society. We are born capable of sensation and from birth are affected in diverse ways by the object around us. Consequently, bringing up children in harmony with nature and its laws so as to preserve the good was central for Rousseau's pedagogic theory. His *Emile* stressed wholeness and harmony, and a concern for the person in the learner. Central to this was the idea that it was possible to preserve the original perfect nature of the child, by means of the control of his education and environment, based on an analysis of the different physical and psychological stages through which he passed from birth to maturity. He appreciated the idea of individualised education.

He argued that the momentum for learning was provided by the growth of the person (nature). The responsibility of the teacher was to facilitate opportunities for learning. He also emphasised the power of the environment for education. It was essential that teachers attend to the environment to which the learner will be exposed. More control will result in more effectiveness. According to him, the child should remain in complete ignorance of those ideas that are beyond his/her grasping.

For him, it was important to develop ideas of the world in our own ways. The teacher should encourage the learners to reason their way through to their own conclusions, and not rely on the teachers or books. The sensations make an impression on him, and he remembers them. From this, without thinking about it, he continually enriches his memory while waiting until his judgment is able to profit by it. It is in the choice of these objects, the presenting of those that he can know and, of hiding from him those that he ought to ignore that constitutes the true art of cultivating in him this first faculty. It forms a store of knowledge that serves his education throughout his life.

Since it is not possible to prevent the child from learning what he sees outside himself, those examples should be presented on his mind in the best suited form for him. He considers teaching as an art of controlling without percepts and to do everything without doing anything at all. A good education aims to make a man reasonable.

He argued for experience against verbal lessons. To exercise their attention, only those things should be told to them in which they are interested at present. The teacher should remain brief but without being obscure or vague.

### *Descartes (1596-1650)*

While modifying the false direction of the mind in the search for scientific truth, Descartes stated some of the great principles of modern pedagogy. The first is the equal aptitude of minds to know and comprehend. But equal capability of mind does not mean equal use of it. According to him, nature is not sufficient in herself; she needs to be guided and directed. Success will depend less on natural qualities, such as imagination, memory, quickness of thought, than upon the rules of intellectual direction imposed on the mind (Compayre, 1889). It means that formation and development of the individual depends mostly on the education rather than the nature. Another Cartesian principle is the substitution of free inquiry and reflective conviction for blind beliefs founded upon authority. He opposed the mechanical processes and exercises of pure memory in the education process, and emphasised the use of rational methods that stimulate the intelligence, clear and distinct ideas, judgment and reflection. The rule of evidence, applied with moderation and discretion, is an excellent pedagogical concept to save the child from being a mere machine. He also distinguished between subjective and objective pedagogy. Subjective pedagogy refers to instructions that led to the development of the internal qualities of precision and measure. Objective pedagogy is instruction that takes place through what is without, through an extended erudition, through an accumulation of knowledge.

### *Malebranche (1638-1715)*

Malebranche was a staunch idealist philosopher. He totally condemned sense instruction. According to him, sensations hinder the metaphysical pursuit of the individual. Therefore, the child should be nourished on abstract truths, as souls have no age and the infant is always capable of ideal contemplation. It is only bad habits which makes the child or the individual incapable of meditation on abstract truths. For this, he also suggested remedy for this that the child should be kept away from fear, desires, hope, pain, pleasures, etc. Therefore, all kinds of sensible rewards should be avoided. But he upholds material punishments in the education of children, which is in contradiction to theory against sense. He believes in the influence of physical environment on the development of the soul. The soul is not an independent and isolate force which develops through an internal activity. So, his pedagogy considers an appropriate environment important for learning and development of the individual.

## Concept of Pedagogy

There is always a challenge to situate our knowledge in our living context. In the field of education, the living context is the classroom.

So, the knowledge is to be situated in the classroom. Though the purpose of education has been broad as well as contextual, there are some universal motives with which the process of education goes on, for instance, the welfare of the learners. The process of education involves two fundamental functions—teaching and learning. The relation between teaching and learning may be stated as—teaching is the act of facilitating learning. However, sometimes learning may take place without teaching. In the field of education, cognitive issues are one of the vital issues. The cognitive issues in education include the way the minds of beings meet each other. The teacher's cognitive issue is to reach the student's minds and the students' cognitive issue is trying to get what is coming from the teacher's mind.

Pedagogy is the science of teaching. It is complex and difficult to define what constitutes pedagogy. Even the definitions of pedagogy appear to be somewhat obscure. Watkins and Mortimer (1999) define it as 'any conscious activity by one person designed to enhance the learning of another'. Alexander (2003) suggests that pedagogy requires discourse: Pedagogy is the act of teaching together with its attendant discourse. It is what one needs to know, and the skills one needs to command in order to make and justify the many different kinds of decisions of which teaching is constituted. Leach and Moon (1999) described a *Pedagogical Setting* as 'the practice that a teacher, together with a particular group of learners creates, enacts and experiences'. Their definition suggests that pedagogy is a joint activity in which the learner has an active role. This offers a different perspective from previous definitions offered and draws in the social interaction between teachers and learners. Pedagogy involves the act of teaching and the rationale that supports the actions that teachers take. It is what a teacher needs to know and various skills that a teacher needs to use in order to make effective teaching decisions. It is what teachers ought to do to fully facilitate and support learning. The responsibility of the education process is to ensure that the children exploit their potentials to fullest. This can be done if proper learning takes place, which in turn is facilitated by teaching. So, the demand is to make pedagogy strong and well-developed.

Pedagogy is the study of the education of the child. The Soviet psychologist and educational reformer, Pavel Petrovich Blonskii regarded education as a deliberate, organised, and prolonged effort which influences the development of an individual. Pedagogy is establishing clearly and precisely how this effort may be organised, what different forms it may take, what techniques it may utilise, and what direction it should assume. For this, it is necessary to understand the laws that govern the development of the individual. Alexander (2004) argues that pedagogy is the act of teaching together with its attendant discourse. It constitutes the knowledge and skills necessary for making and justifying decisions in teaching situation. According to him, the teacher requires knowledge in three main domains: domains that enable teaching (whom, what and how of teaching); domains that formalise and legitimate teaching (requirements and expectations of the institution and local and national authorities); and domains that locate teaching (culture, how an individual relates to others and develops as a person, and how to understand the current and future state of education).

Pedagogy may be considered as both natural and normative science. On the one hand, it is a sub-field of the biological (i.e. natural) sciences since it has responsibility of developing the child. On the other hand, it deals with philosophical or normative sciences since every form of education sets for itself particular ideals, goals, or norms.

A pedagogy can be (1) *general*, as in the strategies, techniques, and approaches that teachers use to facilitate learning in general; (2) *specific to a domain*, such as the application of specific strategies, techniques, and approaches belonging to a domain to the instruction of that specific domain; or (3) *specific to a certain approach to teaching* that may or may not be domain specific, such as work-based pedagogy, problem-based pedagogy, or even constructivist pedagogy.

Pedagogy also includes the ways in which teachers interact with students. It implies issues like how they question and respond to questions, motivate students, use their ideas and respond to their diverse backgrounds and interests. It includes creating the social and intellectual environment and deciding on the types of learning to be engaged. It also includes the decisions about framing the content around a series of tasks or as key ideas and skills that are revisited and built on. Teachers also need to think about how they link and sequence activities and how and what they assess. All this decision-making by the teacher constitute pedagogy.

**Relationship between Cognitive Science and Pedagogy**

A strong relationship is evident between cognitive science and pedagogy. The applications of cognitive science in the educational process are straightforward. The main goal of the education process is to improve learning and performance of the students, which can be done through effective pedagogical intervention. A thorough understanding of the learning processes is vital for the deployment of adequate curricula and teaching methods. Teaching does not constitute only the content and the method of presenting the content but it should also take into account the information processing in the learner, accessing a learner's cognitive structure (prior knowledge) to determine whether it is adequate to process the new information, problems in processing the information and ways of overcoming these problems. A better understanding of the neural underpinnings of learning mechanisms and cognitive functions involved in the educational process (memory, attention, motivation, perception, and metacognition) has obvious implications for effective pedagogy. The most significant implication is the designing of effective learning tools and educational paradigms by using the principles and researches on cognitive science. It is only when the complexity of teaching reaches parity with the complexity of learning that there will be significant improvement in levels of classroom learning and performance (Letteri, 1991). Teaching, to a large part, is based on the assumptions about the mind of the learner. Therefore, it is important for the teacher to determine what children think they are doing and what their reasons are for doing it, apart from knowing what they do. Teaching begins with a teacher's understanding of what is to be learned and how it is to be taught. Though the teacher is responsible for designing learning opportunities for the learners, learning itself ultimately remains the responsibility of the students. Thus, teaching is inevitably based on the notions about the nature of the learner's mind. When the teacher attempts at teaching something to the learners, it is based on the assumption that the learners are either ignorant of something or what they believe is false. Gardner (1991) puts it in his "The Unschooled Mind" as "We must place ourselves inside the heads of our students and try to understand as far as possible the sources and strengths of their conceptions." Modern pedagogy is emphasising more and more on the cognitive paradigm. It is developing a strong view that the child should be aware of her own thought processes. Therefore, it is crucial for both the pedagogical theorist and the teacher to help the child to become more meta-cognitive. It implies that the improvements in pedagogy require the understanding of the learners' mind. Cognitive science is the field which can best help at a comprehensive understanding of the human mind.

Cognitive science researches are concerned with the structure and representation of knowledge in our minds. Pedagogy is concerned with sharing of this knowledge among many brains. The innovative models and theories that have been proposed to facilitate advancement in the field of pedagogy tend to focus on cognitive factors.

Bruner (1999) mentioned about four models of learners' minds. These are—

(a) Imitative Learners—When an adult demonstrates or models a successful or skilled action to a child, that demonstration is implicitly based on the adult's belief that—
- The child does not know how to do x
- The child can learn how to do x by being shown
- The child wants to do x
- That the child may, in fact, be trying to do x

To learn by imitation, the child must recognise the goals pursued by the adult, the means used to achieve those goals, and the fact that the demonstrated action will successfully get the child to the goal. However, learning by a combination of practice and conceptual explanation is more effective for gaining flexible skills than just learning how to perform skillfully.

(b) Learning from Didactic Exposure—Didactic teaching is usually based on the notion that the pupils should be presented with facts, principles and rules of action which are to be learned, remembered, and then applied. It assumes the child to be ignorant of certain facts, rules or principles that can be conveyed by telling. In this teaching situation, abilities are conceived as the ability to acquire new knowledge by the aid of certain 'mental abilities', verbal, spatial, numerical, interpersonal, or whatever. This model presumes that the learner's mind as tabula rasa. The mind accumulates knowledge cumulatively, which implies the importance of prior knowledge. It considers the child's mind as passive, a receptacle waiting to be filled. Active interpretation or analysis does not enter the picture.

(c) Children as Thinkers—According to this model, the teacher is concerned with understanding what the child thinks and how that belief came into being. Pedagogy is to help the child understand better and holistically. Understanding is fostered through discussion and collaboration. The learners are encouraged to express their own views to achieve some meetings of minds with others who may have other views. Such pedagogy of mutuality presumes that both child and adult have their own points of view, i.e. the concept of individuality. Each is encouraged to recognise the others, though they may not agree. The child is assumed to be able to reason, to make sense, both on her own and through discourse with others. This model of education is mutualist and dialectical, more concerned with interpretation and understanding than with the achievement of factual knowledge or skilled performance. Recent researches on inter-subjectivity (how children develop their ability to 'read other minds'), theories of mind, meta-cognition and collaborative learning have enriched this perspective on teaching and learning.

(d) Children as Knowledgeable—The fourth perspective holds that teaching should help children grasp the distinction between personal knowledge, on the one side, and what is taken to be known by the culture, on the other. We come to view personal against the background of what has come to be shared with the historical past. Those presently engaged in the pursuit of knowledge become sharers of conjectures with those long dead. Thus, there is something special about 'talking' to authors, now dead but still alive in their ancient texts—so long as the objective of the encounter is not worship but discourse and interpretation, 'going meta' on thoughts about the past.

It is seen that each model emphasises different educational goals. These models are conceptions of mind that determine how teaching is carried out. In the first model, practice and conceptual explanation have been given importance. The second model considers the learner's mind to be passive. So, it gives importance on putting new knowledge in their minds on the basis of previous knowledge. The third model gives importance to individual difference and therefore, discourse and dialogue are encouraged. The fourth model emphasises on meta-cognition of the learner.

## References

Alexander, R.J. (2003). Talk in teaching and learning: International perspectives. In QCA (Ed.), *New Perspectives on Spoken English* (pp. 26-37). London: QCA.

Alexander, R.J. (2004). Still no pedagogy? Principles, pragmatism and compliance in primary education. *Cambridge Journal of Education, 34* (1), pp. 7-33.

Bruner, J. (1999). Folk pedagogies. In J. Leach and B. Moon (Eds.), *Learners and pedagogy* (pp. 4-20). London: Paul Chapman Publishing.

Compayrs, G. (1889). *The History of Pedagogy*. (W.H. Payne, Trans.) Boston: D.C. Heath & Company. (Original work published 1885).

Cranston, M. (1957). *John Locke: A biography.* London: Longman's Green & Co.

Gardner, H. (1991). *The unschooled mind: How children think and how schools should teach.* New York: Basic Books.

Leach, J. and Moon, B. (1999). Recreating pedagogy. In J. Leach and B. Moon (Eds.), *Learners and Pedagogy* (pp. 265-276). London: Paul Chapman Publishing.

Letteri, C.A. (1991). Cognitive profile: Academic achievement. In M.L. Languis, D.J. Martin, P.J. Naour, and J.J. Buffer (Eds.), *Cognitive science: Contributions to educational practice,* 6, pp. 286-310. Philadelphia: Gordon & Breach Science Publishers.

Tarcov, N. (1984). *Locke's Education for Liberty.* Chicago: The University of Chicago Press.

Watkins, C. and Mortimer, P. (1999). Pedagogy: What do we know? In P. Mortimer (Ed.), *Understanding pedagogy and its impact on teaching* (pp. 1-19). London: Chapman.

# 3

# Cognitive Science as a Field of Study

## Foundation of Cognitive Science

Cognitive science as a discipline comes under the epistemological branch of philosophy. The history of cognitive science is practically equivalent to the history of all intellectual efforts to understand human cognition systematically. This would include the history of epistemology and philosophy of mind as well as history of psychology, cognitive anthropology, linguistics, neuroscience and artificial intelligence. But like of any other discipline, philosophical background forms the foundation of cognitive science.

Epistemology is the branch of philosophy which deals with 'knowledge'. Before going into epistemology, it is necessary to understand what philosophy as a field of study is concerned with. Philosophy is the critical study of the most fundamental questions that arise in the human mind. It asks what the matter of reality is, and what the reality of nature is. Do our perceptions of reality match the actual reality? What does it mean to think? What does it mean to have a mind? How can we know that other minds actually exist? Is there a difference between right and wrong, and if so, how can we prove this? How do we define rules that allow us to apply theoretical ideas of right and wrong in practical situations? What do we mean by the word 'God'? Does God exist? It deals with the concepts as existence, goodness, knowledge and beauty. It asks "Is knowledge possible," and if so, "what is knowledge?" Philosophy is the critical, speculative or analytic study of such issues.

The method of philosophy involves formulating problems carefully based on all known facts, and attempting at logical solutions to them, and engaging in a dialectical process to arrive at the truth. This is same as the method of science but without much dependence on physical experimentation. The method of science proceeds by observation, formulation of a hypothesis, and further experimentation. The method of philosophy proceeds by logical formulation of a problem, argument for a solution, and counter argument. These proceed until a solution (truth) is reached. Philosophy has developed more slowly than other sciences. It is because it is solely dependent on cognitive integrity. It does not have a coherent paradigm for determining what kinds of experimental evidence to accept. Thus, it can be said, philosophy is one's integrated view of the world. It includes an understanding of the nature of existence, man and his role in the world. Philosophy is the foundation of knowledge. It is the standard by which ideas are integrated and understood.

The issues and concerns in philosophy have been divided into three broad categories which forms the branches of philosophy. These are—

- **Axiology**—It explores (i) aesthetics (the study of basic philosophical questions about art and beauty) (ii) ethics (the study of what makes actions right or wrong) (iii) logic (the study of the standards of correct argumentation).
- **Epistemology**—It is the study of knowledge and its nature, possibility, and justification.
- **Metaphysics**—It is the study of the most basic categories of things, such as existence, objects, properties, causality, etc., including ontology.

As the concern of the study is on cognition and knowledge, the focus is on the theory of knowledge—epistemology.

### Concept of Epistemology

It is recognised that the world exists in a particular way or pattern. Gaining knowledge about the world and its nature and pattern is important for man to survive in this world. Philosophy provides the framework to understand the world. It provides the premises by which man can discover truth and use his mind to support his life.

Epistemology is the branch of philosophy that studies knowledge. It is also called the theory of knowledge. It is concerned with the nature and scope of knowledge, its presuppositions and basis, and the reliability of claims to knowledge. The epistemological problem is one of the basic problems of philosophy. It attempts to answer the basic questions: what distinguishes true (adequate) knowledge from false (inadequate) knowledge? What are the necessary and sufficient conditions of knowledge? What are its sources? What is the structure of knowledge; and what are its limits? Epistemology is also concerned with the study of justified belief. It aims to answer questions such as: How we are to understand the concept of justification? What makes justified beliefs justified? Is justification internal or external to one's own mind? Thus, the issues that surround the general problem of investigating the nature and extent of human knowledge are the problems of epistemology. However, in actual terms, the basic epistemological problem is not that of discerning the true extent of human knowledge, but that of deciding which of our ordinary knowledge claims can properly be called examples of human knowledge.

### *History of Epistemology*

Philosophers and scholars have dealt with the epistemological questions from different perspectives. Though there are contradictions in epistemological theories, the history of epistemology shows a clear trend. It is evident from the trend that the first theories of knowledge stressed its absolute, permanent character, whereas the later theories put the emphasis on its relativity, its continuous evolution or development, and its active interference with the world and its subjects and objects. The whole trend moves from a static, passive view of knowledge towards a more and more adaptive and active one.

The history of epistemology may be understood from viewpoints of the Greek philosophers, particularly Plato and Aristotle, along with some other distinguished philosophers like Descartes, Spinoza, Locke, Leibniz, Berkeley, etc.

#### *Plato (428-348 BC) Views on Epistemological*

It is difficult to find Plato's epistemological theory systematically expressed and completely elaborated in any one dialogue. However, the 'Theatus' considers the problems of knowledge. Here, he endeavoured to disprove false theories of knowledge, especially the theory that knowledge is sense perception.

Plato assumed knowledge to be unattainable. If attainable, he believed, true knowledge is that which is 'infallible' as well as 'of the real'. True knowledge must possess both these characteristics. Any state of mind that cannot justify its claim to both these characteristics cannot be true. Plato described our acquisition of true knowledge through his allegory of the Cave, his metaphor of the Divided Line and his doctrine of the Forms.

He presented an allegory to show how humans acquire true knowledge and what it is. According to him, most people lives in the darkness of the cave. Their thoughts are oriented around the vague world of shadows inside the cave, which is actually not true knowledge. The men inside the cave keep thinking the shadows to be their true knowledge of the world. But after coming out of the cave, they gradually realise that the real world is different from the shadows inside the cave. The responsibility of leading man out of the cave into the world of light is beheld on education. Education is not putting knowledge into a person's soul that does not possess it. Knowledge is like vision in that it requires an organ capable of receiving it (Stumpf, 1988). It is important to direct the soul towards the right direction to acquire true knowledge rather than only putting light (knowledge) into the soul so that it can see or perceive the true knowledge.

Plato used the metaphor of the Divided Line to demonstrate the stages or levels of knowledge in a systematic form. According to him, the mind moves through four stages of development in the process of discovering true knowledge. At each stage, there is a parallel between the kind of object presented to the mind and the kind of thought this object makes possible (Stumpf, 1988). A continuous vertical line between the modes of cognition (Imagining, Belief, Thinking, and Knowledge) and the corresponding objects (Images, Things, Mathematical Objects, Forms) suggests that there is some degree of knowledge at every point. The line passes through the lowest form of reality (imagining) to the highest (knowledge).

According to his doctrine of Forms, Plato viewed knowledge as an awareness of absolute, universal 'Ideas' or 'Forms' existing independent of any subject trying to understand them. His theory of knowledge attempted to separate knowledge from opinion. According to him, knowledge originates in sense experience. His basic idea is that—'just as there are objects which the senses experience, so there are objects which the mind experiences'. However, these are not objects but 'Ideas' or 'Forms'. The mind may be said to experience these ideas or forms through a process called 'Intuition'. Thus, Plato gives importance to mind, and not senses in acquiring true knowledge, although he places the origin of knowledge as sense experience.

*Aristotle (384-322 BC) Views*

The literatures authored by Aristotle suggest very little about epistemology directly. But he also conceives of knowledge as involving systematic understanding. He thinks that the findings of a properly developed science can be laid out in connected sequences of explanation. In the 'Posterior Analytics', Aristotle stated explicit conditions for knowledge. It is Aristotle's major work on the structure of scientific knowledge. It is not an account of how we acquire knowledge, but an account of what we must have acquired if we are to consider as possessing knowledge. He advocated that a scientific theory must be demonstrative for expressing genuine knowledge.

Aristotle believes sense perception to be crucial for the process of knowing. But that sense perception by itself does not constitute knowledge. It only shows us particular objects. Genuine knowledge is about universal characteristics of things. Observation by itself neither provides us with the definitions of things, nor does it give us science as such. Science requires the discovery of a premise, a starting point for reasoning. He emphasised upon deduction and demonstrative reasoning. He analysed and systematically organised the basic elements of this form of reasoning which is called syllogism. Syllogistic reasoning assures linking of major and minor premises through the agency of the middle term, thereby producing valid conclusions.

Aristotle's epistemological opinion may be inferred from his discussion of the method of inquiry in empirical science and in philosophy. According to him, humans acquire knowledge by means of a process called 'Induction'. The empirical inquiry proceeds from perceptual observation through induction until experience. The process of induction involves four different steps—

(i) Perception—the acquiring of information through the senses.

(ii) Memory—the ability to retain perceptions in the mind.
(iii) Experience—by perceiving many times in conjunction with memory, experience is formed.
(iv) Knowledge—experience becomes knowledge when the essence of things is understood through this process.

Aristotle recognises observation and experience not only as the basis for forming theories, but also as a means of testing them; and for this purpose he advocates the collections of new observations (Terrence, 2009). It seems Aristotle is little more in the side of sense perception than Plato, in that, he regard senses to aid the mind in acquiring knowledge. He believes that knowledge can be reached through the process of induction which includes perception, memory, experience and knowledge.

*Rene Descartes (1596-1650) Views*

Descartes' views on knowledge were influenced by the time in which he lived. It was characterised by questioning of beliefs held for centuries and more reliance on straightforward observation. He strongly believed that a systematic method is essential for establishing a reliable opinion out of various preconceived opinions.

Descartes defines knowledge in terms of doubt. He understands doubt as the contrast of certainty. As our certainty increases, our doubt decreases and as our doubt increases, our certainty decreases. Knowledge is to be based on complete or perfect certainty. This requires a complete absence of doubt—an indubitability. Descartes' emphasis on doubt, rather than on certainty, marks an epistemological innovation as 'Cartesian method'. His method of doubt involves a determined effort to test our preconceived opinions or prejudices to the limit by applying a series of deliberate skeptical techniques (Cottingham, 2009).

The Cartesian method means certain and easy rules that will lead to not taking anything false to be true. Descartes points out that mind itself is infallible. But it is deflected from the true path of rational reflection by factors like prejudice, passion, the influence of education, impatience and the over-hasty desire to attain results. This deflection makes the mind unable to employ its natural operations correctly. Hence, Descartes believes in the utility of a set of rules. However, these rules presuppose the mind's natural capacities and operations.

Intuition and deduction are natural possessions of our mind. These are mental powers that enable us to arrive at the knowledge of things without illusion. But without regulation, these powers can lead us astray. Therefore, the Cartesian method consists in those rules by which our powers of intuition and deduction are guided in an orderly way. Descartes placed the whole edifice of knowledge upon the foundation of intuition and deduction. By intuition, Descartes means an intellectual activity or vision of such clarity that it leaves no doubt in mind. Deduction is the ability to recognise a special relation between a set of statements (the premises) and a further statement (the conclusion). The relation being that the conclusion must be true, whenever all the premises are true.

Descartes wanted to rest knowledge upon a starting point that had absolute certainty in the individual's own mind. Therefore, knowledge requires the use of intuition and deduction. While intuition gives the first principles, deduction gives the remote conclusions.

*Spinoza (1632-1677) Views*

Spinoza's epistemology is mostly found in his 'Ethics' and in an earlier unfinished work 'Treatise on the Emendation of the Intellect'. According to Spinoza, every idea naturally involves affirmation of its own content. It does not need any validation from any outside entity. An idea can and will be denied or doubted only when the mind has another idea which contradicts or questions the first. He believes the doctrine that truth 'requires no sign' and is instead 'its own standard' (Garrett, 2009). For Spinoza, since the truth of true ideas can be determined directly, the true thought is distinguished from a false one chiefly by an intrinsic denomination along with the extrinsic one. He holds that doubt arises only when the mind has two related ideas, at least one of which is doubtful.

Spinoza added a highly systematic arrangement of principles and axioms to Descartes' method of determining true knowledge. He provided a complete set of axioms or theorems that would explain the whole system of reality in the same way that geometry explains the relations and movement of things.

Spinoza distinguishes three kinds of knowledge—imagination, reason and intuition. He also describes how we can move from the lowest to the highest level. The beginning is to be made through the things most familiar to us. He says, by refining our knowledge of things, we can move from (i) imagination, to (ii) reason, and finally to (iii) intuition.

At the level of imagination, our ideas are derived from sensation. Here our ideas are very concrete and specific, and the mind is passive. Though our ideas on this level are specific, they are vague and inadequate. It is because we know things only as they affect our senses. Spinoza believes that the ideas formed from experience are useful for daily life, but do not necessarily give true knowledge.

The second level of knowledge is reason. This is scientific knowledge. At this level, man's mind can rise above immediate and particular things and deal with abstract ideas, for instance in mathematics and in physics. Knowledge is true and adequate at this level. Spinoza says it is true and adequate because truth validates itself.

The highest level of knowledge is intuition. Through intuition, the whole system of nature can be grasped. At the first level, particular things are seen in a disconnected way. At this level, they are seen as parts of the whole scheme. This kind of knowledge "proceeds from an adequate idea of the formal essence of certain attributes of God to the adequate knowledge of the essence of things" (Garrett, 2009). Intuitive knowledge makes us more and more perfect.

*John Locke (1632-1704) Views*

John Locke's masterpiece, 'An Essay concerning Human Understanding' is an epistemological work. In this work, he aims at discovering what kind of thing God has fitted us to know. It also concerns how we should direct and use our intellect and understandings. His epistemological concerns were to find out the origin, certainty and extent of knowledge. Locke also restricted knowledge to ideas. But his concept of ideas involves the ideas generated by objects we experience, i.e. sensations. He regarded the human mind as 'tabula rasa' (white or blank paper). It implies that he was strictly against innate knowledge. According to him, origin of ideas is experience. There are two forms of experience—sensation and reflection. The ideas are formed through senses (experience of the external world) and reflection upon these ideas (an internal experience). But experience of reflection is not possible until the experience of sensation. Reflection means simply the mind's taking notice of its own operations. But its operations begin when the mind is provided with ideas, and these ideas come from the external world through the senses.

Locke distinguished between simple and complex ideas. According to him, simple ideas are un-analysable and indefinable and the complex ideas are mentally constructible out of simple ones. Simple ideas are received passively by the mind through the senses. They also originate in reflection. In relation to the ideas received through senses, the mind can develop other simple ideas by reasoning and judging. On the other hand, complex ideas are not received passively but are rather put together by the mind as compound of simple ideas. In complex ideas, the emphasis is upon the activity of the mind, which takes three forms as the mind joins ideas, brings ideas together but holds them separate, and abstracts.

Locke also makes distinction between primary qualities and secondary qualities in order to answer the question of how ideas are related to objects. Primary qualities are those that actually exist in concrete form. Secondary qualities produce ideas in our mind that have no exact counterpart in the object.

According to Locke, the extension and validity of knowledge depends upon the relations among the ideas. The ideas that enter the mind may be related to each other in many ways. The validity of knowledge depends upon the perception of the relationships of the ideas to each other. There are three modes of perception—intuitive, demonstrative and sensitive. Each one of these modes leads to a different degree of knowledge regarding reality. Sensitive knowledge can be said as the lowest knowledge. In strict sense, it cannot be considered as knowledge. It gives some degree of knowledge, but it does not give certainty, nor does it extend very far. It gives awareness of the qualities but not of the connections between qualities. Demonstrative knowledge occurs when our minds engage in trying to discover the agreement or disagreement of ideas by calling attention to other ideas. Intuitive knowledge is the highest and certain knowledge that is possible for humans.

### *Leibniz (1646-1716) Views*

Gottfried Wilhelm Leibniz's works does not contain any theory of knowledge. He did not consider the epistemological issues in detail. However, he made important contributions to epistemology.

He can be listed under both rationalist as well as empiricist. In 1684, Leibniz published a short treatise called "Meditations on Knowledge, Truth, and Ideas". There he mentioned a series of characteristic features for human knowledge or cognition—

- Knowledge is either obscure or clear,
- Clear knowledge is either confused or distinct,
- Distinct knowledge is either inadequate or adequate,
- Adequate knowledge is either symbolic or intuitive.

According to Leibniz, clear knowledge means the ability to recognise a thing, that is, the ability to account the characteristic features of that thing. This enables one to give a *nominal definition* of the thing. If all the features that form part of a distinct notion are themselves known, then the cognition is adequate. The knowledge is intuitive, if all the component notions of a complex notion can be considered simultaneously.

Leibniz's account of a priori knowledge infers his rationalistic approach to epistemology. He distinguished between *truths of reason* and *truths of fact* (Stumpf, 1988). A *truth of reason* is a necessary truth, that to deny it, is to be involved in a contradiction. On the other hand, *truths of fact* are contingent, and their opposite is possible. Truths of reason are known purely by logic whereas truths of fact are known by experience. The test of a *truth of reason* is the law of contradiction, and the test for a *truth of fact* is the law of sufficient reason.

Leibniz's account of truth leads to the conclusion that all knowledge is ultimately a priori knowledge. But he himself avoids this conclusion. He claimed that the knowledge of particular contingent truths has its basis in the sense perception. He argued that the knowledge of universal contingent truths cannot be based entirely on simple enumerative inductions but must be supplemented by a priori knowledge. Although the senses are necessary for all our actual knowledge, they are not sufficient to give us the whole of it. For this, he gave the reason that the senses give only instances, i.e. particular or individual truths.

*David Hume (1711-1776) Views*

David Hume was an empiricist. Sometimes his philosophy is seen as skeptical. It was thought to consist in a string of arguments designed to show the impossibility of knowledge (indeed, even of reasonable belief) about many of the things that our common sense view of the world takes for granted. The common sense belief is that there is a world of bodies outside and independent of our minds. These bodies stand in causal relations to one another, which can be discovered through reason or experience. Thus, their behaviour can be predicted, at least to some extent.

He divided perceptions into two types—impressions and ideas. Impressions are more vivid perceptions while ideas are faint images of impressions. He maintains that all our concepts (ideas) are derived, directly or indirectly, from sensations (impressions). It implies his conclusion that impressions cause ideas. There are two kinds of impressions—sensation and reflection. After sensation, ideas are formed. From the ideas, the second kind of impressions is formed, which are the result of reflecting on ideas caused by sensation. Our beliefs are formed as a function of the strength of our impressions. Thinking refers to transition from one idea to another. This transition is a matter of natural propensities, not of reflective, rational calculation. It is governed by three 'principles of association': resemblance, contiguity, and cause and effect.

*Kant (1724-1804) Views*

Immanuel Kant's epistemology is a mixture of empiricism and rationalism. He was trained in rationalist tradition and influenced by empiricist. As such, he emerged as a reconciliator. It is realised in his works that there is a distinction between 'understanding' as the general concept and 'understanding' as a faculty of the human mind. Kant believed that all knowledge cannot be derived from experience, but all knowledge is based on experience. He originates knowledge in intuitions but due to possibility of judgment about things, intuition alone is also not sufficient. According to him, we have some objective knowledge of the world. But this knowledge relies on synthetic, a priori laws of nature. He believes that objective knowledge is gained through the sensibility, which supplies the mind with intuitions, and there is the understanding which produces judgments of these intuitions and considers them under categories. These categories uplift the intuition and produces universally necessary knowledge. This knowledge is gained through sensible intuition. A sensible intuition consists of a sensation and the form (i.e. its relation to other sensations). As the categories are innate in any rational being, so any intuitions thought within a category in one mind will necessarily be subsumed and understood identically in any mind.

The subject matter of cognitive science—'cognition' i.e. knowing—is the central point of epistemological discussions in philosophy. The rivalry between the methodologies of pure reason (rationalism) and sense experience (empiricism), as the means for gaining knowledge, laid the foundation for cognitive science. It is found that almost all the philosophers i.e. Socrates' (469-399 BC), Plato's (427-347 BC), Descartes' (1596-1650), Spinoza (1632-1677) and Leibniz (1646-1716) believe that mind is the source of knowledge either in the form of universal ideas or imagination except Aristotle (384-322 BC) and David Hume (1711-1776). Though Locke (1632-1704) is an empiricist, he advocates that reflection is necessary for knowing the internal world. Kant (1724-1804), a reconciliator, believes that sensibility supplies the mind with intuition. Thus the rationalist approach towards epistemology laid the foundations of cognitive science.

## History of Cognitive Science

The roots of cognitive science may be found in the ancient philosophical thoughts and discussions, particularly epistemological discussions. However, it was formalised into a discipline much later. While studying the historical development of cognitive science, the researcher divided it into two stages for the convenience of understanding—early history of cognitive science (historical developments in its contributing disciplines which may have effected in the emergence of cognitive science) and the formal conception of cognitive science.

### *Early History of Cognitive Science*

The inception of cognitive science took place in the early thoughts of the philosophers and other debates related with mind or knowledge in the branch disciplines of cognitive science, though in subtle form. Though the epistemological discussions in philosophy laid the foundation of cognitive science, the staircases are made by the queries related to cognition in other branch disciplines of cognitive science—psychology, linguistics, anthropology, neuroscience and artificial intelligence.

***Philosophy:*** The roots of cognitive science go back to the thoughts of the early Greek philosophers like Socrates, Plato, Aristotle, etc. and some other great philosophers and scholars like Descartes, Spinoza, Locke, Leibniz, Berkeley, Hume, etc. Their debates on epistemological issues ultimately led to the emergence of a new science—cognitive science.

Socrates' (469-399 BC) view was that knowledge of the cosmos and the ultimate nature of things is unattainable. He argued that wisdom consists precisely in attaining an accurate view of our own ignorance, in a critical ability to deconstruct false beliefs in ourselves and in others. He claimed that this critical, penetrating self-knowledge would lead to the pursuit of virtue.

For Plato (427-347 BC), the mind is said to experience the ideas or forms through a process called 'Intuition'. Knowledge was having justified true belief. He described how the human mind achieves knowledge by means of his allegory of the Cave, the metaphor of the Divided Line and the doctrine of the Forms. According to him, learning or knowledge acquisition in the ordinary sense is impossible. Even if knowledge is attainable, it must of the real.

Aristotle's (384-322 BC) describes the mind in functional terms by regarding it as the part of the soul. The mind enables the soul to know and understand. Therefore, the mind is by nature desirable of knowledge. Aristotle says our mind has a better knowledge of the things close to our senses than of things farther from our senses. So, our mind moves from knowledge of particular things gained through sensation to universal or class ideas, which cannot be gained through sensation. Thus according to him, our mind provides the universal characteristics of things, provided the premises based on our sense perception. Aristotle's idea may be schematically described as—

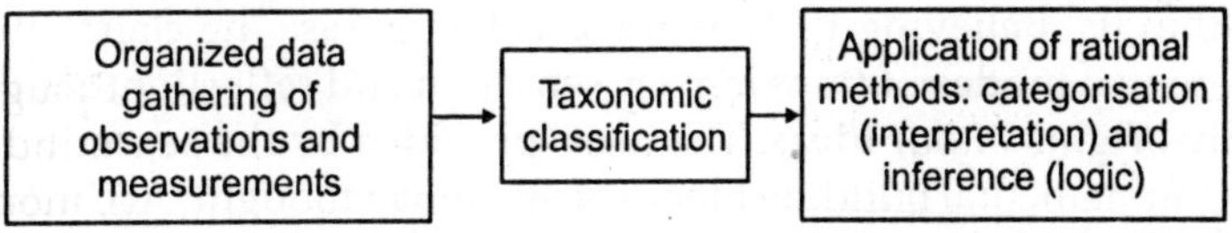


**Fig. 3.1:** Schematic Representation of Aristotle's Epistemological View

Descartes' (1596-1650) regarded the mind to be pure and infallible, if left to itself. The mind is distinct from the body. Its essence is thought. It naturally possesses two powers—intuitions and deduction. Descartes devised the Cartesian method which guides the power of intuition and deduction, so that the mind is not deflected. He placed the whole structure of knowledge upon the foundation of intuition and deduction.

Spinoza (1632-1677) believes that the human mind contains ideas. Some of these ideas—sensory images, qualitative feels, perceptual data—are imprecise qualitative phenomena. Because they are expression in thought of states of the body as it is affected by the bodies surrounding it. The knowledge perceived by the mind from the external world is vague and inadequate. Adequate ideas are formed in a rational and orderly manner. They are true and reveal the essences of things. The mind can deal with abstract ideas. Thus, the mind serves as the guarantee of true knowledge through reasoning and intuition. Spinoza's conception of adequate knowledge reveals an unrivaled optimism in the cognitive powers of the human being (Nadler, 2013).

According to Locke (1632-1704), at birth, the mind is like a blank slate (Tabula Rasa). Human beings experience the external world through the senses and the internal world through reflection. But, experience of reflection is not possible until the experience of sensation, i.e.

Sensation ⟶ Ideas ⟶ Reflection

The foundation of Locke's cognitive model is his division of human thinking into a series of interrelated but distinct processes—each with its own parameters and functions. According to him, all thinking falls into one of the two general categories of sensation or reflection. Sensation describes the way in which our senses convey into the mind several distinct perceptions of things. Reflection is the perception of the operations of our own mind within us. Believing that the mind is tabula rasa, he claims that these two modes of thinking, i.e. sensation and reflection, are the only origins of our ideas. The ideas provided by the senses form the fundamental building blocks of all human thought. According to Locke, all Reflective thought falls into one of the following sub-categories: Memory, Retention, Discerning, Comparing, Composition and Abstraction. The ideas passively received by the mind are simple ideas and ideas produced by compounding of simple ideas by the mind are complex ideas.

Leibniz (1646-1716) is both an empiricist as well as a rationalist. He argued against both materialist and dualist view of the mind. According to him, the world consists solely of one *type* of substance, though there are infinitely many substances of that type. His system sometimes contains ideas of relevance even to contemporary discussions in the cognitive sciences (Kulstad and Carlin, 2013). He believes that everything in this world has a mind or something analogous to a mind. Leibniz calls these mind-like substances 'monads.' While all monads have perceptions, only some of them are aware of what they perceive (he called them souls), and even fewer monads are capable of self-consciousness and rational perceptions (he called them minds). He argued that the mind is immaterial in nature. Therefore, it is impossible to construct a computer that can truly think or perceive like the human mind. These are significant positions of Leibniz in regard to cognitive science.

To explain the workings of our minds, David Hume (1711-1776) introduces the minimal amount of machinery he thinks is necessary to account for the mind's operations. He believes that everything (or every idea) we believe, is ultimately traceable to experience. He uses *perception* to designate any mental content. Perception is divided into two categories, *impressions* and *ideas*. In the *Treatise*, Hume proves his claim that our ideas are copies of our impressions. He gives an account of definition as a series of tests to determine cognitive content. It involves asking about the idea annexed to a particular term. If there is an idea annexed to the term, and it is complex, it has to be broken down into the simple ideas that compose it, and trace them back to their original impressions. If the process fails at any point, the idea in question lacks cognitive content. The mind has the natural ability to associate certain ideas based on three principles: resemblance, contiguity in time and place, and causation.

Kant's model of the mind was the dominant model in the empirical psychology that flowed from his work and toward the end of the 20th century, especially in cognitive science. Three ideas define the basic shape ('cognitive architecture') of Kant's model and one its dominant method. They have become part of the foundation of cognitive science.

1. The mind is complex set of abilities (functions).
2. The functions crucial for mental, knowledge-generating activity are spatio-temporal processing of and application of concepts to, sensory inputs. Cognition requires concepts as well as percepts.
3. These functions are forms of what Kant called synthesis. Synthesis is central to cognition.

Kant's transcendental method is regarded high in the contemporary cognitive science. According to it, to study the mind, the conditions necessary for experience are to be inferred. The core of this method is inference—the method of postulating unobservable mental mechanisms in order to explain observed behaviour. He held that some features of the mind and its knowledge had *a priori* origins. Kant believed that mind can be studied through transcendental method using transcendental arguments.

The 17th to 20th century debate between the rationalists and the empiricists on the origins of knowledge has contributed a lot towards the making of the field of cognitive science. Reflecting the empiricists' emphasis on experience as the source of knowledge, early experimental psychology focussed on phenomena of sensation and perception.

***Psychology***: In the field of psychology, the nature of the subject matter itself was a concern of controversy. It saw great changes during the late 18th century and throughout the 19th century.

Wilhelm Wundt (1832-1920) focussed on understanding the nature of consciousness. He urged psychology to be a 'true quantitative, experimental natural science'. The early psychologists of Wundt's school showed that mental activity can be broken down into more basic operations. Moreover, they developed objective methods for assessing mental activities. However, they also relied heavily on introspection.

But in 1885, Ebbinghaus proved Wundt's concept of psychology as wrong by inventing methods for the quantitative, experimental study of memory. William James (1842-1910) strongly argued that the subject matter of psychology should focus on understanding the functions of consciousness.

In 1896, Mary Whiton Calkins developed paired associate learning. She was the first to discover the paired associates technique involved in memory. Through experimental investigation, she paired colours and numerals together and found that people could remember numerals better when a vivid colour was consistently paired with the same numeral. Overall, she found the amount of exposure affected memory the most. Frequency of exposure (above vividness and how recent one was exposed to stimuli), was found to be the strongest factor for correct recall.

In 1913, behaviourism emerged, advocated by John B. Watson, who argued that psychology should focus on observable and measurable behaviour. Thorndike, Pavlov and Skinner were some psychologists who argued for the behaviouristic nature of psychology. They developed similar methods to study learning in animals.

In 1920, Clark Hull adopted Ebbinghaus' methods to study concept formation. He wanted to exclude all cognitive notions from the description and explanation of behaviour. He felt that the ultimate explanations in psychology should come in neuro-physiological terms. Hull's theory of learning is centreed on the necessity of reinforcement, defined in terms of "drive reduction." The behaving organism is viewed in the context of homeostatic model seeking equilibrium from "drive forces."

Edward Tolman (1932) developed molar approach to behaviour, i.e. the behaviour is guided by the goal determined by the cognitive structure of the organism.

In the early part of the 20th century, the Gestalt psychology (1912) emerged against the behaviourist psychology. They considered mind to play a major role in learning (behaviour modification). They emphasised the role of configuration or organisation in the perceptual field and highlighted the role of insight and understanding in learning or problem solving. A Gestalt psychologist, Kurt Lewin (1917), advocated that locomotion from one region of life space to another leads to change in the cognitive structure.

Jean Piaget (1920s) developed developmental psychology. He believed that real insight to human knowledge can be gained only through the study of its formation and evolution in childhood. He designed a proper framework to understand the structure, functioning and development of the cognitive network of the human mind. According to him, there are two aspects of human mind—cognitive structure and cognitive functioning.

J.S. Bruner (1915) was largely influenced by Piaget. The outcome of cognitive development is thinking. The intelligent mind creates from experience generic coding systems that permit one to go beyond the data to new and possibly fruitful predictions. Cognitive growth involves an interaction between basic human capabilities and culturally invented technologies that serve as amplifiers of these capabilities. Knowledge and understanding can take 3 different forms which are known as the modes of representation. These are—enactive, iconic and symbolic.

D. Ausubel (1918-2008) views knowledge as representing an integrated system. Ideas are linked together in an orderly fashion. The human mind follows logical rules for organising information into respective categories. Cognitive structure is hierarchically organised in terms of highly inclusive concepts under which are subsumed less inclusive sub-concepts and informational data (Ausubel, 1960). Subsumption allows us to absorb new information into our cognitive structures.

In the late 1950s and early 1960s, cognitive revolution took place. However, its root is in Jean Piaget's (1920s) interest in studying cognition and cognitive development in children. Then L. Vygotsky contributed to psychology in Piaget's line incorporating the social element in it. Cognitive revolution mostly developed when the researchers developed new methods to test predictions from computational models, which often specified the order in which specific mental activities take place. It led to the development of information processing approach to mental functioning. It along with the scientific approach to studying mind and belief in internal mental states later gave rise to cognitivism as the dominant model of the mind. At present, the field of psychology is dominated by the cognitivism and information processing models of mind.

***Anthropology***: Anthropology can be traced back to the earliest antiquity, when human beings first began to speculate about their own nature, origins and diversity. But as an explicitly defined field of inquiry, it is a product of the last two centuries of thought in the West. The development of anthropology consists of a complex interweaving of often opposing currents.

Mostly anthropologists have looked primarily at non-Western people. Anthropology began as a kind of natural history, a study of the people encountered along the frontiers of European expansion, and anthropologists have continued to use this approach. However, since 1930s, anthropology has been directly related to the social sciences. It analyzes and compares societies and their ways of life in search of theoretical generalisations, regularities of process and patterns. Thus, anthropology aimed at studying the human differences, which threw light on human nature and universals underlying diversity.

The history of anthropology goes back to the ancient civilisations of Egypt, Mesopotamia, China, India and Central America. It goes back more directly to the European thought of the Enlightment and to philosopher-scholars, notably J.J. Rousseau, who used fragmentary reports of exotic people to reflect on human nature, civilisation and society.

In the second half of the 19th century, the information on primitive people increased and was incorporated into comparative theoretical schemes. The major theme was evolution: reconstructing the development of human cultures from the earliest 'savage' stage of primitive promiscuity, through the progressive evolution of 'barbarism', and finally to 'civilisation' (Shashi, 1992).

The scope of anthropology is very broad and varied. It incorporates the archeological surveys, collection of folklore and mapping the gene sequences of organisms. It is also concerned with the psychic unity of humankind. It assumes that races and people all over the world are same, both in terms of evolutionary biology and manipulation of culture.

In 1735, the Swedish naturalist Carl Linnaeus Systema Naturae (first edition), attempted to differentiate various types of people scientifically. He identified humans as a single species. He did not explicitly rank types of people within a hierarchy. Johann Blumenbach divided the human race into separate and unequal varieties (Ingold, 1994) published 'On the Natural Varieties of Mankind'. Later, the discussion of human difference was shifted from the religious to the natural world. During the early and middle part of 19th century, the American school of anthropology thrived as the champion of polygenism (the doctrine of multiple origins). It sparked a debate between those who believed in the unity of humanity and those who argued for the plurality of origins and the antiquity of distinct types.

In the last part of 19th century and the early part of 20th century, Franz Boas, the father of American anthropology, argued that the distinct cultures of the people around the world should not be viewed within a hierarchy, but holistically and as relative to other cultures. He was a critic of the comparative method, which compared different groups and races within the rubrics of savage, barbarian, and civilised (Baker, 2008).

The second facet to the diversity of anthropological approaches lies in the fact that anthropology is not a single field, but is rather a contingent and unstable blend of subfields, each laden with its own history, theoretical agenda, and methodological preoccupations. In the American tradition, anthropology is distinguished into four subfields—physical, archaeological, cultural and linguistic. In the British tradition, however, there are only three subfields—physical, archaeological and social anthropology.

***Linguistics:*** The earliest known linguistic tradition arose in antiquity, in societies with established traditions of writing. The historical development of linguistics include the Babylonian tradition, the Hindu tradition, Greek linguistics, Roman tradition, Arabic and Hebrew traditions, developments in Europe (from 500 AD to early 19th century) and modern era (from late 19th century). In the Babylonian tradition, word lists are found in Sumerian and Akkadian language. The focus of the Hindu tradition was on grammar covering phonetics and morphology.

The Greek tradition emphasised on the origin of language, parts of speech systems, the relation between language and thought, and the relation between the two aspects of word signs—whether form and meaning are connected by nature or purely by convention. Another important contribution was the syntax. Their philosophical studies incorporated speculation on the nature of their language. The embryonic science of Greeks was passed on to the Romans, whose linguistics studies on Latin were in general the application of Greek thought, controversies and grammatical categories. Like the Greeks, the Romans were aware of word changes in both form and meaning from earlier texts but no significant headway was made in the study of etymology. Their primary interest was in morphology, particularly parts of speech and the forms of nouns and verbs. The Arabic tradition (7th-8th centuries) also focussed on morphology and phonetic descriptions.

In the Hebrew (9th century) tradition, grammatical tradition flourished.

In Europe, the 12th century, the notion of the universal nature of grammar emerged. With the advent of Renaissance (14th-17th century), language studies underwent a change as both local and non-Indo-European languages came under linguistic scrutiny. Once vernacular languages were deemed worthy of study and the world's diversity in linguistics structures was recognised, language studies turned to universal linguistic concepts and to the idea of universal grammar.

An important trend in the 17th century was the effort to compare and classify languages in accordance with their resemblances. The study of etymology also gained momentum. In the early 18th century, comparative and historical linguistics gained more consistency. In the late 19th and early 20th century, modern linguistics emerged. The focus was shifted from historical concerns of changes in language to the idea that a language can be viewed as a self-contained and structured system situated at a particular point in time. Phonetics and phonology were dominant in early modern linguistics.

Thus, in the early part of the history of linguistics, the concern was more about phonetics, morphology and syntax. The schools of linguistics that emerged may be divided under two types—formal and functional—according to whether they adopt an overall focus on form or on function.

*Neuroscience*: Modern neuroscience has deep roots in the history of Western biology, medicine and philosophy. The history of Neuroscience has been shaped by three major debates: mind vs. brain debate (monism/dualism); localism vs. holism; and the nature of neural communication. The brain has been regarded as the location of intelligence since pre-Socratic times, except Aristotle, who regarded heart to be the seat of intelligence. Then the debate turned to localism vs. holism. In medieval Europe, mental faculties were localised in the ventricles of the brain. Rene Descartes, Thomas Willis, Franz Joseph Gall, J.H. Jackson, P.P. Broca, Gustav Fritsch, Korbinian Brodman and Wilder Penfield were the advocates of localism.

Rene Descartes (1596-1650) provided the first idea of reflex action. He thought within a nerve, there are thin threads attached at one end to the sense organs. External stimuli pull on threads to open little gates to the ventricles (reflected) through the same hollow nerves, causing movement by inflating the muscles.

Thomas Willis (1621-1675) took this idea further and related it to actual brain structures. He believed the cortex to initiate voluntary movement whereas the cerebellum is involved only in involuntary movement. He coined the term 'neurology' in 1681.

Emanuel Swedenborg (1688-1772) gave the idea on importance of the cerebral cortex in sensation, cognition and movement. He argued that the cortex was the highest sensory and motor structure of the brain. He also had the idea of somatotopic organisation of motor function in the cerebral cortex. It implies that he localised control of the foot in the dorsal cortex, the trunk in an intermediate site, and the face and hand in the ventral cortex.

Franz Joseph Gall (1758-1828) was a German anatomist and anthropologist who took a naturalistic approach, and saw that objective observation was very important in recognising the different natures and functions of the brain. He concluded that all moral and intellectual faculties were innate; organisation played a major role in the way that these faculties were used; the brain was the driving force of peoples' different propensities and talents; and that the brain was composed of as many organs, as there were faculties. He believed that each region of the brain had a particular function and the size of the region affected the shaping of the skull. The larger regions depicts that these faculties were more developed.

P.P. Broca (1824-1880) was a pioneering neurosurgeon. His work concluded that language was localised to the frontal lobes of the brain. This finding eventually led to Broca putting his full support behind the localisation of function argument.

J.H. Jackson (1835-1911) reasoned that the cerebrum should have basic sensory-motor functions. He also inferred that different parts of the brain must be involved in the control of different muscle groups.

Gustav Fritsch (1838-1907) and Hitzig in 1870 reported in a paper that stimulation of portions of the cerebral cortex elicited movements and that the stimulation sites were somatotopically arranged.

Korbinian Brodman (1868-1918) categorised the brain into 52 distinct areas based on the cellular organisation of the cortex in the respective regions, and therefore helped to support the localist view.

Pierre Flourens (1794-1867) held holistic view of the brain. According to him, other parts of the brain could take over the function of damaged ones.

The electrical nature of the nervous system was discovered in the early 18th century. In the modern period i.e. 21st century, the communication of discrete neurons using electrical and chemical signals is well established and accepted. Today localisationism dominates neuroscience. However, extreme localism and holism is being replaced by 'connectionism', which believes that lower level or motor functions are strongly localised but higher level functions are the results of interconnections between brain areas. Cognitive science encompasses both localism and holism (Abraham Betchel, 2012). It recognises that as the behavioural techniques measure mental states, the neural techniques measure brain states. Neither replaces the other. Neuroscience provides converging evidence for the theories of cognitive psychology. A cognitive theory is best supported if both behavioural data and neurobiological data lead to exactly same conclusion.

***Artificial Intelligence***: The theoretical foundations of AI are philosophy, mathematics, economics, neuroscience, psychology, computer engineering, control theory and linguistics. Philosophers have floated the possibility of intelligent machines as a literary device to help us define what it means to be human. While Descartes saw "mechanical man" as a metaphor, Leibniz seemed to see the possibility of mechanical reasoning devices using rules of logic to settle disputes.

Leibniz and Blaise Pascal designed calculating machines that mechanised arithmetic. With early 20th century inventions in electronics and the post-World War II rise of modern computers, possibilities have given over to demonstrations.

Around the middle of the 20th century, cybernetics emerged, the concept of self-correcting and self-regulating systems (Weiner, 1948). This new science claimed that complex machines have to have control systems (that is, subcomponents of their architecture in charge of governing their inner functioning and their interactions with the external world), and that all such systems are to be considered instances of the same natural kind. Then robotics emerged and robots became powerful vehicles for testing our ideas about intelligent behaviour.

By 1944, Herbert Simon had laid the basis for the information-processing, symbol-manipulation theory of psychology. In the last half of 20th century, we had computational devices and programming languages powerful enough to build experimental tests of ideas about what intelligence is.

Alan Turing's 1950 seminal paper crystallised ideas about the possibility of programming an electronic computer to behave intelligently. There were numerous programmes actually solving problems that only intelligent people had previously been able to solve. Knowledge representation—both the formal and informal aspects—had become a cornerstone of every AI programme. Marvin Minsky's work on network representations of knowledge in frames directed much research. In 1956, John McCarthy, the father of artificial intelligence has been an advocate for using formal representations, in particular extensions to predicate logic.

**Formal Conception of Cognitive Science**

Cognitive science got its formal conception in the 1950s in a conference of scholars of various disciplines. It developed with the contributions of various thinkers in different disciplines in the symposium held on information science at the MIT, Boston on 11th September, 1956. A number of diverse disciplines like philosophy, psychology, computer science, neuroscience, linguistics and anthropology met at the symposium. Alan Newell and Herbert Simon emphasised on demonstrating the machine intelligence and the general laws underlying all thinking (Simon, 1969). Noam Chomsky's idea postulated computational transformations across the morphological units of language (Chomsky, 1957). George Miller discussed the limitations of human information processing. Jerome Bruner stressed that self-reports are crucial to understand complex cognition. In 1958, Colin Cherry and Donald Broadbent proposed that we think in the same terms as simpler information processing devices are described, as a set of input and output channels with known limited capacities (Broadbent, 1958). In 1960, the Centre for Cognitive Science was established at Harvard. In 1969, Ulreic Neisser published his book 'Cognitive Psychology'. The Sloan Foundation established a programme in cognitive science in 1976. The publication of the journal "Cognitive Science" and the first conference of the Cognitive Science Society at the University of California, San Diego in 1977 are regarded as the formalisation of the enterprise as a properly recognised scientific discipline. Thus, an interdisciplinary field of cognitive science was institutionalised. The Sloan Foundation conceived it as "an autonomous science of cognition". Since then, an annual meeting in the form of a conference is held by the Cognitive Science Society, and the developments and prospects in the field of cognitive science are discussed by thinkers and scholars of various disciplines.

## Relationship between Epistemology and Pedagogy

Epistemology is a branch of philosophy. It is the study of knowledge and what it means to know something (Shaffer, 2007). It studies the nature, methods, limitations, and validity of knowledge and belief and addresses questions such as: What is knowledge? How is knowledge acquired? What do people know? Pedagogy, on the other hand, is the art or science of being a teacher, generally referring to strategies or styles of instruction. It is not simply the act or method of teaching, rather it involves creating a proper social, educational and developmental environment which is aimed at facilitating learning based on specific norms and values. It is characterised by the personality, authority and professionalism of the teacher as he/she enters into interpersonal relationships with the learners for helping them to develop.

As a discipline pedagogy is closely related to philosophy. Epistemology is the theory of knowledge and pedagogy is the theory of teaching, the art of taking the comprehension of the knowledge by the teacher to its comprehension by the students. The theories of pedagogy are based on the theories of epistemology. Epistemologies are fruits on the imaginary tree of knowledge while pedagogy is the seed of its replication and transmission. Pedagogy is the way through which the epistemologies are shared and transmitted to the future generations. Personal epistemological beliefs reflect an individual's views about what knowledge is, how knowledge is gained, and the degree of certainty with which knowledge can be held. Pedagogical beliefs refer to preferred ways of teaching by teachers (Chai, 2010). The personal epistemological beliefs of the teacher influence his pedagogy. Hofer and Pintrich

(1997) argued that "beliefs about learning and teaching are related to how knowledge is acquired, and in terms of the psychological reality of the network of individuals' beliefs, beliefs about learning, teaching, and knowledge are probably intertwined". Some other researches have also supported this view. Thus, it can be said that epistemology and pedagogy are closely related to each other. Epistemology is related to pedagogy in three ways—teacher's knowledge about the content, teacher's knowledge about the skills and strategies and teacher's knowledge about his own learning.

## References

Abrahamsen, A., and Bechtel, W. (2012). History and the core themes. In K. Frankish and W. Ramsey (Eds.), *The Cambridge Handbook of Cognitive Science, pp. 9-28*. New York: Cambridge University Press.

Ausubel, D.P. (1960). The use of advance organisers in the learning and retention of meaningful verbal materials. *Journal of Educational Psychology, 51* (5), pp. 267-272.

Baker, L.D. (2008). Anthropology, History of. In J.H. Moore (Ed.), *Encyclopedia of race and racism*, pp. 93-97. USA: Macmillan Reference.

Broadbent, D. (1958). *Perception and Communication.* London: Pergamon Press.

Chai, C.S. (2010). Teachers' epistemic beliefs and their pedagogical beliefs: A qualitative case study among Singaporean teachers in the context of ICT supported reforms. *The Turkish Online Journal of Educational Technology, 9* (4), pp. 128-139.

Chomsky, N. (1957). *Syntactic structures*. Netherlands: Gravenhage.

Cottingham, J. (2009). Rene Descartes (1596-1650). In J. Dancy and E. Sosa (Eds.), *A Companion to Epistemology*, pp. 93-97. Blackwell Publishers Ltd.

Garrett, D. (2009). Spinoza, Benedict (1632-77). In J. Dancy and E. Sosa (Eds.), *A Companion to Epistemology*, pp. 488-490. Blackwell Publishers Ltd.

Hofer, B.K., and Pintrich, P.R. (1997). The development of epistemic theories: Beliefs about knowledge and knowing and their relation to learning. *Review of Educational Research, 67* (1), pp. 88-140.

Ingold, T. (1994). General Introduction. In T. Ingold (Ed.), *Companion Encyclopedia of Anthropology: Humanity, Culture and Social Life.* London & New York: Routledge.

Kulstad, M. and Carlin, L. (2013). Leibniz's philosophy of mind. *Stanford encyclopedia of philosophy*. Retrieved from http://plato.stanford.edu/entries/leibniz-mind/

Nadler, S. (2013). *Baruch Spinoza*. Retrieved December 15, 2014, from http://plato.stanford.edu/entries/spinoza/

Shaffer, D.W. (2007). *How Computer Games Help Children Learn*. New York: Palgrave.

Shashi, S.S. (Ed.). (1992). *Encyclopedia of Humanities and Social Sciences*, 2. New Delhi: Anmol Publications.

Simon, H.A. (1969). *The Sciences of the Artificial*. Cambridge, Massachusetts: MIT Press.

Stumpf, S.E. (1988). *Socrates to Sartre: A History of Philosophy*. McGraw Hill, Inc.

Terrence, I. (2009). Aristotle (384-322 BC). In J. Dancy and E. Sosa (Eds.), *A Companion to Epistemology*, pp. 27-31. Blackwell Publishers Ltd.

Weiner, N. (1948). Cybernetics: Or control and communication in the animal and the machine. Paris (Hermann and Lie), Cambridge, Massachusetts MIT Press.

# 4

# Cognitive Science in Indian Perspective

Modern psychology is scientific which makes its scope very limited. Human behaviour is varied in its nature to a very high degree. Therefore, it is not sufficient to fit it only in the framework of scientific approach. This gives rise to the necessity of studying indigenous psychology. The study of mind was always a concern of the Indian philosophy and psychology. Though the quest about mind has long been in India, but no interdisciplinary effort took place in Indian context. However, we can trace back the roots of cognitive science in the rich history of Indian culture, knowledge, philosophy and psychology. Indian philosophical ideas and theories play a crucial role in cognitive science. Various philosophical theories represent different traditions of exploring the mind. The ancient Indian texts are evident of the gradual development of mathematical, physical, linguistic, and psychological ideas. We find that the ancient Indians were greatly interested in cognitive science where they were so advanced that their insights may yet be useful to modern science.

## Indian Philosophy

India has been a home for many diverse groups of people from all over the world from ancient times. Therefore, Indian psyche is constituted of heterogeneous elements. It comprises of a mixture of beliefs and cultures. In Indian tradition, the four *Vedas*; 108 principal *Upanishads*; the six orthodox systems such as *Pûrva-Mîmânsâ, Uttara Mîmânsâ (Vedânta), Sâmkhya, Yoga, Nyâya, and Vaisesika*; the two heterodox systems—Jainism and Buddhism; *Dharma Shastra, Puranas, Ramayana, Mahabharata, Samhitas* and others are the repertoire of indigenous knowledge and constitute indigenous psychologies. These can be said as Wundt's "mental products", created by the ancient seers and sages, which serve as valuable lenses to understand the Indian psyche.

It is believed that the Vedas contain source of all knowledge—physical or metaphysical. They are the absolute mine containing knowledge repositories transcending time and space. They are considered as the supreme authority. Therefore, they had a profound influence upon one of the greatest and most ancient civilisations of the world. The word 'Veda' literally, means knowledge or the ultimate knowledge. The Vedic literature comprises of *Samhitas, Brahmanas, Aranyakas* and *Upanishads*. These literatures are considered to be direct revelations from God, embodying the supreme truth that could not be gained by any efforts of the human mind. Broadly, the Vedic scriptures comprise four great works, viz. *Rig Veda, Yajur Veda, Sama Veda* and *Atharava Veda*. *Upanishads* or *Vedanta* may be considered as the concluding parts of the Vedas. The philosophy of this school arose from where the Vedas ended, i.e., from the Upanishads. Sri Samkara's interpretation of it is considered to be the most powerful one, and his philosophy of *Advaitavada* is considered to be the representative of the Vedanta Philosophy. Vedanta believes in monism and its metaphysics is in accordance with this principle. They do not consider the world to be ultimately real.

The Buddhist school of philosophy came into being as a result of the enlightenment attained by Gautam Buddha. There are three central doctrines of the Buddhist philosophy which are well-recognised. The first doctrine is 'the Four Noble Truths'. The four noble truths are that there is misery; that there is a cause of misery; that there is cessation of misery; and that there is a path leading to the cessation of misery. The second doctrine is that of '*Pratityasamutpada*' or dependent origination. It says that everything in this world arises depending on the cause and is, therefore, impermanent. It is contained in the second noble truth. Buddha believed that suffering, which resulted due to ignorance, led to the endless cycles of birth and death. Only knowledge can break this cycle and liberate us. The third doctrine is well known as the Eight-fold Noble Path. It prescribes the following eight steps, which lead to enlightenment—right view, right intention, right speech, right action, right livelihood, right effort, right mindfulness and right concentration. This theory is contained in the fourth noble truth.

Jaina philosophy comes under the heterodox class of Indian philosophy, in the sense that it does not confirm *Vedas* as the ultimate authority. Realistic, relativistic, pluralistic, and atheistic are the qualities of the Jaina philosophy. It believes in the validity of perception, inference, and testimony as means of knowledge. It believes in *Syadavada,* or the theory of relativity of knowledge. They believe that reality has innumerable aspects. Human knowledge is finite and cannot comprehend them all. Therefore, our judgements can never be absolutely affirmative or negative but only relative, i.e., as viewed from a particular viewpoint out of the infinite possible ones. Related to this doctrine is their theory of *Anekantavada,* i.e., the theory of plurality of reality, which asserted that reality is neither absolutely permanent nor constantly changing. It is permanent with respect to substance since matter exists forever, but qualities are its accidental features, which come into being and perish. The Jaina metaphysics is pluralistic and divides all substances into souls (*jiva*) and non-soul (*ajiva*), and both are separately and independently real. It lays great emphasis upon the principle and practice of equality. It has found expression in non-violence. Non-violence received supreme importance and wide and practical application in Jainism. Non-violence consists in sincere and earnest exertion of oneself for the application of the principle of equality as far as possible in every field of life. It also deduced the law of *Karma* from the doctrine of equality of selves. The law of *karma* holds that all physical, mental and other distinctions between oneself and another are only adventitious, that is, due to karma, and not intrinsic. It maintains that the present is created in accordance with the past and that the future is created on the basis of the present.

The Samkhya School of philosophy was founded by Kapila. It believes in dualistic realism—the existence of two mutually independent ultimate realities, viz. *Prakrti* and *Purusa.* The essentially conscious *Purusa* is intelligent. It is the self, which is other than the body, the senses and the mind. It is a witness to the change going on in the world, but is itself eternal and not subject to change. Samkhya advocates the multiplicity of *Purusa. Prakrti* is unconscious and eternal. It is the first principle of the world. It is always changing and is meant to be enjoyed by the *Purusa*. It is constituted of the three *gunas* of *sattva, rajas,* and *tamas,* which are held in perfect equilibrium at the beginning of evolution. They consider earthly life as painful and liberation as cessation of all pain. Knowledge of distinction between the self and the not-self does not itself liberate us, but send us on the path of liberation, which is achieved through the spiritual training gained by the practice of Yoga.

Nyaya and Vaisesika schools are allied systems of philosophy. Both schools have similar views on causation, God, and liberation, while differing on a few. Nyaya School of philosophy is believed to be founded by Gotama while Vaiseshika was founded by Kanada. Nyaya subscribes to atomistic pluralism and logical realism. It asserts that there is suffering because the soul is in bondage due to ignorance of reality. The only way to end this suffering is by attaining liberation through knowledge. Therefore, Nyaya undertakes to establish the right ways of knowing. Vaiseshika is devoted primarily to metaphysics and ontology. It found its epistemological and logical counterpart in Nyaya. Considering how important the right knowledge of reality is for liberation, Vaiseshika devotes itself to the exposition of reality.

Mimansa School of philosophy was founded by Jaimini. It aimed at providing reasons in defence and favour of the ritualism prescribed by the *Vedas*. Their entire epistemology and metaphysics is formed to support this aim. They contend that the *Vedas* are self-existing and eternal. They are free of error and we should submit to their authority without questions. They claim that the rituals mentioned in the *Vedas*, when performed without prejudice, destroy the *karmas* and lead to liberation after death. Apart from the reality of the physical world, they also insist on the reality of the souls. The soul is considered to be immortal. There is no place for God in the Mimamsa philosophy. There is a shift from their idea of liberation as attainment of bliss to liberation as cessation of suffering.

Yoga School of philosophy was founded by Patanjali. It was closely allied with Samkhya, and accepts its epistemology and metaphysics. Yoga may be regarded as the practical side of Samkhya philosophy. It believes that discriminative knowledge (i.e. *vivekajnana*) is necessary for liberation and it can be attained through the practice of Yoga. There are eight steps prescribed for its practice, which emphasise internal and external cleansing, self-discipline physical fitness, and meditation, which result in alertness and mental strength.

## Cognitive Science in Indian Philosophy

Cognitive science was born in the western countries as a well-established discipline in the 1950s, but we can surely find its traces in the Indian knowledge system long back. The ancient Indian texts are evident that the study of mind has always been interesting for the Indian philosophers and psychologists. The pillars of the Indian philosophy such as the *Vedas* and the Indian schools of philosophy have interpreted about mind in various ways. Therefore, an attempt to trace the roots of cognitive science in the Indian philosophical system and the way they have described about the role, place and importance of our mind is inevitable in discussing the history of cognitive science.

In traditional Indian thought, psychology was never a subject independent of philosophy. Jadunath Sinha was the first scholar to attempt a constructive survey of Indian psychology. According to him, Indian psychology was based on introspection and observation. It was not empirical or experimental, but was based on metaphysics. He discussed the nature of cognition, perception and emotion in the light of various schools of Indian philosophy like Buddhism, Jainism, Samkhya, Vedanta, etc. He regarded cognition to be one of the three fundamental modes of consciousness, the other two being affection and conation. Sensation, perception, memory, imagination and thinking are the kinds of cognition.

Indian psychology regards mind to be very powerful. But difference lies among individuals in using the powers of mind. It is because some individuals are not aware of their power of mind. Some people are aware of it but are not able to express their power of mind, because of weak will power and disintegrated emotions. Thus, it relates mind with emotions. Swami Vivekananda was one of those philosophers who regarded mind as an important factor of an individual's life. He considered mind to be an infinite library of the universe, as the source of all knowledge in the world is the mind. But sometimes it is covered, and when it is slowly discovered, it is called as the process of learning. According to him, the mind is the subtle part of the body.

According to Indian psychology, the mind is the instrument of perception. It believes that an unstable and unsteady mind cannot perceive things correctly. The behaviour patterns of an individual are affected by their mental conditions. To realise the ultimate truth, a stronger mental development than the ordinary mental health is required. A transparent mind is required to see the reflection of our soul or the real or higher self. An idealistic civilisation is possible only when the mind is focussed on the permanent reality within us. Indian psychologists say that the primary objective of life is the ultimate realisation of the divinity of man, or the manifestation of the divinity that is already in him (as said by Swami Vivekananda). According to Patanjali, there are five states of mind: *kshipta* (extreme restless state when the mind has tension and many emotional conflicts and longings); *mura* (inert stage in which the mind has lower conscious and unconscious passions, such as anger, lust and so forth); *vikshipta* (state in which the mind is partly concentrated at times); *ekagra* (concentrated state); niruddha (superconscious state). These states of mind have been explained by Swami Vivekananda as (Akhilananda, 1952):

> *The Chitta (mind) manifests itself in the following forms—scattering, darkening, gathering, one-pointed and concentrated. The scattering form is activity. Its tendency is to manifest in the form of pleasure or pain. The "darkening" form is dullness which tends to injury... The "gathering" form is when it struggles to centre itself. The "one-pointed" form is when it tries to concentrate and the concentrated form is what brings us to Samadhi.*

Indian psychologists' recognise that although the present condition of mind is created by the past thoughts and actions, the present changed mode of living and thinking effectively transforms the mind.

Though there are differences of opinion among the different schools of Indian philosophy regarding the sources of cognition or knowledge, all the systems of Indian philosophy have emphasised perception as the source of valid cognition or knowledge. For the Charvaka philosophy, perception is regarded as the only source of valid cognition. The Buddhist and the Vaisesika philosophy accept both perception and inference as sources of knowledge. The Samkhya philosophy accepts perception, inference, and verbal testimony; the Nyaya accepts perception, inference, comparison, and verbal testimony. The Mimansa philosophy accepts presumption in addition to the four sources accepted by the Nyaya. Another school of Mimansa and the Advaita Vedanta accept non-apprehension (*anupalabdhi*) in addition to the previous five sources of knowledge. The Jaina philosophy accepts two more sources of valid cognition, namely, the use of a type of counterfactual conditional, and memory (Shaw, n.d.).

If we attempt to trace cognitive science in Indian psychology, we have to take hold of its roots in the diverse traditions of knowledge deliberated upon in various texts (*Shastra*), as well as the practices, artifacts and meanings embodied in various forms (Dalal and Misra, 2010). It is a result of rigorous observation, experimentation and reflection, continuous contemplation and sharing of personal accounts of inner experiences. It is dynamic, progressive and self-determined.

## Cognitive Science in Vedic Philosophy

The *Vedas* deal with the knowledge framework from a holistic perspective with universal application. The *Vedas* present different dimensions of knowledge encompassing *Jnana, Vijnana, Samjnana and Prajnana.* In Vedic view, the mind and the outer world is complementary in nature. This complementary nature makes it possible for our minds to comprehend the universe. In the *Katha Upanishad* and the *Bhagavad Gita*, the mind is called as the driver who holds the reins to the horses (senses), but next to the mind sits the true observer, the self (Kak, 1997). Yajnavalakya estimated long before Plato the importance of intuition. Intuition may be distinguished as pre-reflective and post-reflective, sub-conceptual and supra-conceptual, and sub-mental and supra-mental. The *Upanishads* throw much light on the development of vital and higher mental intuition, but their great services lie in going beyond them and in emphasising supra-mental intuitions. According to *Samkara Vedanta*, cognition is not perceived by another cognition but by itself. Thus, it is self-luminous. A mental mode may either apprehend an external object, when it is modified into the object, or it may apprehend itself. There is direct and immediate consciousness of a cognition; a cognition is directly apprehended by itself. Moreover, a cognition cannot be the object of another cognition as a cognition is not of the nature of an unconscious object. A cognition is conscious, while an object is unconscious. They believe in six means of valid knowledge, viz. perception, inference, comparison, testimony, presumption, and non-cognition. As the Vedas cover extensively the various dimensions of mind, knowledge and intellect, they are of vital importance for proper research in the domain of cognitive science.

## Cognitive Science in Buddhist Philosophy

The Buddhist tradition has throughout its history given attention to the workings of mind. For example, the *Dhammapada*, discusses about the power one's perception of a situation has in determining the emotional quality one experiences in that situation. Understanding the working of mind is considered important to progress on the path and the achievement of awakening (*bodhi*) (Payne, 2002). Throughout Buddhist thought, one frequently finds the phrase "body, speech, and mind" which describes the existential totality of human beings. This view can be understood as emphasising the embodied nature of human existence, establishing at least a prima facie similarity with the embodied-enactive approach to cognitive science. Buddhism believes in perception and inference as the means of valid knowledge. It also believes in testimony, but reduces it to inference. Buddha recommended avoiding extremes and following the middle path, which leads to knowledge, enlightenment, and, consequently, nirvana or liberation.

Nagarjuna, the famous Buddhist monk believes in the acquisition of knowledge through the six sensory organs—eye, ear, tongue, skin, nose and the mind. The first five senses are the gates of our knowledge of the outside world. These senses strictly confine themselves to their own particular spheres and do not overlap each other. The *Abhidhamma Pitaka* upholds the view that pure sensation is vague and hazy. To have a correct knowledge of the world around us, the mind must be active. Boundary line for the things perceived must be set resulting in perception followed by imagination. The Buddhist philosophy believes that cognition is self-luminous; it apprehends itself but not an external object as there is no such object. Cognition is not apprehended by the self because there is no self at all.

## Cognitive Science in Jain Philosophy

In Jaina philosophy, *jnana* is an intrinsic property of the *Jiva*. As such the process of knowing must be interpreted to be the process of the manifestation of the intrinsic nature of the *Jiva*. *Jnana* or knowledge is of five different kinds according to the stages of the spiritual development of the soul, viz. *mati, sruta, avadhi, manah-paryaya and kevala*. *Mati jnana* refers to the ordinary process of sense experience. *Sruta jnana* is the knowledge revealed by the scripture. *Avadhi jnana* corresponds to what is known as clairvoyance. It is a kind of extra sensory perception, not ordinarily available to all persons, though it is latent in everyone. *Manah-paryaya jnana* refers to the knowledge of thoughts in other minds. *Kevala jnana* refers to the infinite knowledge which the soul attains as the result of complete liberation or *moksa* (Chakravarti, 1958).

According to the Jaina philosophy, cognition is perceived by itself in apprehending its object; it is not perceived by any other cognition. Manikya Nandi defines valid knowledge as the determinate cognition of itself and an object, which has been known before. It has practical efficiency and pragmatic utility. It apprehends itself and an object as it really is. It believes that cognition in itself is valid, since it cannot contradict itself. It is valid or invalid in relation to its object. Valid knowledge is of two kinds—immediate knowledge and mediate knowledge. Immediate knowledge is distinct consisting apprehension of an object with its specific qualities without the mediation of any other knowledge. Mediate knowledge is indistinct, devoid of perceptual vividness.

## Cognitive Science in Samkhya Philosophy

According to Samkhya, knowledge involves four factors: the knower (*pramatr*), the known (*prameya*), the means of knowledge (*pramana*) and the valid knowledge (*prama*). Kapila defines valid knowledge as determinate knowledge of an object not known before. According to Vijnanabikshu, the pure self is the knower (*pramatr*); the mode of *buddhi* modified into the form of the object is the means of knowledge (*pramana*); relfection of the mode of *buddhi* with the form of the object in the self is valid knowledge (*prama*); the object apprehended by the mode of *buddhi* reflected in the self is the known (*prameya*). The knowledge of the self, which is the result of the mode of *buddhi*, is valid knowledge.

The organs of sight, hearing, touch, taste and smell are the gates of our knowledge. Samkhya accepts three sources of valid knowledge: Perception, inference and scriptural testimony. It believes that the *manas* (mind), the *Mahat* (intellect=*buddhi*) and the *purusha* play a role in 'producing' knowledge. *Mahat* evolves as a result of predominance of *sattva*. Since it is an evolution of *Prakriti*, it is made of matter. But it has psychological, intellectual aspect known as *buddhi* or intellect. *Mahat* or intellect helps man in judgment and discrimination. It helps to distinguish between the subject and the object. *Mahat*, by its inherent association with *sattva*, possesses qualities like luminosity and reflectivity. *Manas* or the mind in co-ordination with the sense-organs, receives impressions from the external world, transforms them into determinate perceptions and conveys them to the experiencer or the ego. These percepts are carried to the *Mahat*. By its own applications, *Mahat* gets modified. *Mahat* takes the form of the particular object. This transformation of *Mahat* is known as *vritti* or modification of *buddhi*. A cognition is considered as a psychic function or a function of the psyche or *buddhi*. Therefore, a cognition cannot apprehend itself; nor can it apprehend an object. It is apprehended by the self. It is the self that apprehends an object, and apprehends the cognition of the object.

## Cognitive Science in Nyaya-Vaisesika Philosophy

According to the Nyaya-Vaisesika philosophy, cognition is an object of perception; but it is not perceived by itself but by another cognition through the internal organ, mind, just as we perceive an external perception through the external senses. Gautama holds in his *Nyayasutra* that we derive particular knowledge of things through perceptions arising from specific organs (Dasgupta, 1949). The *pramanas* are the means by which individuals attain accurate cognition. The four *pramanas* are perception, inference, analogical reasoning, and testimony (Dasti, 2012). Perceptual cognition arises by means of the connection between sense faculty and object, is not dependent on words, is non-deviating, and is determinate. The absence of simultaneous cognition from all of the senses indicates the presence of a faculty—the *manas*—which governs selective attention. It processes the information of the senses and governs mnemonic retrieval and a perceptive awareness of mental states. An inferential cognition is preceded by perception. The fundamental characteristic of inferential cognition is that it is a cognition which follows from another cognition owing to their being conceptually connected in some way. Analogy makes an object known by similarity with something already known. Testimony is the assertion of a qualified speaker of information apprehended by the initial cognition to an epistemically responsible hearer. Nyaya epistemologists speak of cognition (*jnana, buddhi, upalabdhi, pratyaya*) as generally immediate awareness states of a mind-independent (according to Nyaya) external reality. Ontologically, cognitions are considered properties (*gunas*) of individual selves (*atmans*). Memory dispositions, when triggered, generate cognition about the past.

The Vaisesika agrees with the Nyaya in its doctrines of valid knowledge (*prama*) and its extrinsic validity and invalidity. It accepts only perception and inference as valid independent pramanas. It reduces comparison and verbal testimony to inference. Valid knowledge is what apprehends the real nature of its object. Invalid knowledge is what apprehends an object as it is not in its real nature. Validity of knowledge is produced by the excellence (*guna*) of its causes and invalidity of knowledge is produced by the defects (*dosa*) of its causes. The Vaisesika, like the Nyaya, adopts the realistic test of correspondence of knowledge with its object and the pragmatic test of practical efficiency.

## Cognitive Science in Yoga Philosophy

The Yoga philosophy calls it *citta*, what is called *Mahat* or *Buddhi* in Samkhya. *Citta* stands for all that is psychological in man and is the seat of all experiences and repository of their residual effects (Paranjpe, 1984). It may be generally translated to the mind as it refers to the living principles of human life, the senses, the ego and the intellect.

The Yoga philosophy advocates realism. It holds that external objects are real. They are apprehended as they are in themselves by mental modes. There is correspondence between the mental modes and their object. The modes of *buddhi* are modified into their forms. The forms of cognitions correspond to the forms of their objects. Novelty, correspondence, non-contradiction and service ability are the marks of truth. The *pramanas* are the means of valid knowledge. Patanjali, like the Samkhya, recognises three *pramanas*—perception, inference and testimony.

According to the *Yoga Sutras of Patanjali* "the stilling of the changing states of the mind" is Yoga (Bryant, 2009). It is believed that we are essentially an all-perfect entity totally free from any imperfection and not subject to any undesirable, imperfect, negative experience whatsoever. The subject-matter of the science of Yoga is how to give back to us once again that perfect state in which we are always there. The imperfect-experience condition which is distressing, going up and down, arises due to our association with *Prakriti* or Nature that is ever unsteady. *Prakriti* is made up of many things—the five elements, the *Prana,* the senses, and the mind in its different modes, each mode having its own variations. This association with *Prakriti* has to be broken to regain the independent status of everlasting joy. The philosophy of Yoga provides solution for this. The first two steps of Raja Yoga given by Patanjali are clear indications of the emphasis of Indian psychology. *Yama* (ethical observation and mental control) and *niyama* (physical cleansing and dietetic restrictions and some forms of mental training) are purification processes for higher mental development (Akhilananda, 1952).

The mind has got many variations—*Vasanas, Samskaras,* imaginations, anger, passion, greed, hatred, envy, jealousy, worry, selfishness, attachment. The intellect has its own variations—clear perception, unclear perception and wrong perception. According to the Yoga Sutra, varieties in perception of a single object depend upon the varieties of the constitution of minds. The various stresses through which the minds of individuals pass determine the variety in cognition and perception of objects. This may be due to the variety in the nature of the minds themselves. This means the impression formed by the object upon minds is not always uniform on account of the different receptive capacities of the perceiving minds. The moods of the mind—the *vrittis* of the *manas*—influence the reaction which they set up in respect of the impress that the object makes upon them, so that even if the object is the same, the perceptions and cognitions may be variegated.

## Cognitive Science in Mimansa Philosophy

Mimansa philosophy attaches a lot of importance to the verbal testimony. Jaimini accepts the 'word' or the '*shabda*' as the only means of knowledge which is necessarily the Vedic word (according to Jaimini). This system strongly contends that since the Vedas are *apaurusheya* (not authored by an individual), they manifest their own validity. There are two schools of Mimamsa philosophy—the Prabhakara School and the Kumarila school. The Prabhakara School accepts the validity of perception, inference, comparison, testimony, and postulation. Prabhakara also regards apprehension (*anubhuti*) as a means of valid knowledge. He identifies *pramana* with *prama* (valid knowledge), and regards cognition as manifesting itself, and not as inferable from the cognisedness of its object. According to him, all cognitions as cognitions are valid, and their invalidity is due to their disagreement with the nature of their objects. The Kumarila School adds non-cognition to this list of *pramanas*. It regards a cognition as a means of valid knowledge (*pramana*) because it is apprehension. Kumarila regards cognisedness (*jnatata*) produced by a cognitive act as its result (Sinha, 1985). According to him, novelty, non-contradiction and correspondence with the object are the tests of truth. He recognises the intrinsic validity and the extrinsic invalidity of knowledge. The validity of knowledge arises from the essential nature of its causes unaffected by defects, and is known by the knowledge itself. Savara and Kumarila recognise six *pramanas* viz. perception, inference, comparison, testimony, presumption and non-apprehension.

## Indian Cognitive Science in Modern Perspective

Thus we can see that the Indian philosophy and psychology have long ago described what cognitive science endeavours to discuss in modern times. The concepts of cognitive science are weaved in the Indian philosophy and psychology. We can find a lot of discussion on cognition, though the term 'cognitive science' was not in use. The *Vedas* have emphasised on the intuitive knowledge and have elaborate discussions on intuition, mind and intellect. The Buddhist philosophy has also registered mind as the sixth sense which allows us to have correct knowledge of the world. It has emphasised on imagination after perception. The Jaina philosophy has interpreted knowledge as the intrinsic property of the individual. Samkhya philosophy also believes that mind and intellect plays a great role in producing knowledge. The Nyaya philosophy holds that the mind processes the information carried by the senses. The Yoga philosophy believes that different nature and constitution of mind leads to differences in perception of the external world.

The Vedanta, the Buddhist and the Mimamsa philosophy regarded cognition as self-luminous. But according to the Vedanta, a cognition cognises itself and according to the Buddhist, a cognition is not apprehended by any other cognition and Mimamsa believes that cognition is not inferable from the cognisedness of its object. While Samkhya and Nyaya-Vaisesika believes that cognition is not perceived by itself, according to Jainism, cognition is perceived by itself in apprehending its object. According to Yoga philosophy, our mind cognises the objects as it really is.

An elaborate study of the Indian philosophy reveals that every major problem in cognitive science, from the nature of subjectivity to the possibility of conscious computers is casted differently in Indian approach to cognitive science. Now the question is to engage with the issue of how Indian philosophy will transform the practice of cognitive science. Indian philosophy based cognitive science should break the co-dependence of cognitive science with syntactic symbolic metaphors as well as mechanical technologies. According to the Indian philosophies, knowledge can be part of our nature and yet be utterly grounded in experience. It can be noted that the basically empiricist attitude of Indian philosophy almost avoids the 'rationalist-empiricist divide' that prevail in modern western philosophy and cognitive science. The field of cognitive science can be taken to deeper understanding based on the Indian philosophical concepts.

In Indian philosophical perspective, knowledge is considered as an integrated concept. It is an action or reaction or response to a particular situation with a view to face the challenges of the life. Therefore, knowledge cannot be fragmented or partial. The information can never be considered as knowledge in Indian philosophical perspective. Further, information is converted into knowledge when it is manifested with understanding. Again the level of understanding may vary from individual to individual. The cognitive science deals with that level of understanding. Again, knowledge merges into wisdom. Here the question comes—'Can wisdom be transformed or transmitted?' Certainly, the answer is no. Logical analysis reveals that if the connotative concept is increased the denotation is decreased. The Indian philosophy looked into knowledge as *vidya* and there are two types of *vidya* such as *apara vidya* and *para vidya. Apara vidya* can be equated with knowledge, even with wisdom. But *Para vidya* is the highest or supreme knowledge which has neither substitute nor any procedure to measure it. If we look into cognitive science in tune with the development of memory and understanding or image through the light of the Indian philosophy then we think, a comprehensive idea can emerge which can resolve the debates among the various schools of cognitive sciences.

## References

Akhilananda, S. (1952). *Mental Health and Hindu psychology.* London: George Allen and Unwin Ltd.

Bryant, E. (2009). The Yoga Sutras of Patanjali: A new edition, translation and commentary. In *Internet Encyclopedia of Philosophy—A Peer Reviewed Academic Resource.*
Retrieved from www.iep.utm.edu/*yoga*/?

Chakravarti, A. (1958). Jainism: Its philosophy and ethics. In S. Radhakrishnan (Ed.), *The Cultural Heritage of India,* I, pp. 414-433. Kolkata: The Ramakrishna Missison Institute of Culture.

Dalal, A.K. and Mishra, G. (2010). The core and context of Indian psychology. *Psychology and Developing Societies,* 22 (1), pp. 121-155.

Dasgupta, D.C. (1949). *Educational Psychology of the ancient Hindus.* Calcutta: Motilal Banarasi Das.

Dasti, M.R. (2012). Nyaya. In *Internet Encyclopedia of Philosophy—A Peer Reviewed Academic Resource.*
Retrieved from *www.iep.utm.edu/nyaya/?*

Kak, S.C. (1997). On the science of consciousness in ancient india. *Indian Journal of History of Science,* 32 (2), pp. 105-120.

Paranjpe, A.C. (1984). *Theoretical Psychology: The Meeting of East and West.* New York and London: Plenum Press.

Payne, R.K. (2002). Buddhism and Cognitive Science: Contributions to an enlarged discourse. *The Pacific World Journal,* 3 (4), pp. 1-13.

Shaw, J.L. (n.d.). *Sources of knowledge.*
Retrieved from www.philosophyandculture.org/PDFs/05_03_Jay_Shaw.pdf?

Sinha, J. (1985). *Indian Psychology: Cognition,* I. Calcutta: Motilal Banarasi Das.

# 5

# Cognitive Science and Education

This chapter presents an analysis of the components of cognitive science which have implications in the field of education. The components have been analysed by studying them from cognitive science perspective, their cognitive theories and their pedagogical implications. Both cognitive science and education are very broad fields and incorporates a wide spectrum. It is realised that it is difficult to discuss all the components of cognitive science relevant to education at one place. Therefore, the discussion has been limited to some areas of cognitive science which have been identified as relevant to education, i.e. Learning, Problem Solving, Creativity, Intelligence and Attention.

## LEARNING

To understand the educational process, it is necessary to understand learning. The understanding of learning requires knowing about problems of representation, of input (perception), of output (performance), and of thought and inference. Learning has been understood with appropriate depth only recently. It is more than simple accumulation of knowledge. Though accumulation of knowledge is indeed one form of learning, but there are other things that must be considered. It includes restructuring one's knowledge, reformulating the basis of understanding as a result of new concepts and new experiences, tuning of behaviour, acquiring of skills and understanding to the extent of expertise, smoothness, efficiency, and effortlessness.

Kimble defined learning as "relatively permanent change in behavioural potentiality that occurs as a result of reinforced practice."

Gardner Murphy believed learning to cover "every modification in behaviour to meet environmental requirements."

Learning is a process rather than a product. It involves 'change in behaviour' which is relatively 'permanent' resulting from 'experience'. This means in learning process, there should be some kind of change in the behaviour of the individual, be it positive or negative. But this change should be relatively permanent, temporary changes are not considered as learning. And this change must result due to experience or practice, not due to fatigue or sickness or drugs, etc. Psychologists define experience as the product of interactions between individual and the environment. However, the question remains as 'how long new information is retained so as to be considered as permanent or as a learnt behaviour'. Learning is a goal-directed process i.e. we modify our behaviour largely to adapt ourselves to our environment. It is a construct or an idea that cannot be observed overtly. But it can be inferred from the behaviour of the individual. It is difficult to define learning universally as it has been explained from different perspectives by various philosophers and psychologists which led to formulation of a large number of theories of learning. It can be said that a paradigm shift has taken place from the associationist theories to the cognitive theories and now to a whole enterprise of more complex and sophisticated learning programmes.

## Learning in Cognitive Science

Cognitive science attempts to understand learning in a broader sense and from an interdisciplinary perspective. From the philosophical viewpoint, empiricism and rationalism provide valuable background for comparing and classifying modern learning theories. According to empiricism, our concepts or ideas come from sense impressions. Knowledge comes from experience, from experience to impression and then to idea. Rational or a priori knowledge of a proposition is also regarded as necessary—being result of an *a priori* judgment. No experience can ever grant such judgements truth but only assumed as strictly universal. A psychologist understands learning as the modification of behaviour as a result of experience or training. Two major types of learning are generally distinguished, depending on the level at which the psychological processes are integrated into the cognitive system—elementary (stimulus-driven) learning and complex (representation mediated) learning (Houde, 2003). In cognitive neuroscience, it is conventional to distinguish between two types of learning, according to whether implicit or explicit memory is involved. Each type calls upon different brain structures. Skill learning involves an adaptive modification of behaviour achieved through task repetition. Learning that takes place in intentional memorisation situations is called intentional learning (Decety and Koenig, 2003). Artificial intelligence (AI) studies the mechanisms to enable a machine to learn. It aims at building machines capable of adapting and acting more efficiently. Another task of artificial intelligence is simulating certain aspects of human or animal learning. Such simulations improve our understanding of the learning process (Ganascia, 2003). It can be said that cognitive science regards learning as a change in the cognitive abilities rather than in behaviour. However, the change in cognitive abilities is explicit in the behaviour of the individual.

## Learning in Education

Leaning is a key concept in the field of education. All the efforts in an educational system are ultimately directed towards improving the efficiency of learning. But due to various factors, learning becomes mere accumulation of knowledge or rote memory or cramming or getting good grades in the test. Learning is largely seen as a product rather than a process. Therefore, it is necessary to understand learning and the cognitive processes underlying learning. In pedagogy, it is important to consider the cognitive capabilities that the learners should have and not to develop only knowledge. Further, it is also important to determine how pedagogy will be designed to facilitate the cognitive processes underlying learning. There are 12 cognitive processes underlying learning—prediction, modeling, experimentation, evaluation, diagnosis, planning, causation, judgment, influence, teamwork, negotiation and describing (Schank, 2011). Pedagogy should be designed based on these cognitive processes.

## Cognitive Processes Underlying Learning

Roger Schank (2011), a contributor in the making of the field of cognitive science, defined "learning as improvement in one's cognitive processes". He listed 12 cognitive processes underlying learning—prediction, modeling, experimentation, evaluation, diagnosis, planning, causation, judgment, social influence, teamwork, negotiation and describing. The first four may be grouped under conceptual processes, next four under analytic processes and the last four under social processes. All these are considered as cognitive processes in the sense that the steps of these processes are based in thought rather than in action.

*Prediction*: Learning to predict requires repeated practice in each domain of knowledge. This is experiential learning by trial and error. The cognitive issue is building up a large case base according to expectation (prediction) failures.

*Modeling*: Processes need to be learned in order to effectively participate in them and in order to propose changes in them. This can be learned through designing it, modifying it and participating in simulations of it. This is termed as modeling.

*Experimentation*: Learning to analyse what has worked out and what has not and why is an important aspect of a rational life. These things can be learned by living and talking about our experiences, thus creating a database stories that we can rely on later. The cognitive task here is story creation, comparison, indexing and modification.

*Evaluation*: Learning to make judgments is about learning to notice, to describe, and to appreciate. Making value judgment requires understanding what our values are. These are learned consciously.

*Diagnosis*: Diagnosis means both reasoning from evidence and understanding what constitutes important evidence. In diagnosis, both the process and the domain knowledge is important. People learn to do diagnosis and to understand what causes what, consciously. This is knowledge that can be taught by experts as a part of the process of diagnosis.

*Planning*: Learning to plan has two components—being able to create a plan and being able to modify an existing plan for new purposes. The first one is important to learn how to do, but it is the latter ability that makes one proficient at planning. Planning from first principle is very difficult. Mostly people just modify an old plan by remembering the mistakes in the previous plans and making improvements upon them. One can modify plans from one domain of knowledge to use in another but this is not easy and requires a level of abstraction that is very important to learn.

*Causation*: A cause has been defined as that which produces something, or as the origin or motive of an action, or as that which explains why something occurs or comes into existence. Aristotle's theory of causation held that there are four kinds of causes—efficient causes (which brings about changes), material causes (on which the changes occur), formal causes (distinctive shapes or forms or properties belonging to the final results) and final causes (purposes or aims). Causal knowledge is knowledge fixed to a domain of inquiry. It is important to discuss the cases with others because it helps in indexing them in the mind, enabling retrieval whenever needed.

*Judgment*: There are two forms of judgments—through experience (without knowing the reasons) and through reasoning based on evidence. To learn to make objective judgments, one needs constant feedback either from a teacher or a colleague or from reality. They should be able to analyse their successes and failures and articulate their reasoning.

*Influence*: Here, influence means understanding how others respond to our behaviour and recognising consciously and unconsciously how to improve the process. Conscious awareness about mistakes can help in learning to behave differently.

*Teamwork*: It refers to understanding our own as well as others' roles and responsibilities as members of a team. It is learning how to achieve goals in a group, consciously allocating roles, managing inputs from others, coordinating actors and handling conflicts.

*Negotiation*: It refers to making a deal. That is to analyse the positive and negative sides of a deal and consciously selecting a better option than the other.

*Describing*: It refers to creating and using conscious descriptions and analysis of situations to identify faults. Describing is important in order to get help from people who may know more about the situation than we do. It is important even to put the small incidences in order so as to understand the situation better.

## Theories of Learning

Psychologists have tried to understand 'learning' by explaining it through behaviourism (classical and operant conditioning). But some psychologists disagreed to the behavioural explanation of learning. These psychologists (at first, the gestalt theorists) explained it as a cognitive process. After this, many cognitive theories were proposed.

The cognitive theories of learning are backed by rationalism rather than empiricism. They emphasise on the changes in mental processes that people use in their efforts to understand the world. From a cognitive perspective, learning is a change in a person's mental structures resulting in demonstration of different behaviours. These "mental structures" include schemas, beliefs, goals, expectations, and other components. Cognitive learning theories stress the importance of mental processes and focus on what is happening in the learner. An underlying principle of all cognitive theories is that the mental processes allow learners to actively interpret and organise information. The cognitive theories are based on some general assumptions—

(a) Cognitive processes are the focus of study.
(b) Knowledge is organised.
(c) Though objective and systematic observations of behaviour should be the focus of scientific inquiry, inferences about unobservable mental processes can often be drawn from such behaviour.
(d) Learning involves the formation of mental associations that are not necessarily reflected in overt behaviour changes.
(e) Individuals are actively involved in the learning process.
(f) Some learning processes may be unique to human beings.
(g) Learning is a process of relating new information to previously learned information.

Many cognitive theories have emerged after the Gestaltists established themselves as a diversion from the traditional connectionist approach on the account of difficulty in explaining the learning process or behaviour involving higher cognitive abilities. Here, a brief account of the cognitive theories has been presented.

### *Gestalt Theory*

Three German psychologists—Max Wertheimer, Kurt Koffka and Wolfgang Kohler developed a new approach of studying behaviour. This approach considered learning as the result of organisation of perception (insight) by the learner. The German word 'Gestalt' means form, pattern, structure—an integrated whole. The basic idea underlying this theory is that a thing cannot be understood by the study of its constituent parts but by the study of it as a totality or whole. Learning is not interpreted by random steps, not by trial and error, not by conditioning, but interpreted as purposive, exploratory and creative. While learning, the learner perceives the situation as a whole and after seeing and evaluating the different relationships takes the proper decision in an intelligent way.

### *Tolman's Theory*

Though E.C. Tolman was a behaviourist, he combined the advantages of cognitive theories and connectionist theories. His theory includes aspects like knowledge, thinking, planning, inference, purpose and intention. He developed molar approach to behaviour, in place of molecular approach. Molar behaviour is purposive and goal oriented. It means that behaviour is guided by the goal determined by the cognitive structure of the organism. He developed the concept of "cognitive map". It refers to acquisitions, representation and use of spatial information to perform tasks. According to him, learning is an affair of sign gestalt, formation, refinement, selection and invention.

### *Lewin's Cognitive Field Theory*

Kurt Lewin, another gestalt psychologist emphasised more on the development of behaviour and motivation than on previous experiences of the learner for developing insight. He gave concepts like life space, topology, valence, etc. to understand the mental structure. According to him, learning is behaviour, locomotion from one region of life space to another. This leads to change in cognitive structure which is learning. Lewin's psychological interest was in the motivating conditions of person-environment situations. Whereas behaviourists study psychology as a series of events, the 'field' in 'field psychology' implies that psychologically interpreted everything happens at once. 'Field' is defined as 'the totality of coexisting facts which are conceived of as mutually interdependent'.

### *Piaget's Theory*

According to Piaget, human infants do not start out as cognitive beings. Instead, out of their perceptual and motor activities, they build and refine psychological structures. He proposed knowledge as a process, a set of actions that a person may perform. For him, to know something is to act on that thing, which can be either physical or mental or both. He believed that children move through four stages of development—sensory-motor, pre-operational, and concrete operational and formal operational. Three important characteristics of this theory are (a) it is a general theory, (b) the stages are invariant, and (c) the stages are universal.

### *Bruner's Theory*

Jerome S. Bruner developed a cognitive model of learning. His theory explains how subject matter can be best learnt practically. Bruner's theoretical framework is based on the theme that learners construct new ideas or concepts based upon existing knowledge. Learning is an active process which includes selection and transformation of information, decision making, generating hypotheses, and making meaning from information and experiences. According to him, three issues should be considered in the teaching-learning process—nature and ability of learners, the structure of knowledge and the nature of knowledge acquisition process. He provided some modes of representation, i.e. specific ways of presenting the subject matter by which learning becomes easier. These are—enactive mode, iconic mode and symbolic mode. These play a vital role in learning.

### *Ausubel's Theory*

According to David Ausubel, if learners have properly internalised the material learnt, they can easily reproduce it. The more the material is presented to the learner systematically, the more the process of internalisation will be facilitated. Learning is internalised by progressive differentiation process and integrative reconciliation process. His work focussed on verbal learning. He dealt with the nature of meaning, and believes that the external world acquires meaning only as it is converted into the content of consciousness by the learner. Meaning is created through some form of representational equivalence between language and mental context. It involves two processes—reception and discovery. The subsumption theory advocates that when information is subsumed into the learner's cognitive structure it is organised hierarchically. For meaningful learning to take place, a stable cognitive structure is essential.

### *Vygotsky's Theory*

Like Jean Piaget, Lev Vygotsky also believed that children are active seekers of knowledge, but he considered them in a wider context. According to his theory, rich, social and cultural contexts profoundly affect children's cognition. He believed that all higher cognitive processes develop out of social interaction. A special concept, the Zone of Proximal (or potential) Development (ZPD), explains how this happens. It refers to a range of tasks that the child cannot handle alone but can accomplish with the help of adults and more skilled peers. According to Vygotsky's theory of learning, cognitive development is influenced by social factors, cultural factors and language.

### *Constructivism Theory*

This theory propounds that the learners construct their understanding of the topics they study, rather than recording understanding delivered from others. Constructivism refers to the idea that learners construct knowledge for themselves—each learner individually (and socially) constructs meaning—as he or she learns. It emphasises that new learning is interpreted in the immediate context of current understanding. There is no single unified view of constructivism. Constructivists disagree on the nature of knowledge and the importance of different elements in the knowledge construction process. There are mainly two viewpoints.

1. Cognitive Constructivism: It is based on Piaget's work. It focusses on individual, internal constructions of knowledge. Social interaction acts only as a catalyst for individual cognitive conflict.

2. Social Constructivism: It is strongly influenced by Vygotsky's work. It suggests that knowledge exists in social context and is initially shared with others instead of being represented solely in the mind of an individual.

The constructivist theory is based on the following principles—

1. Learning is an active process in which the learner constructs meaning out of sensory input.
2. Learning consists both of constructing meaning and constructing systems of meaning.
3. The construction of meaning takes place in the mind. But it is necessary to provide activities which engage both the mind as well as the hands.
4. Learning is influenced by language used.
5. Learning is a social activity and is intimately associated with social interaction.
6. Learning is contextual—it is influenced by our lives, relationships, beliefs, prejudices and fears.
7. Learning takes place upon the base of previous knowledge. It is not possible to assimilate new knowledge without having some previous knowledge to build on it.
8. Learning is not instantaneous—it requires some time for significant learning to take place.
9. Motivation is a key component of and plays a significant rôle in learning.

### *Information Processing Theory*

Information processing is a cognitive theory that examines the way knowledge enters and is stored in and retrieved from memory. This model has three major components—

(i) Information stores: These are repositories that hold information. These are analogous to a computer's main memory and hard drive. It includes sensory memory, working memory and long term memory.

(ii) Cognitive processes: It refers to the cognitive processes that move information from one store to another. These involve attention, perception, rehearsal, encoding and retrieval.

(iii) Metacognition: It refers to knowing about and having control over our cognitive processes. It integrates the cognitive processes so as to use them strategically.

*Learning Systems:* The learning systems are the contribution of artificial intelligence. These are software programmes which are capable of learning. A computer programme is said to learn from experience E with respect to some class of tasks T and performance measure P, if its performance at tasks T, as measured by P, improves with experience E (Mitchell, 1997). The main characteristics of the new generation of learning programmes are that they are basically problem-solving programmes, capable of undertaking heuristic search, with a reasonable storehouse of methods like generate-and-test and means-end analysis.

BACON is a learning system that discovers empirical laws by using two complementary techniques. The first is the detection of regularities in data. The second is construction of new attributes in terms of more primitive ones. The first technique leads to useful generalisations and also directs the second technique. Together the two lead the search for more data which could lead to further generalisations.

In 1964, Bobrow developed a computer programme named "STUDENT". It was designed to solve algebra word problems. Its performance was compared to that of human problem solvers by Paige and Simon. They intended to describe human behaviour while solving algebra word problems. Further testing determined that STUDENT could not account for human solution processes that rely on semantic knowledge. Its limitations led to the development of UNDERSTAND. According to Hayes and Simon (1974), UNDERSTAND was based on two assumptions—

(i) To understand a written problem, the text is read and encoded both semantically and syntactically; and
(ii) A representation must be made of the newly encoded information.

The resulting representation must include a problem space. A problem space consists of the set of problem elements, the initial state, the goal state, an operator or a set of operators and the restrictions under which the operator may be applied. UNDERSTAND reads the problem text, then rereads it, to semantically and syntactically analyse the structure and match it against a set of requirements specified as input for the General Problem Solver. Hayes and Simon (1974) contended that an individual solves a problem using two interactive processes, an understanding process and a solving process. The understanding process generates a problem space from the problem text, and the solving process uses the problem space to search for steps toward solving the problem. Even though the solving of a problem follows the understanding, the model shows that these are not sequential stages, but rather, interactive stages. These two processes are not sequential, rather interactive.

Another contribution of AI in the field of learning is Dendral. Its primary aim was to study hypothesis formation and discovery in science. It chose a specific task in science for this—to help organic chemists in identifying unknown organic molecules, by analysing their mass spectra and using knowledge of chemistry. The software programme Dendral is considered the first expert system because it automated the decision-making process and problem-solving behaviour of organic chemists.

The Automated Machine (AM), another learning programme was developed by Doug Lenat. It works by generating and modifying short Lisp (programming language) programmes. These are then interpreted as defining various mental concepts. The system has elaborate heuristics for choosing which programmes to extend and modify. It is chosen on the basis of the experiences of working mathematician in solving mathematical problems. It is composed of many data structures called "concepts" and "heuristic rules" and a simple flow of control.

Thus we can see that mere conditioning cannot explain all types of learning. Some psychologists explained learning on the basis of cognition or cognitive processes. Cognitive processes include creating mental representations of physical objects and events, and other forms of information processing. Cognitive learning is the result of sensory. It is defined as the acquisition of knowledge and skill by mental or cognitive processes; the procedures for manipulating information 'in our brain'. It is a powerful mechanism that provides the means of knowledge, and goes beyond simple imitation of others. The cognitive theories of learning developed starting from the concept of insightful learning to constructing meaning and to the modern, sophisticated learning programmes. While gestalt psychologists explained learning on the basis of insight, Tolman described it as a molar behaviour which works on sign gestalt, Kurt Lewin went on to describe it on the basis of psychological field. Piaget related cognitive development to biological development. Bruner emphasised constructing new knowledge on the basis of prior knowledge. David Ausubel emphasised the importance of internalisation of meaning for learning. While constructivism itself grew as a very attractive topic for the contemporary psychologists, Vygotsky emphasised more on social constructivism. Recently, the information processing theory has gained much popularity. The importance of the information processing concept in learning has led to development of various learning programmes or systems, which are usually based on problem solving.

## Pedagogical Implications of Learning

Learning theories may be looked at as a continuum running from behaviourist through cognitive/social to constructivist. It is understood from the continuum that the cognitive processes although unobservable are real and can precede, influence and modify behaviour. Learning itself is not directly observable. It is evident from a change in knowledge, which in turn makes a change in behaviour possible. Moreover, humans are social beings. Their cognition is not isolated and they also learn by observation and imitation. Social interaction facilitates the organisation of cognition. Learning is a process of knowing and knowing is a form of action. In learning, the knower engages positioning themselves in relation to the knowable. When engagement occurs, they become more or less transformed person. Pedagogy is the science and practice of the dynamics of knowing. In general, the cognitive theories of learning have the following implications on the educational process—

1. Cognitive processes influence learning.
2. With growth, children become capable of increasingly more sophisticated thought.
3. People organise the things they learn.
4. New information is most easily acquired if it is associated with previous knowledge.
5. People control their own learning.

Ivie (1998) explained pedagogy on the basis of Ausubel's learning theory and arranged instruction in a sequence of five logical steps—(1) ascertaining if the student already possesses relevant concepts in his or her cognitive structure; (2) providing appropriate advance organisers, which are used to anchor the new material within established cognitive structure; (3) presenting the new material in an organised fashion, checking to make sure the student is subsuming the new information under appropriate organisers; (4) providing sufficient practice (drill) so that the material is thoroughly learned, becoming an integrated part of the student's cognitive system; and (5) guiding the student through a problem solving situation that utilises higher order thinking skills. Kumar and Gupta (2009) supported for pedagogy based on cognitive constructivism, in which the role of the teacher is to facilitate discovery by providing the necessary resources and by guiding learners as they attempt to assimilate new knowledge to old and to modify the old to accommodate the new. Teachers must take into account the knowledge that the learner currently possesses when deciding how to construct the curriculum and to present the sequence, and structure new material. The role of the teacher in Piaget's theory is to provide a classroom full of interesting things to encourage the children to construct their own knowledge and to have the ability to explore. Direct experience, making errors, and looking for solutions are vital for the assimilation and accommodation of information. Whiteley (2006) addressed the issues of implementing Socratic Method and Bloom's taxonomy of cognitive domain in Virtual Classroom Setting. According to him, the Socratic approach can be effectively used to help learners to achieve the higher order learning level of Bloom's Taxonomy of cognitive domain. In this method, the teacher's role is to direct the learners in the right direction, but without providing the answers. Rittle-Johnson and Star (2007) found that comparing and contrasting varied solution methods to the same problems helps in learning mathematics. It requires written record of all-to-be compared solution methods, preferably with solution steps aligned; explicit opportunities to identify similarities and differences in methods; instructional prompts to encourage learners to consider the efficiency of the methods. Comparing contrasting solutions seemed to support gains in procedural knowledge because it facilitated learners' exploration and use of alternative solution methods. Comparison of multiple solutions helped them move beyond rigid adherence to a single solution method to more adaptive and flexible use of multiple methods. However, this method was not found to be helpful in gaining conceptual knowledge.

Apart from these, we may draw pedagogical implications of each cognitive theory of learning—

- The pedagogical implications of the Gestalt theory directs towards emphasis on insight. The teacher should present the picture of whole subject matter in the class first, and then he should come to its parts. This theory advocates for adopting problem solving approach in the class. The teacher should provide appropriate problem situations to the learners. The teacher should relate the present knowledge with the past knowledge, because the insight of the learner is based upon his past experiences. Ivie (1998) has also supported that the teacher should look for the status of previous knowledge in the cognitive structure of the learner. This theory advocates for developing reasoning, thinking and imagination powers and thus the creative potentials of the learners. So, the teacher should always encourage these.
- The pedagogy implied by Tolman's theory is that the teacher should make the behaviour of learners purposive and goal directed during the whole teaching learning process. The goals should be set beforehand and the behaviour of the learners should be directed towards the goals. The teacher should use reward and punishment for reinforcing behaviour. Gestalt principles should be followed in order to make the teaching material meaningful i.e. more importance should be given to whole learning than to part learning. Ivie (1998) and Kumar and Gupta (2009) have regarded organised pattern of the learning material important for effective learning. Providing cues by the teachers help the children to proceed further to solve the problems. Cognitive mapping helps an individual to know the progress of the tasks performed. So, the teacher should help the learners to structure the cognitive map.
- Lewin's learning theory implies that proper psychological as well as physical environment should be provided to pupils in the class in order to help them cross the barriers and develop insight in them. The teacher should help different pupils in formulating their respective goals

keeping in view their needs and capacities. The teacher should strengthen the valence by making the goals attractive for learners and by raising their aspiration level. The teacher should use reward and punishment procedure regularly. The teacher should make efforts to reduce tension of learners as much as possible, as tension may lead them away from their goal.

- The concepts of assimilation, accommodation and equilibration provided in Piaget's cognitive development theory suggest the importance of the optimal conditions for an individual's learning and development. Thus the pedagogy implied is to encourage children to discover for themselves through spontaneous interaction with the environment, which has also been stated in the study by Kumar and Gupta (2009). Teachers should provide a rich variety of activities designed to promote exploration. A classroom following Piaget's learning theory does not try to speed up development. Instead, he believed that appropriate learning experiences build on children's current level of thinking. The teacher should plan activities for individuals and small groups rather than just for the total class. It highlighted the importance of drives and motivation in the field of learning and development. It has utilised the concept of equilibration for this purpose. Moreover, teacher must understand the processes children use to get to the answer in addition to checking the correctness of the answer.
- The pedagogy based on Ausubel's theory suggests more emphasis on internalisation of the meaning of the content. Systematic presentation of the content or the learning material facilitates internalisation. The teacher should use didactic, expository methods of teaching. Most notable contribution of Ausubel's learning theory is the advance organiser. It is a tool or a mental learning aid to help learners integrate new information with their existing knowledge, leading to "meaningful learning" as opposed to rote memorisation. The study conducted by Ivie (1998) suggests that opportunity for adequate practice should be given to the learners for integrating the new knowledge in cognitive system and appropriate advance organisers

should be used. Mayer and Wittrock (2006) identified instructional methods that are intended to promote meaningful learning, such as providing advance organisers that prime appropriate prior knowledge during learning, asking learners to explain aloud a text they are reading, presenting worked out examples along with commentary, or providing hints and guidance as learners work on an example problem. Meaningful learning also helps in transfer of problem-solving.

- Bruner's theory regards children as active problem solvers. They can explore difficult subjects by themselves. The teacher's responsibility is to expose them to the opportunities to explore. This theory believes that children can be taught any subject at any stage of development in a way that fits the child's cognitive abilities. The teacher should encourage intuitive and analytical thinking capacity of the children. Instead of giving external competitive goals like grades or class ranking, the teacher should develop interest in the subject matter, as it is the best stimulus for learning. The teachers should structure the knowledge in such a way that enables the learner to most readily grasp the information. Understanding the fundamental structure of a subject makes it more comprehensible. Details are better retained when placed within the context of an ordered and structured pattern. The teacher should also take care of effective sequencing, as sequencing or lack of it can make learning easier or more difficult. No one sequencing will fit every learner, but in general, the sequence should be in increasing difficulty. Another implication is that the teacher should select and pace the rewards and punishments appropriately.
- The pedagogy implied by Vygotsky's theory is to use information about the two levels of Vygotsky's zone of proximal development in organising classroom activities. The two levels are 'what a child can do independently' and 'what the child can do when assisted by an adult or more competent peer'. It can be done in the following ways:

- ➢ Instruction should be planned to provide practice in the zone of proximal development for individual children or for groups of children.
- ➢ Cooperative learning activities should be planned with groups of children at different levels who can help each other learn.
- ➢ Scaffolding should be a component of pedagogy, where the adult provides hints and prompts to the learner at different levels.

Therefore, the teacher must plan activities that encompass not only what children are capable of doing on their own but also what they can learn with the help of others. A significant application of Vygotsky's theory is 'reciprocal teaching'. In this method, teacher and learners collaborate in learning and practicing four key skills: summarising, questioning, clarifying, and predicting. It particularly improves learners' ability to learn from text. Gradually the teacher's role is reduced and the learner becomes independent. Another implication that can be drawn from Vygotsky's theory is 'collaborative learning'. Here, the group members should have different levels of ability so that more advanced peers can help less advanced members (McLeod, 2007).

- According to the information processing theory of learning, a well-developed schema helps to incorporate the new knowledge in an organised manner and to reduce the load on working memory. So, this theory implies that the teacher should focus on relationships among the items of information that the learners are expected to learn. The organisation of information is very important in promoting learning. The teacher can organise the information in several ways—charts, matrices, hierarchies, outlines, graphs, tables, flowcharts, maps, etc. Developing procedural knowledge to the point of automaticity has important implications for teaching. The teachers should provide the learners with as many opportunities as possible to practice in a variety of contexts for reaching the automatic stage. The teacher can make use of chunking (process of combining separate items into larger, more meaningful units), automaticity (mental operations that can be performed with little awareness or conscious effort, essential for higher cognitive skills) and dual processing (verbal instruction supplemented with visual representations) to overcome the limitations of working memory. Attracting and maintaining learner's attention are crucial first steps in teaching. Teachers should plan their lessons so that the learners attend to what is being taught and ignore irrelevant stimuli. Background knowledge in the form of schemas affects perception and subsequent learning. The teacher can check learners' perceptions by asking open-ended questions. The teachers can also use organisers to capitalise on imagery—the process of forming mental pictures, which also facilitate problem-solving. Teachers can make use of tools like teacher questioning, examples, analogies and mnemonic devices to encourage learner elaboration. The teacher should develop the metacognitive abilities of the students to enable them to effectively use strategies—plans for accomplishing learning goals. Teachers should be aware of the wide and varied background knowledge of the students. The challenge of dealing with this wide variety can be addressed by—asking students what they know about the topic the teacher is planning to teach; providing background experiences with rich examples and representations; using open-ended questions to assess students' perception; and using the experiences of students in the class.

- The constructivist theory believes that learning can be only through construction of meaning. It implies:
  - ➢ The teacher has to focus on the learner in thinking about learning (not on the subject/lesson to be taught).
  - ➢ There is no knowledge independent of the meaning constructed or attributed to experience by the learner.

Learners mostly use examples to construct their understanding. So, the teacher should provide them with a variety of examples and representations of content. Social interaction facilitates learning. Interactions along with the teacher's support keep the learners active. Providing the appropriate amount of support is a very sophisticated process, so as not to reduce the learners' active role in the learning activity. So, the teacher needs to take care of this. Learners' constructions are most meaningful to them if they can relate their learning to the world outside the classroom. The teacher should relate the theoretical knowledge with the surrounding of the learner. For example, identifying the longitude and latitude of their school or writing a persuasive essay for a school or class newspaper, designing an advertisement for a particular group or their own school, etc. Representation of content is important in the construction of understanding. The contents which are difficult to represent with concrete materials or in actual situations, can be illustrated using technology.

- Learning systems are helpful for generalisation, problem solving, decision making, etc. Teachers in classroom need to understand the underlying processes in these processes and try to make them effective in the classroom. The learning systems are also designed to serve the purpose of improving the learning of the students in the pedagogical situation. The learning system, Bacon, for example, implies that the teacher should help the students in finding out the common elements in the contents and generalisation and construction of new meaning based on earlier ones. UNDERSTAND implies that problem solving requires understanding the problem and then finding a solution. The teacher should at least try to ensure to the level of understanding. Dendral is a learning system for decision-making and problem solving.

## PROBLEM SOLVING

Problem solving is a critical cognitive activity that pervades many aspects of our day-to-day lives. It is a higher order cognitive ability. In order to understand problem solving, it is important to decide what constitute a 'problem'. Goldstein (2005) tried to give a complete definition of a problem as "a problem occurs when there is an obstacle between a present state and a goal and it is not obvious how to get around the obstacle". Hayes (1989) defined problem solving as "transforming a given situation into a desired situation or goal". According to Mayer and Wittrock (2006), problem solving is "cognitive processing directed at achieving a goal when no solution method is obvious to the problem solver". So, 'problem' is a situation in which there is a difference between one's current state and one's desired or goal state, without any clear way of getting from one to the other. Searching for the way to move from the current state to the goal state is 'solving' the problem. Problem solving is the process that an organism implements in order to try to get from the current state to the desired state. It refers to any activity in which both the cognitive representation of prior experience and the components of a current problem situation are reorganised in order to achieve a designated objective (Ausubel et al., 1978). It is the analysis and solution of tasks or situations that are complex or ambiguous and that pose difficulties or obstacles of some kind. It is the analysis and transformation of information towards a specific goal (Lovett, 2003). It is thinking in terms of some problems and solutions, that is, thinking is stimulated by some problems, which arises when the individual selects a goal and something obstructs him to reach the goal. Skinner (1968) defined it as "a process of overcoming difficulties that appear to interfere with the attainment of a goal". A problem situation has three major components: an initial state (the present situation), a goal state (the desired situation) and strategies (for getting from the initial state to the goal state). Apart from these three components, it also includes prior knowledge and experiences and decision making ability of the individual. Thus, problem solving is the process, by which a person represents the goal to be accomplished, determines a procedure for reaching the goal, executes that procedure, and evaluates the success of the solution attempt (Novick, 2003).

## Problem Solving in Cognitive Science

Problem solving is a major component of cognitive science. It is studied in several disciplines of cognitive sciences, particularly in psychology, where it is addressed in conjunction with cognitive functions such as attention, control, learning, reasoning and so on using a symbolic or connectionist approach (Ghallab, 2003). Problem solving may occur inside a mind, inside a computer, in some combination of both, or in interaction with an external environment. Studying how humans solve problems comes under *cognitive psychology*. In psychology, problem solving is understood as a deliberate and purposeful act on the part of an individual to realise the set of goals or objectives by following some systematic step for removal of the obstacles in the path of the realisation of these goals. It is an important area in the field of Artificial Intelligence (AI). Artificial Intelligence (AI) studies how computers solve problems. The researches on AI have both borrowed from and contributed to research on human problem solving. It includes a number of important conceptual and algorithmic contributions. It produced systems, applied to different tasks that can solve problems at the level of professionally trained humans. These AI programmes are usually called expert systems. While the computer's process appears to be more systematic and even compulsive, the human's process is more intuitive. The expert systems are modified as and when new knowledge becomes available. The field of neuroscience provides the neurological and mental processes involved in problem solving. The areas of the brain involved in this process are—occipital lobe (processing of visual information and eye movement), temporal lobe (short term memory and sorting new information), parietal lobe (processing somato-sensory information), pre-motor area (initiating and modifying movements), hippocampus (formation of new memories and finding shortcuts and new routes between familiar places) and prefrontal cortex (planning and executing strategies). These areas, while being the major areas used during problem solving, are not a definitive list.

**Problem Solving in Education**

A major goal of education is to help students learn to use what they have learned to solve problems in new situations. Problem solving occupies an important position in the teaching learning process. It comprises a fundamental component of education because teachers are interested in improving students' ability to solve problems. Another reason for its significance in education is the difficulty level of problem solving. Most often students have very poorly developed problem solving abilities and they approach problems in haphazard ways (Reif, 2008). Teachers always try to improve the problem solving abilities of the learners, but their efforts often turn out to be inadequate. Though they are able to solve particular problems, difficulty arises in generalisation. That is, they can solve similar problems but cannot use the knowledge gained from previous problem solving process to solve a new kind of problem. Therefore, it is a challenge for the teachers to improve problem solving abilities of the learners. For this, it is necessary to understand better the cognitive processes underlying good problem solving and to develop pedagogy to teach problem solving effectively. Some other questions posed for the educational system, which can be answered on the basis of cognitive science researches are: whether problem-solving courses should attempt to teach problem solving as a single skill or as a collection skills; whether problem-solving courses should focus on the product or process of problem solving; whether problem solving should be taught as a general course or within specific domains; whether problem solving should be taught before or after students have mastered corresponding lower-levels.

### Cognitive Mechanisms in Problem Solving

Problem solving involves the operation of the various representational and executive mechanisms. Gagne (1980) provided a description of the cognitive activities that appear to be involved in problem solving which include intellectual skills, verbal knowledge and cognitive strategies. Intellectual skills are those capabilities that develop as a result of cognitive growth. It is the ability of the individual to generalise basic skills such as number concepts, and to understand and use rules when confronted by problems. Verbal knowledge or declarative knowledge refers to the meaningful organisation of large bodies of general and specific knowledge. Cognitive strategies are cognitive tools that enable us to select and operate upon intellectual skills. It involves skills that enable them to comprehend symbol systems and rules governing the relationship between objects and events.

Mayer and Wittrock (2006) distinguished among four major cognitive processes in problem solving: representing, in which the problem solver constructs a cognitive representation of the problem; planning, in which the problem solver devises a plan for solving the problem; executing, in which the problem solver carries out the plan; and self-regulating, in which the problem solver evaluates the effectiveness of cognitive processing during problem solving and adjusts accordingly. During representing, the problem solver seeks to understand the problem, including the given state, goal state, and permissible operators, and the problem solver may build a situation model—that is, a concrete representation of the situation being described in the problem. Mayer and Wittrock (2006) listed five kinds of knowledge in order to be successful problem solvers: facts (knowledge about characteristics of elements or events); concepts (knowledge of a categories, principles, or models); strategies (knowledge of general methods); procedures (knowledge of specific procedures); and beliefs (cognitions about one's problem-solving competence) or about the nature of problem solving. Facts and concepts are useful for problem representation, strategies are needed for planning a solution, procedures are needed for executing the plan, and beliefs can influence the process of self-regulating.

### Strategies of Problem Solving

Psychologists and educationists have devised some strategies to solve problems in an economical and effective way. A strategy means a systematic plan for generating possible solutions that can be tested to see if they are correct. The main advantage of cognitive strategy is that they permit the problem solver to exercise some degree of control over the task at hand. They allow individuals to choose the skills and knowledge that they will bring to bear on any particular problem. Two important strategies of problem solving are—

1. *Algorithm*: An algorithm involves systematically exploring and evaluating all possible solutions until the correct one is found. Here, every possible step is listed till the correct solution of the problem is found. It is a set of rules which is systematically applied in a specific order, to all possibilities and their outcomes. But it is not applicable for complex problems. It is expensive in terms of time and energy.
2. *Heuristics*: It is a problem solving strategy in which hypotheses about problem solutions are generated and tested in a time saving and systematic way. It is based on informal, intuitive and speculative strategies. Heuristics

are cognitive short-cuts for guiding operator selection in problem solving. Heuristics is applied in a problem space—the universe of all possible actions that can be applied to solve a problem. Its limitation is that it does not guarantee an acceptable solution. Some commonly used heuristics are—means-end analysis (looking for the action that will lead to the greatest reduction in difference between the current state and goal state), working forward (starting at the beginning and trying to solve the problem from the start to the finish), working backward (starting with the desired result and trying to work backwards until the initial state is attained), using analogy (making use of experiences, training and practice to find a solution for similar problems), sub goal analysis (the complex goal is divided into easily attainable sub-goals), generate and test (simply generating alternative courses of action, not necessarily in a systematic way, and then notices in turn whether each course of action works). The simplest heuristic is *repeat-state avoidance* or *backup avoidance*, whereby individuals prefer not to take an action that would take them back to a previous problem state. But this is not helpful when a person has taken an inappropriate action and actually needs to go back a step or more.

In Fredericksen's (1984) review of cognitive theory and problem solving, he listed details of how a general class of problems might be addressed which included the following:

(a) Get the complete picture without being concerned about the small details
(b) Withhold judgment until all relevant information has been gathered
(c) Simplify the problem using words, diagrams, symbols or equations
(d) Try changing the way the problem is presented
(e) State questions and vary the form of the question
(f) Remain flexible in approach and challenge the assumption being made
(g) Try working backward

(h) Work toward sub-goals that are part solutions
(i) Use analogies and metaphors
(j) Verbalise the problem

Bransford *et al.*, (1986) suggested a simple problem solving sequence in the form of an easily learned mnemonic—IDEAL—Ideal, Define, Explore, Act and Look. In 1957, Newell and Simon developed the General Problem Solver, a computer programme. It used means-ends analysis to find solutions to a range of *well-defined problems*.

Another important strategy is the Basic Problem Solving Strategy which includes two general guidelines—decomposing tasks (decomposing complex tasks into simpler sub-problems) and successive approximations (not to attempt the problem in one single major effort, but in successive approximation). This strategy decomposes the solution process into several successive phases—

(a) Describing the problem—In this phase, a clear description of the problem, its initial state and the goal state are produced.
(b) Analysing the problem—The problem is put into a form which will facilitate the subsequent construction of its solution by identifying the useful knowledge, analysing the problem more theoretically and providing a more analytic description of the problem.
(c) Constructing the solution--This is the most important and complex phase. Here the problem is decomposed into carefully chosen sub-problems which are then successively solved leading to the actual solution.
(d) Assessing the solution—It is assessed whether the solution obtained in the preceding phase is correct and useful by providing some general criteria for checking the solution. If the solution is not satisfactory, the problem solver must go back to revise it appropriately.
(e) Exploiting the solution—This phase suggests reflecting about the problem so as to exploit one's work for future purposes. This is not necessary for the solution of the problem but will help the problem solver in future problem solving.

## Approaches to Problem Solving

### *The Behaviourist Approach*

The behaviourists viewed problem solving as a *'reproductive'* process. That is, organisms faced with a problem applied behaviour that had been successful on a previous occassion. Successful behaviour was itself believed to have been arrived at through a process of trial-and-error. Thorndike's law of effect greatly influenced the behaviourist view of problem solving.

### *The Cognitive Approach: The Gestalt Theory*

The Gestalt psychologists believed that a problem occurs because of the way in which a situation is initially perceived, and that its solution emerges suddenly from reorganising it in such a way that its real structure becomes apparent. They argued that problem solving was a *'productive'* process. In particular, in the process of thinking about a problem, individuals sometimes "restructured" their representation of the problem, leading to a flash of insight that enabled them to reach a solution. According to them, insight problems require problem solvers to go beyond associations among various parts in order to perceive the problem as a whole. They speculated on a few ways in which insight might occur like extended unconscious leaps in thinking, greatly accelerated mental processing or some kind of short-circuiting of normal reasoning processes. The research by the Gestaltists revealed many interesting problem-solving results. However, the approach taken was descriptive so it did not constitute a systematic exploration of the processes of problem solving.

## Information Processing Theory

Some contemporary psychologists have borrowed ideas from research on artificial intelligence to understand problem solving. They consider the mind as analogous to a computer programme which operates in discrete steps (information processing) to reduce the difference between existing states and sub-goals. On this basis, the problem space theory of problem solving was proposed by Allen Newel and Herbert Simon in their book *Human Problem Solving (1972)*. The theory is based on a human-computer metaphor in which problem solving involves carrying out a series of mental computations on mental representations. In this theory, people solve problems by searching in a *'space'*. The problem space consists of the initial (current) state, the goal state, all possible states in between and a set of operators that can be applied to move from one state to another. The problem begins in the initial state, an operator is applied that generates a new state and so on until the goal state is reached. Operators are the actions that people take in order to move from one state to another. The problem spaces can be very large. So, the significant issue is how people navigate their way through the possibilities or how do they choose operators. There are three ways in which operators can be acquired: trial-and-error (behaviourist account of problem solving), direct instruction and analogies (using elements in examples from one domain to aid problem solving in another domain). For example, a common search heuristic is means-ends analysis, in which an operator is applied that will satisfy the problem-solver's current goal. If there is a constraint that blocks the application of the operator, then a goal is set to remove the constraint, and thus it proceeds. Information processing theory informs educational programmes aimed at teaching strategies for solving problems. However, this theory is criticised on the basis that the problem space concept and the derived search methods can only be applied to well-defined problems.

In the second half of 20th century, two main approaches to problem solving arose in Europe, one initiated by Donald Broadbent and the other one by Dietrich Dorner. Both the approaches share an emphasis on relatively complex, semantically rich, computerised laboratory tasks, constructed to resemble real-life problems. However, they differ in their theoretical goals and methodology. Broadbent's approach emphasised the distinction between cognitive problem-solving processes that operate under awareness versus outside of awareness. It typically employed mathematically well-defined computerised systems. On the other hand, Dorner's approach was more concerned with the cognitive, motivational, and social components of problem solving. It utilises very complex computerised situations that contain up to 2,000 highly interconnected variables. Almost simultaneously, in North America, researchers began to investigate problem solving separately in different natural knowledge domains based on Herbert Simon's work on 'learning by doing' in semantically rich domains. Thus the focus of the researches in problem solving was shifted from extracting a global theory of problem solving to development of problem solving within a certain domain i.e. on the development of expertise.

## Pedagogical Implications of Problem Solving

The pedagogical implications of cognitive science on problem solving involve the strategies of the teachers to teach problem solving in the classroom, i.e. what to teach and how to teach. To facilitate problem solving among the students the teacher has to ensure that the learners have the ability of—decision-making, recovering from impasses and pursuing a systematic approach. Teaching problem solving focusses upon how to derive maximum information from the problem as presented, how to formulate a suitable strategy for its solution, enact that strategy, and monitor performance until the goal is achieved. Two important things to be considered here are what to teach and how to teach. Ashman and Conway (1989) have listed a number of skills required to enhance problem solving skills, i.e. what to teach. These are—

- Teaching cognitive processes (strategies and executive mechanisms underlying successful performance in any specific task).
- Teaching how to deal with the structure of the problems (for example, using appropriate strategies or plans to deal with ambiguities in the instructions).
- Teaching the recognition of patterns within the problem (looking for relationships and rules based upon experience and practice).
- Teaching problem solving procedures (systematically applying steps to search, scan organise, set goals, plan and monitor).
- Teaching the knowledge base (forming the information network required to complete the task).
- Teaching development of knowledge structures (how information is organised to ensure that success generalizes to other situations).
- Providing practice with feedback (reinforcing performance and the development of insight).
- Using models of instruction (using approaches that systematically address problems).

An effective approach to problem solving requires—a problem solving strategy and well organised domain knowledge. The most important aspect in pedagogy is to focus on decision processes. These should be taught within the framework of a systematic problem solving strategy. However, perhaps the most widespread approach to training in problem solving is to instruct the learner in various general principles that have emerged from theoretical analysis of the thinking process and from comparative observations of successful and unsuccessful problem solvers (Ausubel et al., 1978).

Proficiency in problem solving is best achieved in recognising the essence of a given problem and the application of the proper problem solving heuristics. The teacher may facilitate problem solving in the learners by—

- *Using mental models:* Limjap (2002) recommend use of mental models in problem solving. It involves using diagrams or drawings used to represent the structure of the concept. Using this, the learner is able to map the essence of the model into the essence of the concept, and match or transfer specific conceptual aspects of one domain into another. This cognitive process promotes reflective abstraction.
- *Focus on process and not the product:* Limjap (2002) believes that the focus of instruction should not be on the product but on the process of problem solving. Proficiency in problem solving is best achieved in recognising the essence of the problem and the application of the proper heuristics.
- *Using intuition and logic:* Barb and Quinn (1997) advocate that the teacher should emphasise on developing the students' problem solving skills and refining their strategies using intuition and logic. The ultimate goal of this instructional method is to help learners build a good knowledge base in solving world problems.
- *Using variable problem contexts:* According to Bernardo (1997), presenting concepts in variable problem contexts enables the students to appreciate the meaning and use of a particular concept or procedure in a variety of contexts. Teaching strategies that promote analogical transfer should be used. For example, presenting students with a

context problem and then asking them to make their own problem using a different context.

- *Using text editing skills:* Problem solvers are asked to identify missing information from problems or point out information that is irrelevant to the problems. This activity enhances the problem solvers' awareness of their own thinking process. Such awareness helps learners identify their points of strengths and weaknesses and regulate their own ways of knowing (Limjap, 2002).
- *Using guided instruction in the use of metacognitive strategies:* This was supported by a number of scholars, particularly, Bernardo (1997) and Schoenfeld (1987). The teachers model the metacognitive processes in problem solving when they present solutions to their students. The teacher thinks aloud and exhibits the whole process of arriving at the correct solution. This demonstrates the complexity of the process involved in solving problems and the fact that there are many possible ways of arriving at the correct solution.
- *Factors influencing problem solving:* Simone (2008) identified four factors which favoured successful problem solving—identifying the main problem/issue; having higher quality problem definition; relating the solution to the problem well and using resources more effectively. So, the teacher should give importance to each of these factors.
- *Importance of concrete thinking:* The teacher should not underestimate the fact that novices find abstract thinking difficult. Though teachers commonly present an abstract principle and then an example to illustrate the principle, the students use this example to refine how the principle works. Specific (content-based) thinking is important both for the novices and the experts (Ross, 2007).
- *Sufficient time:* The teacher should give enough time for wrestling with the problem and to ask question wherever, whenever and whatever necessary in an effort to understand it. If the teacher gives the solution immediately, the pupils do not get time to exercise their mental faculties.
- *Sufficient time for understanding the problem than for finding solution:* The teacher should teach the learners to spend

significant time in describing and analysing a problem before trying to construct its solution. Pupils mostly put their attention and effort in searching for the solution while ignoring the description and analysis of the problem.

- *Proper representation of the problem:* It is very necessary to put the problem in front of the students in such a manner that they can grasp what it means or to guide them to proper representation of the problem at hand.
- *Facilitating analogy:* Facilitating analogy between a previously solved problem and a current problem by giving solvers a hint to think back to the previous problem and making the source and target problems superficially similar.
- *Meaningful learning:* Max Wertheimer (1959) made the classic distinction between learning by rote and learning by understanding. According to him, the rote method of instruction leads to good performance on retention tests (i.e., solving similar problems) and poor performance on transfer tests (i.e., solving new problems). In contrast, learning by understanding leads to good retention and good transfer performance. He claimed that rote instruction creates reproductive thinking—applying already learned procedures to a problem—whereas meaningful instruction leads to productive thinking—adapting what was learned to new kinds of problems.

Apart from these, there are some programmes which have been designed to teach problem solving skills to the learners—the Productive Thinking Programme developed by Martin Covington, Richard Crutchfield, and Lillian Davies, Instrumental Enrichment developed by Reuven Feuerstein, and Odyssey described by Raymond Nickerson. Although none of these programmes is currently popular, but courses based on these four criteria are likely to be successful.

It can be seen that cognitive science focusses more on the internal representation of both the problem as well as the solution. Moreover, it emphasises that while teaching problem solving, the solution process is more important than the solution itself. The students should not be taught to find solutions to a particular problem or type of problem but they should be encouraged to generate solutions for different types of problems on the basis of solution processes of the problems encountered earlier. Their metacognition should be guided and they should be given sufficient time to ponder over the problem. Moreover, the teacher should always keep in mind that the problem solving process of the experts and the novices differ substantially.

## CREATIVITY

The human mind is wonderful in many ways and one of these is its capacity to generate novel ideas, which is commonly known as creativity. Creativity is one of the most highly valued qualities of human beings which enormously affect all spheres of life. The nations which learn best how to identify, develop and encourage creativity in their people, are always in an advantageous position. Creativity is an important contributor in changing history and in re-shaping the world. It essentially relates to potential of an individual for generating new ideas, forms and practices. Creativity is the result of the convergence of basic cognitive processes, core domain knowledge, and environmental, personal, and motivational factors which allow an individual to produce an object or behaviour that is considered both novel and appropriate in a particular context. It is the capacity to produce something that is both new and adaptive (Lautrey and Lubart, 2003). It is a complex phenomenon as it is determined by a wide range of factors. It requires a multifaceted approach even to understand it partially. However, the degree and quality of creative expression is relative. It varies from individual to individual and from age to age, as one grows in years, experience and maturity and thus enhances the status of an individual (Roy, 2001).

Guilford defined creativity as a staunch exponent of cognitive functioning. His sole emphasis was on the model of structure of intellect. He drew a distinction between convergent and divergent thinking. Convergent thinking is converging different ideas into one single point while divergent thinking means opening up different options from one single point. The former involves aiming for a single, correct solution to a problem, whereas the latter involves creative generation of multiple answers to a set problem. A structure can be developed from his explanations of creativity as follows—

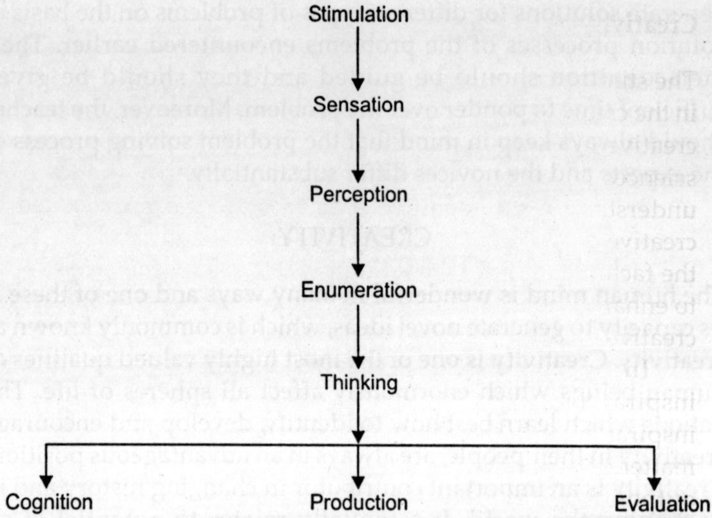


**Fig. 5.1:** Schematic Representation of Guilford's Ideas on Creativity

The figure shows that the process of creative thinking starts with a vibration in the brain cell (stimuli) which leads to sensation, perception, enumeration and thinking. The ultimate products are cognition, production and evaluation.

Barlett defined creativity as an adventurous thinking or a getting away from the main track, breaking out of the mould, being open to experience and permitting one thing to lead to another.

According to Spearman, creativity is the power of human mind to create new contents by transforming relations and thereby generating new correlates.

Torrance conceives creativity as composed of constellation of general abilities, personality variables and problem solving traits, which he considered, can be enhanced through memory, adaptability, self-discipline, introversion, divergent thinking ability and supportive climate.

Sigmund Freud's psychodynamic approach to creativity suggests that creativity arises as a result of frustrated desires for fame, fortune and love. The energy that was previously tied up in frustration and emotional tension in the neurosis is sublimated into creative activity. However, he later retracted this view.

Thus, creativity can be called as the novel, original, useful and genuine cognitive output of divergent thinking.

## Creativity in Cognitive Science

The study of creativity in psychology has sparked a new interest in the creative cognition approach where the idea is to understand creative processes using the methods and concepts of cognitive sciences (Lautrey and Lubart, 2003). Cognitive science tries to understand what cognitive processes are most associated with creative outcomes, the extent to which machines can be creative, the factors that limit creativity, the techniques that are supposed to enhance creativity, and the sources of individual differences in creative performance.

In philosophy, there are two theories of creativity—inspirationist theory and rationalist theory. According to the inspirationist theory, genuine creativity is largely, if not entirely, a matter of inspiration—the sudden, involuntary, and inexplicable outpouring of innovative ideas and actions, the source of which is a sacred instance (a spirit or muse) or the unconscious mind. The rationalist theory believes that all creativity is ultimately reducible to a form of calculation or more or less deliberate problem solving. However, there are many intermediate theories in between these two extremes.

In linguistics, creativity is related to generativity (Abeille, 2003). Linguistic creativity is our faculty to understand or produce an apparently unlimited number of new words and new sentences. In generative grammar, proposed by Noam Chomsky (one of the leading contributor in the cognitive science conference in 1956), linguistic creativity is governed by formal grammar. A formal grammar is defined as a finite set of rules which, when applied to an equally finite set of vocabulary words can generate a potentially infinite set of well-formed sentences.

According to Joel Chan, a cognitive scientist at the University of Pittsburgh, from neurological point of view, creativity is "a collection of cognitive abilities and tendencies, that, when applied to a problem or pursuit, results in the creation of something that is appropriate to the problem/pursuit, and also new/original in some sense" (Christensen, 2013). The processes (or factors) behind creativity are attention, analogy/metaphorical thinking, network organisation of memory, forgetting, imagination, environment and experiences.

In artificial intelligence, creativity of machines is the main discussion. A number of attempts have been made to get computers to function creatively. An important goal of such computational approaches is to develop a better understanding of human creativity through simulation.

In the 1990s, various approaches in cognitive science that dealt with metaphor, analogy and structure mapping converged, and a new integrative approach to the study of creativity in science, art and humanities emerged under the name 'conceptual blending'. According to conceptual blending theory, elements and vital relations from diverse scenarios are "blended" in a subconscious process, which is assumed to be ubiquitous to everyday thought and language.

## Creativity in Education

Creativity has been identified as a key component for survival and resilience. It provides the foundation for art, science, philosophy, and technology. Education holds the responsibility to develop and foster creativity among learners. If education aims at generating productive human beings, it is necessary to understand and nurture their creative potential. The educational system supports them in the process of discovering and enjoying their creative potential. Understanding, identifying, and nurturing creative potential is relevant in education and therefore should be taken into account when developing education programmes, strategies, and policies to achieve quality education (Chavez-Eakle, 2010). To inspire, stimulate and sharpen the creative mind, good education, proper care and provision of opportunities for creative expression are essential. All these can be given only by the teachers, parents and the society. They are required to help the learners in nourishing and utilising their creative abilities to the utmost. This can be achieved by acquainting the teachers and parents with the real meaning of the creative process, the cognitive processes underlying creativity and the ways and means of developing and nurturing creativity.

## Nature of the Creative Process

The nature or basic structure of creative process or processes has been controversial. The controversies concerns whether the expression "the creative process" refers to a single type of process or activity, the extent to which creative activity can be adequately described as a type of problem solving or means-end-analysis, etc. However, even if there are controversies, its nature can be simply described as—

- Creativity is universal. It is not confined to any individual, groups of individuals, caste, colour or creed, age, location or culture. The difference is in the degree of demonstrating creativity.
- Creativity is both innate and acquired. The child is born with some creative abilities as well as the influence of cultural background, experiences, education and training in the nurturing of creativity cannot be denied.
- Originality and novelty are the most important natures of creativity. However, there are questions on the concept of originality.
- Creativity is a relative concept. There are no absolute standards for assessing the creativity of a product. A creative piece is evaluated and its degree of creativity is determined in relation to others of its kind.
- Creativity is a departure from the stereotyped, rigid and closed thinking. It encourages and demands complete freedom to accept and express the multiplicity of responses, choices and lines of action.
- Creativity should have some utility value. It means that the product of the creative process should be such that it will be useful in some way to at least a group of people, if not all.
- Creativity and intelligence are conspicuously related. They do not necessarily go hand in hand. One is not the essential pre-requisite of the other. However, a minimum level of intelligence is required for successful creative expression.

## Theories/Models of Creativity

Scholars have differing views about 'what is creativity'. Many theories and models have emerged in the attempt to understand creativity more intensely and comprehensively. Models of creativity differ from each other in their scope, in the factors they emphasise, and in the tendency to state creativity as stable or flexible. At first, creative behaviours were regarded as a reflection of differences in individual personalities. Beginning from Guilford, creativity began to be viewed as a set of traits which, though stable, were influenced by motivation and temperament (Brown, 1989). Creativity was seen as a result of a set of traits such as problem sensitivity, fluency, flexibility, complexity, evaluation, the use of novel ideas, the ability to break down existing symbolic structure, and the general tendency to organise ideas into larger patterns. Slightly differing from Guilford, Torrance viewed creativity as the combination of ability, skill and motivation (Ford and Harris, 1992). There are two types of theories or approaches to creativity—componential theories of creativity and cognitive models. The componential theories hold that creativity occurs when a variety of biological, cognitive and social factors merge or interact. They provide a global account of the factors that interact to determine the creative impact of novel ideas. The cognitive models focus more narrowly on the way in which basic cognitive processes operates on existing knowledge structures to produce novel ideas. They focus on the acts of problem identification and solution-generation as the keys to creative production.

### *Taylor's Level Theory of Creativity*

According to the level theory, creativity may be described as existing at five levels in an ascending hierarchy. A person is said to be creative to the extent that he is able to reach these levels. The five levels are the following—

(a) Expressive creativity—This stands for spontaneous expression without reference to originality and quality of the product.

(b) Productive creativity—At this level, a person is able to produce something innovative.

(c) Inventive creativity—This level is marked by the presence of ingenuity with a clear emphasis on novel use of old things.

(d) Innovative creativity—At this level, one is able to develop new ideas or principles with the help of highly developed abstract conceptualising skills.

(e) Emergentive creativity—This fifth and highest level of creativity is rarely achieved. The most abstract ideational principles or assumptions underlying a body of art or science are made to use of at this level of creation.

### *Freud's Psychoanalytic Theory of Creativity*

The school of psychoanalysis considers creativity to be a means and product of one's emotional purging. Creativity is considered as an opportunity for sublimation and catharsis. Psychoanalysis proposes that creativity wells up from unconscious drives. Though there are differing opinions about how this occurs, various psychoanalytic schools of thought generally suggest that creativity is a by-product of primary processes. The link between primary processes (specifically sexuality), and creativity is important. It suggests that there is an energy (biological creativity), which can be sublimated into higher psychological processes when the primary gratification urges of the id are inhibited. Freud takes a pathological view of the creative process. He felt that only unhappy people experienced daydreams and fantasies, which are an integral part of the creative process. To Freud there was great similarity between neurosis and creativity. He felt both originated in conflicts stemming from wish fulfillment and biological drives. He considers creativity as attempts for the expression of their repressed desires, mostly sexual in nature. According to him, the creative process is an alternative to neurosis, that is a defence mechanism protecting against neurosis, leading thus to the production of a socially acceptable source of entertainment and pleasure. The unconscious plays a major role in the act of creation. That is, the act of creation is made possible by the libido, the energy of the id, and by a defence mechanism—sublimation. Thus, psychoanalytic theory explains creativity as sublimation of sexual drives. It is not an act in itself, but rather mental relief from pain, anxiety, or sexual tension.

### *Arieti's Theory of Creativity*

Silvano Arieti (1914-1981) was a professor of psychiatry at New York Medical College. His theory represents the contemporary views about the nature and meaning of the terms creativity, the creative process and creative output. This theory believes that both creativity and mental illness involve the transformation of reality and therefore are parallel to one another. However, the distinction lies in that while creative persons aim to change reality for broader, useful and social purposes and self-actualisation, psychotics want to transform reality within the framework of their private world regardless of serving any useful purpose to themselves or the society. Therefore, creative persons cannot be called as mentally ill. In fact, a creative person enjoys good mental health which energises his cognitive abilities to create something unique or novel. Arieti considers the creative process as a 'magic syntheses of the two modalities', the primary process and the secondary process and may thereby be termed the 'tertiary processes'. According to him, there are four stages of the creative process—

(a) *Primary*: It includes a non-judgmental, non-disciplined playing with images, symbols, inner expressions of our inner lives. (Memory, traces of past perceptions, subjective experiences and impressions). Images are the "first germ of creativity" and give birth to intuition and empathy. All these happen in the right hemisphere of the brain.
(b) *Secondary*: It corresponds to conscious cognition or to logic—a process of choosing, deciding and putting order and form into our imaginations. These are the actions of the left hemisphere of the brain.
(c) *Tertiary*: It refers to the sum of the other processes which is greater than the sum of the parts; and the ability to differentiate similarities from manifold experience.
(d) *Fourth*: The artist knows he is an artist when his creative piece is socially appreciated. In this way all energy becomes connected again and the artist's ultimate vocation, to return energy to the universe by way of transformed matter, is accomplished.

### *Finke's Theory of Creative Cognition and Geneplore Model*

In 1992, the Geneplore model was proposed by Ronald A. Finke and his colleagues. It is based on the creative cognition approach to understand creativity. This approach attempts to understand creativity scientifically by adapting the concepts, theories, methods and frameworks of cognitive psychology. It precisely characterises the fundamental cognitive operations that produce creative and non-creative thoughts. Creative cognition emphasises that creative capacity is an essential property of normative human cognition (Ward, Smith and Finke, 1999). Creative activities, in general, can be described as an initial generation of possible ideas or solutions followed by extensive exploration of those ideas.

This model considers both generative and exploratory cognitive processes and provides a useful framework within which to describe basic cognitive creativity. It characterises the development of novel and useful ideas as resulting from interplay between generative processes and exploratory processes. Two processing stages suggested in this model are—

- *Generative phase*: Here, mental representations called pre-inventive structures are generated. Generative processes such as retrieval, conceptual combination, and analogical reminding are assumed to result in ideas. These ideas vary in their apparent novelty, aesthetic appeal or other factors that would influence the creative person's perception that how far they can solve the current problem. People can use such properties to determine which ideas to develop by way of exploratory processes that modify, elaborate and consider the implications, assess the limitations, or otherwise transform the ideas. They may be untested proposal or even a mere germ of idea, but they hold some basic criteria of creativity—originality and appropriateness.
- *Exploratory phase*: Here, the pre-inventive structures are interpreted in meaningful ways. It includes the search for novel or desired attributes in the mental structures, the search for metaphorical implications of the structures and potential function of the structures, the evaluation of structures from different perspectives or within different contexts, the interpretation of structures as representing possible solutions to problems, and the search for various practical or conceptual limitations that are suggested by the structures.

### *Amabile's Model*

The Componential theory of creativity was developed by Teresa Amabile (1950) in 1983. In her model, creativity is considered as a constellation of personal characteristics, cognitive abilities and processes, and social environment factors. Creativity is the production of a novel and appropriate response, product, or solution to an open-ended task. Here, appropriateness implies valuable, correct, feasible or fitting to a particular goal. Moreover, it must be open-ended (heuristic). The theory describes the creative process and the various influences on the process and its outcomes. It is based on the assumptions that there is a continuum from low, ordinary level of creativity to the highest levels of creativity and that there are degrees of creativity in the work of any single individual, even within one domain. The level of creativity that a person produces at any given point in time is a function of the creativity components operating, at that time, within and around that person (Amabile, 2013).

Level of Creativity = fn (Components of creativity)

According to Amabile, there are four components of creativity—three within the individual and one outside the individual. The first three are domain-relevant skills, creativity-relevant processes and task motivation. The component outside the individual is the social environment.

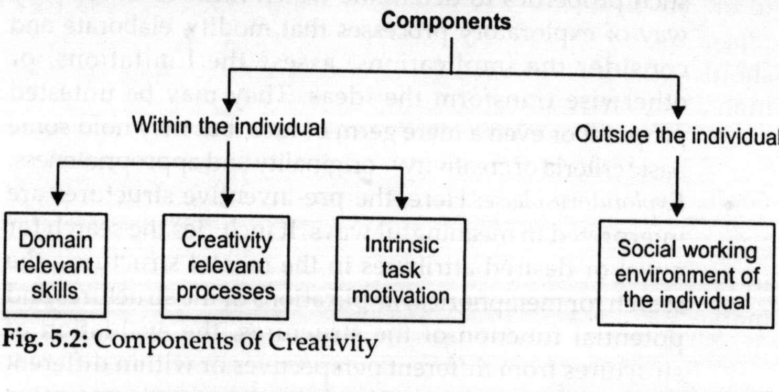


**Fig. 5.2:** Components of Creativity

- Domain relevant skills—These include knowledge, expertise, technical skills, intelligence and talent in the domain in which the problem solver is working. They comprise the raw materials upon which the individual can draw throughout the creative process.
- Creativity-relevant Processes—These include a cognitive style and personality characteristics that are conducive to independence, risk-taking and taking new perspectives

on problems, as well as a disciplined work style and skills in generating ideas, ability to use wide, flexible categories for synthesising information and a tolerance for ambiguity.

- Intrinsic task motivation—It refers to the motivation to undertake a task or solve a problem because it is interesting, involving, personally challenging, or satisfying. People are most creative when they are intrinsically motivated towards that task.
- Social environment—It includes factors like attitude of the people towards new ideas, risk-taking behaviours, non-conformity, openness, freedom, support, recognition, etc. These factors may serve either as obstacles or stimulants to creativity.

According to the componential theory, all these components affect the creative process. The process consists of some sub-processes like identifying the problem and its nature, preparing to solve the problem by gathering information and improving any required skills, generating ideas for solving the problem, testing or validating the chosen solution, and communicating that solution to others. However, the sequence is flexible. The sub-processes repeat themselves till a creative outcome is attained. Creativity should be highest when an intrinsically motivated person with high domain expertise and high skill in creative thinking works in an environment highly supportive for creativity.

### *Graham Wallas's Model*

Graham Wallas (1858-1932) in his work *Art of Thought*, published in 1926, presented the stage model of the creative process. In this model, creative insights and illuminations may be explained by a process consisting of 5 stages—

(i) *Preparation* (preparatory work on a problem that focusses the individual's mind on the problem and explores the problem's dimensions)

(ii) *Incubation* (where the problem is internalized into the unconscious mind and nothing appears externally to be happening)

(iii) *Intimation* (the creative person gets a "feeling" that a solution is on its way)

(iv) *Illumination* or insight (where the creative idea bursts forth from its preconscious processing into conscious awareness)
(v) *Verification* (where the idea is consciously verified, elaborated, and then applied)

Sometimes, these five stages are treated as four stages regarding "intimation" only as a sub-stage. According to Wallas, creativity is the process which allowed humans to quickly adapt to rapidly changing environments, thereby contributing in the human evolutionary process.

### *Gruber's Model*

Howard E. Gruber (1922-2005), the foremost contemporary interpreter of the creative process, has regarded creativity as the merging of personal knowledge, affect and purpose. Gruber demonstrates that creation is not the result of "a set of properties that a person has in a certain moment and carries around with him." He gives importance to 'how' of creativity than to 'what' of creativity. His approach towards creativity is developmental. Accordingly, he regards creativity as the result of developmental changes in knowledge systems. These changes results from different situations that a person encounters over time. He viewed the subject as being creative based on an interpretation that takes into account changes over time. His "evolving systems" approach is based on three basic propositions—

1. Each creative person is a unique configuration.
2. It is a challenge in the field of creativity research to determine means of describing and explaining each unique configuration.
3. A theory of creativity that chooses to look only at common features of creative people is missing the main point of each life and evading the responsibility of research on creativity (Gruber and Davis, 1988).

The methodology developed by Gruber is described in (Brower, 2003) as being characterised by the following six features—

(a) Viewing the individual's work in a continuum rather than in discrete.

(b) Paying attention to a person's organisation of related systems, e.g., knowledge, purpose, affect, physical world.
(c) Identifying sources of deviation amplification.
(d) Starting with someone whose creativity is unquestionable.
(e) Emphasising micro-genesis.
(f) Hermeneutical distanciation.

*Greene's Model*

Richard Tabor Greene, a pioneer in the field of creativity research, attempted a very comprehensive model of creativity. He listed seven types of models, with six models in each type. That is, total 42 models. The seven types of models are arranged in such a way that there is a progression from global, complex, collections of many things to local, particular, specific small numbers of things moving from number one to seven.

(1) Catalog type: It includes models that are collections of large numbers of factors affecting creativity or constituting creation itself.
(a) Recommendations (b) Traits (c) Question finding (d) Darwinian system (e) Combined thought type (f) Garbage can
(2) Blend type: It also concerns numerous factors. It includes (a) Culture mixing (b) Discipline combinatories (c) Trait balancing (d) Paradox balancing (e) Scale blending (f) Fractal marketing
(3) Social type: It concerns less numerous sets of factors and includes
(a) Community of ideas (b) System model (c) Social computation (d) Social movement (e) Space sharing (f) Participatory art and design
(4) System types: It also concerns less numerous sets of factors. It includes
(a) Non-linear systems (b) Darwinian (c) System effects (d) Surprise (e) Adjacent beyond (f) Population automation
(5) Purity type: It contains less number of factors
(a) Sub-creations (b) Productivity (c) Performance (d) Influence (e) Investing (f) Info design
(6) Self-type: It also contains few factors.

(a) Courage (b) Anxieties channelled (c) Extended self-development (d) Interest ecstasy (e) Career invention (f) Performance creativity

(7) Mind type—It contains fewest of all factors.

(a) Insight (b) Cognitive operators extremes (c) Making sense (d) Hint type recognition (e) Experience realisation forms (f) Representational topologies

As the mind type models are most relevant to the present study, we will consider only these models of creativity and discuss them in brief. Under mind types, there are six models.

1. The *Insight Model* of creativity attributes two parts—the accumulation of failed trials and the sudden appearance of insights or illuminations that show the way to creativity. It breaks these down into steps in a process of insight building and occurrence. Insights occur on various size scales and therefore, are fractal in nature. There may be smaller insights within larger insights and short term insights within long term ones.
2. The *Cognitive Operator Extremes Model* is a model of ordinary cognitive operations carried to extremes, of speed, accuracy, breadth, depth, and so on. It emphasises on cognitive skills. Creativity results when one or more cognitive operations are deployed to the extremes.
3. The *Making Sense Model* regards creativity as the ability to create new things, meanings, senses, explanations, procedures and ways of work as they find the existing beliefs, values, procedures and ideas inadequate. They see flaws and faults with even the most commonly accepted ideas and concepts.
4. The *Hint Type Recognition Model* considers creativity as a large scale thorough-going dislocation of perception. It is attention focussed on clues, connections and sequence of these clues, circular arguments and other traces of partial understanding of reality. It is based on inverted perception. This inverted perception results in creativity.
5. According to the *Experience Realisation Forms Model*, creativity is giving form to already realised experiences.

It involves tapping into more direct, unmediated layers of experience, thought, and perception.

6. The *Representational Topologies Model* regards creativity as changes of representations. There may be various viewpoints with respect to different individuals, fields, or areas of knowledge. These viewpoints remain rudimentary till these are turned into meaningful representations, thus resulting in creativity.

However, Greene draws on seven models among the 42 models to frame his own model of creativity—the 4 Cycle model. The seven models included in the 4 Cycle model are: Traits model, Question finding model, Darwinian system model, Insight model, Population automaton model, Sub-creations model and Culture mix model. These seven models represent a combination of all the types of models with three models from the catalog type and one each from the others. Thus, it can be seen that Greene's model of creativity is a vast, comprehensive and detailed model. Among them, the mind type model consists of six models. These models have explained creativity based on insight, cognitive operations, meaning, perception, experience and representation.

It should be noted here that the theories of creativity are not exhaustive. There are many more theories. However, as it is not possible to mention all the theories, the researcher has presented only the theories which are appealing to the present study. To summarise, Taylor explained creativity in a level of hierarchy—expressive, productive, inventive, innovative and emergentive; the school of psychoanalysis considers it to be an opportunity for sublimation and catharsis; according to Arieti, it is a synthesis between the primary process and secondary process; for Finke, it is generation and exploration of ideas; Amabile understood it in terms of components—personal characteristics, cognitive abilities and processes and social environment; Wallas understood creativity as a process of five stages—preparation, incubation, intimation, illumination and verification; Gruber regards it as the merging of personal knowledge, affect and purpose; Greene attempted to give a comprehensive and detail account of creativity by considering all the factors related to creativity.

## Pedagogical Implications of Creativity

Creativity is universal, though not equal in all. It is not the exclusive property of the rare and genius only, but a tender bud that resides in varying measures within every child. It can be taught, enhanced and nurtured (Elshout, 1995). This must be realised and believed by the teacher. And accordingly, the pedagogic practice should be sensitive, stimulative and imaginative. There should be great emphasis on learning creativity in domain or subject-matter contexts and in helping students see the potential use of creativity in real life-situations. Developing creativity should be viewed as a long-range process leading to adult creative achievement and self-fulfillment (Elshout, 1995).

Hamza and Griffith (2006), Cole, Sugioka and Yamagata-Lynch (1999), McWilliam (2007) and Lin (2011) consider 'an open as well as challenging environment', 'collaboration—both student-student and teacher-student', and 'appreciation of the learner's individuality' as inevitable for fostering creativity. Use of techniques like brainstorming, thumbnail sketches, synaptic, matrixes, etc. is helpful for developing creativity (Hamza and Griffith, 2006; Cole, Sugioka and Yamagata-Lynch, 1999). The teacher should stand back in the classroom but always be in a supportive position (Cole, Sugioka and Yamagata-Lynch, 1999; Lin, 2011). Direct instruction should be avoided, rather teaching should be experimental and error-welcoming (Cole, Sugioka and Yamagata-Lynch, 1999; McWilliam, 2007). Less emphasis should be given on grading and standardisation and the standard for assessment should be based on creativity (Cole, Sugioka and Yamagata-Lynch, 1999; McWilliam, 2007; Lin, 2011). For this, apart from traditional examination system, self-assessment and peer assessment (McWilliam, 2007) and giving assignments (Cole, Sugioka and Yamagata-Lynch, 1999) are appropriate.

The teacher's own orientation about creativity is important. He should be sufficiently professionally and emotionally secure to depart from traditional methods and conclusions, open to receive various non-conformities. He should teach children not the subject matter. He should seek new methods of presentation.

Creativity requires a free environment to be fostered. Most often teachers breed conformity and passivity by expecting routine, fixed responses from children and thus kill the potential creativity.

The teacher should allow adequate freedom to the children in responding to a situation. They should be encouraged to think out as many ideas as they can for the solution of a problem.

Creativity is fostered by self-confidence and therefore, the teacher should try to build up confidence among the learners. Lack of confidence develops shyness which hinders fostering of creativity. The self-confidence of the learners can be built up by respecting the individuality of each learner.

The teacher should teach the learners to develop a positive attitude towards every work and towards the failures which may come on the way. If the failures make them disappointed they may be reluctant to attempt again and thus impede creativity.

Creative expression requires appropriate opportunities and atmosphere. This can be given by the teacher by taking full advantage of the curriculum. Not only does the creative person reveal his interest and aptitude in a wide variety of fields, but perceiving new interrelationships among different fields is a mark of creativity. There should be variety for curricular choice and activity. Co-curricular activities can be used for providing opportunities for creative expression. Existing creations and creators, local and global, should be exhibited to the students.

Rather than teaching the children to memorise and recite facts, the teacher should try to engage them in creative problem solving, as this has a direct link to an increase in creative learning. It can be done by activating multiple senses and enabling children of different learning styles to succeed. It opens up more doors in the brain and allows more ways for learning. Moreover, children struggle to articulate things in a verbal or written manner. They might find better success in it using their hands and their minds to explore a particular topic.

Team teaching is also helpful in fostering creativity in classroom. It is a teaching technique in which the pupils are exposed to a variety of subjects and their interrelationships and a variety of teachers and teachings.

Another technique that can be used by the teachers to foster creativity is brainstorming. It is a group technique. It consists of having group members who suggest ideas as rapidly as possible, prohibiting criticisms, encouraging speaking out, and evaluating at a later session, holds possibilities that have not yet been thoroughly tested.

Gaming technique also helps the children in the development of creative traits. It means teaching the learners through games having some creative value. This technique provides learning experiences in a relaxed, spontaneous and evaluative situation.

Another factor influencing creativity is social interaction. Creativity is characterised by optimum growth in social interaction. The teacher may observe pupil interaction and use sociometer to get clues about the degree of interaction. Accordingly, the teacher can help the students in socialising when necessary.

Moreover, there are various programmes which have been developed to teach creativity (Elshout, 1995). Creative problem solving is one of the most widely promulgated models for teaching creativity. Isaken and Treffinger (1985) published a comprehensive set of training materials. Their work builds upon the materials for creative problem solving developed by Parnes. Parnes (1975) reviewed the history of and research on creativity and concluded that it is eminently teachable and the skills generalised to usefulness in real-life situation. Perhaps the most widely known creativity training system is deBono's CoRT programme (1976). This programme consists of a set of training materials used by the teachers and students in the classroom. Another famous creativity programme, the Purdue Creative Thinking Programme (Feldhusen, 1983) is a set of 36 units of instruction on the skills and personal factors of creativity.

## INTELLIGENCE

Intelligence is a very relative term that has been defined variously. According to Webster's New World College Dictionary (3rd edition), intelligence is 'the ability to learn or understand from experience, ability to acquire and retain knowledge; mental ability...' Some experts like Edwin Boring, defined intelligence operationally, simply as 'what intelligence tests test'. It relies on tests to define intelligence and ultimately is circular (Sternberg, 2003).

Wechsler defined intelligence as "the capacity to understand the world and the resourcefulness to cope with its challenges". He also suggested that "intelligence is the capacity to act purposefully, to think rationally, and to deal effectively with the environment" (Wechsler, 1958).

Some of the critical elements of intelligence, as decided by some experts (Lewis Terman, Edward Thorndike, Ulric Neisser and Douglas Detterment), particularly in two symposia (in 1921 and 1986), are—(a) adaptation in order to meet the demands of the environment effectively, (b) elementary processes of perception and attention, (c) higher level processes of abstract reasoning, mental representation, problem solving, decision-making, (d) ability to learn, and (e) effective behaviour in response to problem situations.

However, we can find at least two major consensual definitions of intelligence. First, from "Intelligence: Knowns and Unknowns" a report of a task force convened by the American Psychological Association in 1995:

> Individuals differ from one another in their ability to understand complex ideas, to adapt effectively to the environment, to learn from experience, to engage in various forms of reasoning, to overcome obstacles by taking thought. Although these individual differences can be substantial, they are never entirely consistent: a given person's intellectual performance will vary on different occasions, in different domains, as judged by different criteria. Concepts of "intelligence" are attempts to clarify and organise this complex set of phenomena.

Another widely accepted definition of intelligence is given by "Mainstream Science on Intelligence," a treaty signed by 52 intelligence researchers in 1994: a very general mental capability that, among other things, involves the ability to reason, plan, solve problems, think abstractly, comprehend complex ideas, learn quickly and learn from experience.

Thus, intelligence can be seen as a sort of mental energy of an individual in the form of mental or cognitive abilities, available with an individual that enables him to handle his environment in terms of adaptation to face novel situations as effectively as possible. This includes ability to learn, think rationally, solve problems and make decisions effectively.

In Indian philosophy, intelligence is regarded as the soul of civilisation and all human progress and culture. Kautilya defined it as the capacity for works. Jamini, in his Purvamimamsa Sutra, mentions of the peculiar character of the intellect of certain persons. The Vedanta Sutra regards intelligence as a strong power which is dormant in infancy. It grows and develops gradually with years, reaching perfection in adolescence. The Buddhist source also supports this view. The Rigveda tells us of the mental inequalities existing in different personalities. Gotama, in his Nyayasutra, mentions about three distinct levels of intelligence such as—laukika or ordinary abilities below average, average intelligence, and pariksaka or superior intelligence, ability to make independent investigations by means of arguments and proofs. The Nirayavaliyao, the eleventh Jaina canon mentions four talents such as intuitive or 'autpattiki', disciplined or 'vainayiki', the talent acquired by practice or 'karmaja' and the developed talent or the talent reaching perfection in the maturity of age called 'parinamiki'.

## Intelligence in Cognitive Science

Intelligence is so much proximally related to cognitive science that the main aim of the field of cognitive science is to understand 'intelligence' or various intelligent systems. 'Intelligence', we can say, is the centre of attraction in cognitive science. Roger Schank, a well-known cognitive scientist defined intelligence as "the ability to diagnose well, to plan well, and to be able to understand what causes what" (Schank, 2011). From cognitive science point of view, all types of intelligence are considered—human, animal and machine. The contributing disciplines of cognitive science aids in their own ways towards a common goal of understanding intelligence. In psychology, intelligence has been treated in various ways by various psychologists. But for everyone, the inherent goal was to understand the psychological bases of intelligence. Psychology contributes to cognitive science by giving various cognitive theories of intelligence which explains the cognitive processes underlying intelligence. According to Luger, the field of cognitive psychology is dedicated to finding the common set of principles underlying all instances of intelligence (Luger, 1994). In linguistics, intelligence refers to an enhanced ability of an individual to use one or several languages to convey spoken or written communications to others. People who have a high degree of this type of intelligence usually impart information in a refined manner. They have an ability to teach and explain things to others.

Thus cognitive science takes the cognitive processes underlying linguistic intelligence from the field of linguistics. Anthropology contributes the evolution of intelligence in general, and particularly, in humans. Neuroscience studies the neurological factors that may be responsible for the variation of intelligence within a species or between different species. Artificial intelligence is a field which not only studies but also applies intelligence in machines. Cognitive science as a field of study attempts to understand intelligence considering it from all these points of view.

## Intelligence in Education

Intelligence is relevant to the field of education in two senses. First, the education system has to be designed in such a way as to cater to different levels and types of intelligence of the students. Second, if intelligent can be developed, the education system holds the responsibility of developing it. The teacher has to deal with students of different levels and types of intelligence in the classroom. And accordingly adjust his pedagogical methods. The teacher can do this efficiently only if he understands 'what intelligence is' and the underlying cognitive processes of intelligence. According to Schank (2011), the educational system should aim at "making people more intelligent" rather than only strengthening their knowledge-base. If we consider intelligence in this sense, intelligence becomes the main focus of the whole education system. The teacher has to design his pedagogy with the aim of improving intelligence based on the cognitive processes underlying intelligence.

## Theories of Intelligence

The theories of intelligence have evolved through a succession of paradigms. The major paradigms have been those of psychological measurement (often called psychometrics); cognitive psychology, which concerns itself with the mental processes by which the mind functions; the merger of cognitive psychology with contextualism (the interaction of the environment and processes of the mind); and biological science, which considers the neural bases of intelligence. Broadly, the theories of intelligence may be divided into two types—factor or psychometric theories and cognitive theories. The factor/psychometric theories are—monarchic theory, multifactor theory, two factor theory, group factor theory, sampling theory, hierarchical theory and structure of intellect theory. The cognitive theories include Cattell and Horn's theory, Jensen's theory, Champion and Brown's theory, Sternberg's Information Processing theory and Gardener's Multiple Intelligence theory. While the traditional theories of intelligence focus on measuring and quantifying intelligence, the cognitive theories focus on examining the cognitive processes which cause intelligent or unintelligent behaviour.

### *Psychometric Theories*

Psychometric theories have generally sought to understand the structure of intelligence. Underlying the psychometric theories is a psychological model according to which intelligence is a composite of abilities measured by mental tests. It is additive, and therefore, it is assumed that less of one ability can be compensated for by more of another ability in test performance. Such theories have generally been based on and tested by the use of data obtained from paper-and-pencil tests of mental abilities that include analogies, classifications and series completions.

The first of the major psychometric theories was that of the British psychologist Charles E. Spearman. He noticed the fact that: People who did well on one mental ability test tended to do well on the others, and people who did not do well on one of them also tended not to do well on the others. Spearman devised a technique for statistical analysis, which he called factor analysis and believed to provide an analysis of the underlying sources of these individual differences. Spearman's factor analyses of test data suggested to him that just two kinds of factors underlie all individual differences in test scores. The first and most important factor is the general factor or 'g', which is said to pervade performance on all tasks requiring intelligence. The second factor is specifically related to each particular test and is named as specific factor or 's'. But Spearman could not explain exactly what the general factor might be. However, in 1927, he tried to explain it by labelling it as "mental energy".

The American psychologist L.L. Thurstone disagreed not only with Spearman's theory but also with his isolation of a single factor of general intelligence. Thurstone argued that the appearance of just a single factor was an artifact of the way Spearman did his factor analysis and that if the analyses were done in a different and more appropriate ways, seven factors would appear which Thurstone referred to as the "primary mental abilities." The seven primary mental abilities identified by Thurstone were

(i) verbal comprehension (involved in the knowledge of vocabulary and in reading);
(ii) verbal fluency (involved in writing and in producing words);
(iii) number (involved in solving fairly simple numerical computation and arithmetical reasoning problems);
(iv) spatial visualisation (involved in mentally visualizing and manipulating objects, as is required to fit a set of suitcases into an automobile trunk);
(v) inductive reasoning (involved in completing a number series or in predicting the future based upon past experience);
(vi) memory (involved in remembering people's names or faces); and
(vii) perceptual speed (involved in rapidly proofreading to discover typographical errors in a typed text).

However, some other psychologists such as Philip E. Vernon and Raymond B. Cattell, suggested another possibility. In the view of Philip Vernon, abilities are hierarchical. Vernon's model postulates *g* to be at the apex of the generality-to specificity hierarchy followed by two factors verbal-educational (*v:ed*) and spatial-mechanical (*k:m*). This is followed by minor group factors, namely numerical and verbal ability as components of *v:ed* and spatial and mechanical ability as components of *k:m*. Finally, at the bottom of the hierarchy, follows the specific components of these minor group factors.

Some psychologists were even against the hierarchical theory. An American psychologist, J.P. Guilford, proposed the structure-of-intellect theory. He classified the intellectual abilities into a systematic framework or structure. His view is that each intellectual ability has its own uniqueness and some kind of intellectual ability is necessary for executing some task. In his structure-of-intellect, he divided the intellectual abilities into three broad categories—operation, content and product. There are five kinds of operations, four kinds of contents, and six kinds of products. These various facets of intelligence combine multiplicatively, for a total of 5x4x6, or 120 separate abilities.

The psychometric theories were criticised for their inability to say anything substantial about the processes underlying intelligence. Moreover, the number of abilities was going up with each successive psychometric theory. They were unable to honour parsimony, one of the important features of a scientific theory. The cognitive psychologists proposed a solution to these problems, which was to study directly the mental processes underlying intelligence.

### *Cognitive Theories*

The era of psychometric theories of intelligence was dominated by individual differences in people's test scores. Lee Cronbach's view that 'some psychologists study individual differences and others study commonalities in human behaviour but never do the two meet' has led to the development of cognitive theories of intelligence. He pleaded for unity of these 'two disciplines of scientific psychology'. Underlying most cognitive approaches to intelligence is the assumption that intelligence comprises a set of mental representations (e.g., propositions, images) of information and a set of processes that can operate on the mental representations. A more intelligent person is assumed to represent information better and, in general, to operate more quickly on these representations than does a less intelligent person. The fundamental unit of analysis in cognitive theories is: a mental process acting upon a mental representation in all the models.

### *Sternberg's Information Processing or Triarchic Theory*

At a time when two extreme viewpoints were prevalent regarding intelligence—intelligence in terms of a single general factor and intelligence in terms of multiple factors—Robert J. Sternberg, an American psychologist suggested an alternative approach to studying the cognitive processes underlying human intelligence. He proposed a middle-of-the road view between the two extremes in the study of intelligence. Sternberg viewed intelligence as multifaceted, and so-called general ability is viewed as part of the array that might require higher cognitive processes. According to his theory, "the processes of human intelligence are universal but their instantiations in behaviour are contextually bound" (Sternberg, 1999).

Sternberg's definition of intelligence is "a mental activity directed toward purposive adaptation to, selection and shaping of, real world environments relevant to one's life" (Sternberg, 1985). The information processing approach is the manner in which one proceeds to perform a mental task or solve a problem, gathers information and makes use of this information for completing the task or solving the problem in hand. Sternberg believed that information processing takes place following certain steps—encoding, inferring, mapping, application, justification and response.

The triarchic theory suggests three aspects of intelligence—analytical, creative and practical. Analytical abilities are involved in analysing, evaluating, critiquing, and comparing and contrasting things. Secondly, creative abilities are involved in creating, exploring, discovering, inventing, imagining and supposing. Thirdly, practical abilities are involved in applying, using, implementing and putting into practice. These three aspects along with tasks involved and examples of each of these abilities are presented in the table below.

**Table 5.1:** Sternberg's three aspects of intelligence with tasks and examples

| *Abilities* | *Tasks* | *Examples* |
|---|---|---|
| Analytical abilities | analysing, evaluating, critiquing, and comparing and contrasting things | Choosing the best option, criticising a theory or a personality, comparing between two things or ideas |
| Creative abilities | creating, exploring, discovering, inventing, imagining and supposing | Writing short stories with unusual titles, drawing artwork based on novel topics, creating advertisements for dull products |
| Practical abilities | applying, using, implementing and putting into practice | Everyday practical reasoning problems, solving practical mathematics problems, planning routes using maps |

His Triarchic theory is also based on three sub theories—

(a) Componential Sub theory—He advocated that the intellectual functioning of an individual is decided mainly by the components. There are three components serving distinct functions—

Meta-components: These are executive processes used in problem solving and decision making that involves the majority of managing our mind. They tell the mind how to act.

Performance components: These are the mental processes used for the execution of a task, such as task perception, relation perception, applying relations to another set of terms, etc.

Knowledge acquisition components: These are the processes used in acquiring new information. It can be used to synthesise old ideas in some original and creative ways.

(b) Experimental sub theory—This theory proposes that intelligence represents the ability or capacity of an individual to deal with new tasks, problems and situations by adopting an information processing approach with as little conscious efforts as possible.

(c) Contextual sub theory—It deals with the mental activity involved in attaining fit to context. Through the processes of adaptation, shaping and selection, individuals create an ideal fit between themselves and their environment.

### *Cattell and Horn's Theory*

Cattell, in 1971, suggested that general ability can be subdivided into two further kinds of abilities, fluid and crystallised. Fluid abilities are the reasoning and problem-solving abilities measured by tests such as the analogies, classifications, and series completions described above. Fluid intelligence is the capacity to think logically and solve problems in novel situations, independent of acquired knowledge. It is the ability to analyse novel problems, identify patterns and relationships that underpin these problems and the extrapolation of this using logic. It is required for learning and problem solving, especially scientific, mathematical and technical problem solving.

Crystallised abilities can be said to derive from fluid abilities. These include vocabulary, general information, and knowledge about specific fields. Crystallised intelligence is the ability to use skills, knowledge, and experience. But it is not memory or knowledge, though it relies on accessing information from long-term memory. It is not innate; rather it is specially learned and dependent on education and culture. It can be identified through one's stock of vocabulary, general knowledge, the knowledge of customs, traditions and rituals, manner of behaving in the society, handling of machines and tools, craftsmanship and art, computation and keeping of accounts and various other such tasks requiring knowledge, experience and practice. These two types of intelligence intermingle and interact to produce overall intelligence.

John L. Horn, an American psychologist, added to this theory that crystallised ability more or less increases over the life span, whereas fluid ability increases in the earlier years and decreases in the later ones.

### *Jensen's Theory of Mental Functioning*

Arthur Jensen gave a working definition of intelligence as the 'g' factor of an indefinitely large and varied battery of mental tests. According to his theory of mental functioning, the functioning of one's mind depends upon the type and degree of intelligence one possesses. He demonstrated clear cut genetic differences in the average intelligence of races and social classes. He suggested that two genetically based levels of intelligence exist—associative abilities include ability to remember, reproduce, identify, discriminate, synthesise, associate, assimilate, transfer and apply, etc. while conceptual abilities involve ability to carry out higher order of thinking, reasoning, analysing and the capacity of problem solving.

Moreover, Jensen suggested that intelligence of an individual consists of two dimensions—intellectual breadth and intellectual altitude. Intellectual breadth consists of the intellectual fund of general information, vocabulary, practice and skill of handling tools and machines, ways and manners of behaving in society, etc. It depends upon the environment, attitude, values, interests, experiences and training. Intellectual altitude consists of high level cognitive abilities like abstract and divergent thinking, logical reasoning, imagination and conceptualisation, problem solving, etc. Thus, the intellectual ability of an individual is built up on the base provided by his intellectual breadth and height maintained by his intellectual altitude.

*Gardner's Multiple Intelligence Theory*

Howard Gardner viewed intelligence as 'the capacity to solve problems or to fashion products that are valued in one or more cultural settings'. His theory argues that intelligence does not adequately encompass the wide variety of abilities humans display. He challenged the notion of general intelligence. Instead, he gave a broad base to the concept of intelligence and its measurement by providing a multiple frame. He described intelligence or cognitive competence as a set of an individual's multiple abilities, talents and mental skills related to a multiple number of domains of knowledge in a particular cultural setting. He originally identified seven core intelligences: linguistic, logical-mathematical, spatial, bodily kinesthetic, musical, interpersonal and intrapersonal. In 1999, he added an eighth, the naturalistic intelligence and work continues on the ninth category—existential intelligence.

*Linguistic Intelligence*: It involves sensitivity to spoken and written language, all kinds of linguistic competence—abilities, talents and skills. Components are syntax, semantics and pragmatics as well as written or oral expression and understanding. Examples: verbal persuasion, writing a term paper skillfully.

*Logical-mathematical Intelligence:* It consists of the capacity to analyse problems logically, carry out mathematical operations, and investigate issues scientifically. Components include deductive reasoning, inductive reasoning, scientific thinking, logical puzzles,

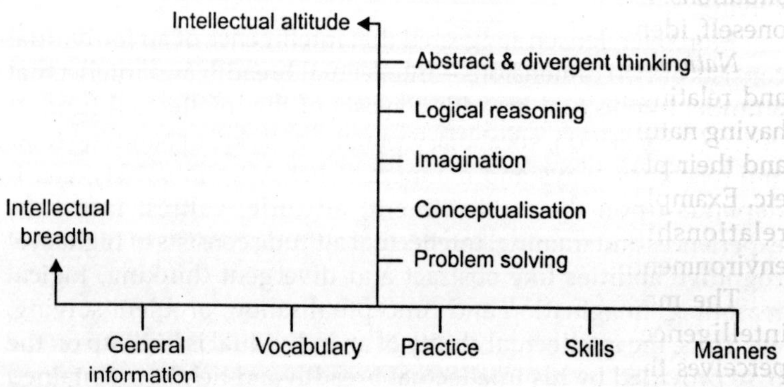


Fig. 5.3: Two Dimensions of Intelligence

calculations, etc. Examples: solving mathematical problems easily and accurately, developing and testing hypotheses.

*Spatial Intelligence:* It involves the potential to recognise and use the patterns of wide space and more confined areas, representation and manipulation of spatial configuration and relationship. Examples: Completing a difficult jigsaw puzzle, assembling a complex appliance.

*Musical Intelligence:* It involves skill in the performance, composition and appreciation of musical patterns. It includes capacity for pitch discrimination, sensitivity to rhythm, texture and timbre, etc. Examples: Singing, playing a musical instrument, composing tunes.

*Bodily Kinesthetic Intelligence:* It involves body movement and doing—using one's body or its various parts to perform skillful and purposeful movements. It is the ability to use mental abilities to coordinate bodily movements. Examples: Dancing, gymnastics, etc.

*Interpersonal Intelligence:* It involves interaction with others—abilities to understand individuals other than one's self and one's relation to others, and also ability to act productively, based on understanding of others. Examples: Sensing when to be tactful, sensing 'subtext' or implied message in a person's statements.

*Intrapersonal Intelligence:* This area has to do with introspective and self-reflective capacities—ability to know own self. It includes knowledge and understanding of one's own cognitive strengths, styles and mental functioning, as well as one's feelings, range of emotions and skills to utilise one's fund of knowledge in practical situations. Examples: Noticing complex of ambivalent feelings in oneself, identifying true motives for an action in one.

*Naturalistic Intelligence:* This area is related to nature, nurture and relating information to one's natural surroundings. People having naturalistic intelligence have greater sensitivity to nature and their place within it, the ability to nurture and grow things, etc. Examples: Identifying species of plants or animals, noticing relationships among species and natural processes in the environment.

The most fundamental difference between the views on intelligence held by Gardner and Sternberg is in how each perceives the way intelligence operates in the world. Sternberg takes a "horizontal" view of intelligence (Gardner, 1999). That is,

Sternberg believes that each component of intelligence will operate on any material. While, Gardner takes a "vertical" view of intelligence, arguing that specific intelligences operate on specific materials. If an individual is appreciating a poem, for instance, two intelligences are operating at the same time—musical and linguistic.

*Newell and Simon's Theory*

Some cognitive scientists have pursued different paths in the study of human intelligence, like building of computer models of human cognition. Two leaders in this field have been the American psychologists Allen Newell and Herbert A. Simon. In the late 1950s and early 1960s they worked with a computer expert, Clifford Shaw, to construct a computer model of human problem solving. It was called the General Problem Solver. It could solve a wide range of structured problems. Their programme relied heavily on a heuristic procedure called "means-ends analysis," which, at each step of problem solving, determined how close the programme was to a solution and then tried to find a way to bring the programme closer to where it needed to be. In 1972, Newell and Simon proposed a general theory of problem solving, much of which was implemented on the computer.

Most of the problems studied by Newell and Simon were very well structured. It involved discrete steps that would lead from the beginning to the end of a problem. The biggest problem for a computer programme (or even for a human) is in deciding which of the innumerable steps will contribute most towards solving the problem.

A common observation in all of the cognitive theories is their primary reliance on the serial processing of information. It is assumed that people process chunks of information one at a time, seeking to combine the processes used into an overall strategy for solving a problem. But some psychologists challenged the idea. They suggested that cognitive processing is primarily parallel. According to them, humans actually process large amounts of information simultaneously. It has long been known that the brain works in such a way, and it seems reasonable that cognitive models should reflect this reality. However, it was difficult to distinguish between serial and parallel models of information processing. This difficulty was solved by subsequently advanced techniques of mathematical and computer modeling. And this led to proposal of 'parallel distributed processing' models of mind by various researchers like David E. Rumelhart and J.L. McClelland. These models postulated that many types of information processing occur at once, rather than just one at a time.

*PASS Theory*

The Planning, Attention-Arousal, Simultaneous and Successive (PASS) theory of intelligence was first proposed in 1975 (Das, Kirby and Jarman, 1975). It challenges g-theory on the grounds that the brain is made up of interdependent, but separate, functional systems. It proposes that cognition is organised in three systems and four processes—

(1) Planning—It involves executive functions responsible for controlling and organising behaviour, selecting and constructing strategies, and monitoring performance.
(2) Attention process—It is responsible for maintaining arousal levels and alertness, and ensuring focus on relevant stimuli.
(3) Simultaneous and Successive processing—It comprises two processes to encode, transform, and retain information. Simultaneous processing is engaged when the relationship between items and their integration into whole units of information is required. Successive processing is required for organising separate items in a sequence. These four processes are functions of four areas of the brain. Planning is broadly located in the front part of our brains, the frontal lobe. Attention and arousal are combined functions of the frontal lobe and the lower parts of the cortex, although the parietal lobes are also involved in attention. Simultaneous processing and Successive processing occur in the posterior region or the back of the brain. Simultaneous processing is broadly associated with the occipital and the parietal lobes while Successive processing is broadly associated with the frontal-temporal lobes.

*David Perkins Theory*

David Perkins analysed a number of different educational theories and approaches to education in his book *Smart Schools* (1992). His analysis strongly supports Gardner's theory of multiple intelligences. He provided strong evidence that education can be considerably improved by more explicit and appropriate teaching for transfer, focussing on higher-order cognitive skills, and the use of project-based learning. He argued that IQ has three major components or dimensions.

1. *Neural Intelligence.* This refers to the efficiency and precision of one's neurological system. There is general agreement that neural intelligence has a "use it or lose it" characteristic. It is clear that neural intelligence can be maintained and, indeed, increased, by use.
2. *Experiential Intelligence.* This refers to one's accumulated knowledge and experience in different areas that lead to expertise in a particular area. Experiential intelligence is based on accumulated knowledge and experiences in a time period, in both informal and formal learning environments. People who live in "rich" learning environments have a significant intelligence advantage over people who grow up in less stimulating environments. Therefore, experiential intelligence can be increased by rich and stimulating environments.
3. *Reflective Intelligence.* This refers to one's broad-based strategies for solving problems, for learning, and for approaching intellectually challenging tasks. It includes attitudes that support persistence, systemisation, and imagination. It includes self-monitoring and self-management. It is like a control system that helps to make effective use of neural intelligence and experiential intelligence. The habits of mind included under reflective intelligence can be learned and improved through approaches like metacognition.

The American psychologists Earl B. Hunt, Nancy Frost, and Clifford E. Lunneborg, in 1973, showed one way in which psychometrics and cognitive modeling could be combined. They showed that individual differences in cognitive tasks were related (although rather weakly) to patterns of individual differences in psychometric intelligence test scores. They argued that the basic cognitive processes might be the building blocks of intelligence.

**Pedagogical Implications of Intelligence**

Intelligence has been always an interesting subject for the teachers as well as the students. However, its discreet nature makes it difficult for everyone to have an accurate or perfect definition of it. This subject attracts the teachers as he has to understand and measure the intelligence of his students as well as of himself to design his pedagogy appropriately. Of all the cognitive theories of intelligence, the theory of multiple intelligences is most relevant to the field of education, particularly to pedagogy.

Fogarty (1998) provided some guidelines which are derived from various theories of intelligence and have classroom implications. These are—emotional safety and care for all learners; rich learning environment in which science equipment, art supplies, tools and workbenches, toys and building blocks, optical illusion posters, etc. are present; teaching of mind-tools and skills of life which include critical thinking skills, creative thinking skills, social skills, technological skills, visual skills, skills in the performing arts, and skills of the elite athlete; develop skillfulness of the learners through formal teaching-learning structures, independent readings, research, dialogue, discussion, articulations of peer coaching, mentoring, or internships and with experiences; provide challenges through experience of doing, i.e. inviting the learner to become an integral part of the teaching learning process; target multiple dimensions of intelligence, i.e. learning is structured in naturally integrated ways that call upon various intelligences; transfer learning through reflection; assessment measures should be balanced and integral to all other interactions.

Haier and Jung (2008) posed some prospects of neuroscience research for education. The neuroscience findings point to ways of assessing the strengths and weaknesses of individual brains so that education can be more precisely targeted to individual students. They also speculated that if neural factors may increase the growth of regional gray matter or white matter, drugs may be developed to stimulate them and target specific cognitive abilities like intelligence. Another prospect is whether brain information in general, and for specific individuals, can improve education from the baseline of current practices. They view to translate new information from the field of neuroscience in the field of education through collaborative work of educators and brain researchers.

Sternberg's theory has three major implications for educational psychology. First, all types of intelligence should be taught. Students need to capitalise on their strongest abilities as well as to develop the abilities in which they are weak. Second, students' strongest abilities are directly related to their learning styles. So, the teachers should know the learning preferences of their students and, try to capitalise on them. Third, assessment system should be diverse to assess variable abilities.

Gardner's multiple theory of intelligence is well adapted to today's classrooms which are full of diversities—both in terms of students and the curriculum.

1. The most important pedagogical implication of Multiple Intelligence theory is the organisation of teaching to allow multimodal delivery in response to diversity in students' talents and activities. Teachers need to expand their repertoire of techniques, tools, and strategies beyond the typical linguistic and logical ones (Armstrong, 2000). Gardner defines a skilled teacher as "a person who can open a number of different windows on the same concept" (Gardner, 1993).
2. This theory holds the fact that there is more than one way to be "smart." It is not important to label student's talents or intellectual strengths. It may be more important simply to provide important learning and knowledge in several ways drawing on more than one possible form of intelligence or skill.
3. Engagement in more authentic methods of assessment than traditional educational testing (Dixon and McPhee, 2001).
4. Multiple Intelligence theory is based on the concept of individual differences. Teachers who employ Multiple Intelligences techniques in the classroom also recognise the importance of the chalkboard and lecture in their pedagogy. According to Gardner, using various pedagogical approaches allows the teacher to reach more students in more effective ways.

## ATTENTION

Human mind is the most complex system on earth. Most of its features are unique. One of such features is to attend to particular stimuli in the environment while ignoring some others. Our sensory systems are continually exposed to various sights, sounds, smells, and other signals from the external environment. Moreover, mental representations of events that just occurred seconds ago, to events from the distant past, to events only imagined in the present or future are also active. A very early definition of attention given by William James is: "It is the taking possession in the mind, in clear and vivid form, of one out of several simultaneous possible objects or trains of thought. Focalisation and concentration of consciousness are of its essence. It implies withdrawal from some things in order to deal effectively with others" (James, 1890). It is the cognitive process of selectively concentrating on one aspect of the environment while ignoring other things. It has also been referred to as the allocation of processing resources. It is involved

**Table 5.2:** Pedagogical Implications of Gardner's theory (Armstrong, 2000)

| *A child who is highly...* | *will tend to think...* | *enjoy...* | *and learn from...* |
|---|---|---|---|
| **Linguistic** | in words | reading, writing, storytelling and word games | books, journals, dialogue, stories and debate |
| **Logical-Mathematical** | by reasoning | experiments, puzzles and calculations | chemistry sets, trips to the planetarium and science museums |
| **Spatial** | in images | drawing, visualising and doodling | paints, clay or play dough, videos, art museums and movies |
| **Bodily-Kinesthetic** | through physical sensations | dancing, running, building, manipulating objects and gesturing | role playing, sports and hands-on instruction |
| **Musical** | in rhythm and melodies | signing, playing music, drumming and listening | singing, concerts and playing musical instruments |
| **Interpersonal** | by exchanging ideas with others | leading, organising and parties | friendship, clubs, group games and mentors |
| **Intrapersonal** | in relation to their feelings and goals | reflecting, planning, meditating and dreaming | spending time alone, independent study and making choices |
| **Naturalist** | through the environment and natural forms | pets, growing plants and nature hikes | observing through binoculars and microscope, and interaction with plants and animals |

in the selective directedness of our mental lives. It is related to the organisation and management of individuals; in the exercise and selection of what one is accustomed to and how one is accustomed to it, attention becomes knowledge of the self that embodies regulatory practices (Sobe, 2004). According to Ross, "Attention is the process of getting an object of thought clearly before the mind."

Thus, attention is the process of concentrating on specific information from the environment while ignoring other information. It is a process carried out through cognitive abilities and helped by emotional and conative factors to select something out of the various stimuli present in one's environment and then to bring it to the centre of one's consciousness in order to perceive it clearly for deriving the desired result.

In all the concrete attentive acts, two processes of sensorial adjustment and ideational preparation coexist—

(a) Adjustment of the sensory organs—The sense organs and the bodily muscles are adjusted most energetically in the sensorial attention. Even intellectual attention is accompanied with some degree of excitement of the sense organs.
(b) Ideational preparation—The preparation of the ideational centre exists wherever our interest in the object—be it sensible or ideal—is derived from, or in any way connected with, other interests, or the presence of other objects, in the mind. This is more relevant to intellectual attention, as the thing attended to here is an idea, an inward reproduction or conception.

### Attention in Cognitive Science

Initially, the term 'attention' was under the purview of philosophy which later came under psychology. Different philosophers have put forward their views on it. Aristotle noticed that everything that our sense organs sense is not perceived clearly. Augustine interpreted attention as an effort of the soul. Descartes distinguished active attention from passive attention. Leibniz discussed the relation between attention, perception and consciousness. Thus the empirical concept of attention was formed. Attention is also a topic of philosophical interest because of its apparent relations to a number of other philosophical phenomena like consciousness, *will and* understanding of *other minds*. In psychology, attention is interpreted as the cognitive activity of selecting a particular stimulus out of numerous stimuli in the environment. It encompasses various cognitive activities that are carried out on representations and involve amplification and attenuation mechanisms. Such mechanisms temporarily change the efficiency of our mental processes and have behavioural consequences (Camus, 2003). Neuroscience studies the neural basis of attention. Analysis of the neural characteristics of attention brings out the predominant role played by certain structures. These structures are organised into complex circuit or network that is responsible for the fundamental features of attentional processes. A central question is how the brain learns to detect relevant sensory features while ignoring irrelevant ones in order to successfully guide behaviour. At the neuronal level this process corresponds to the tuning of a cell's response profile, via synaptic modification, to become sensitive to the relevant features of a given category. Thus attention is the cognitive system that controls the quantity and quality of information that enters the individual's mind. The information that is selected enters the individual's cognitive system and then undergoes further processing.

**Attention in Education**

Attention is a prerequisite to learning and a basic element in classroom motivation. It is even believed that attentional skills are central to successful learning. Helping students to "pay attention" has always been a central concern of the teachers. So, attention may be related to education in two ways. Learning requires the students to pay attention to the task at hand. And attention as a skill may also be taught to the learners. Teachers must understand the basic mechanisms and processes that regulate attention. As William James put it "An education which should improve this faculty (attention) would be the education par excellence." Attention is closely related to the processes and products of learning, and therefore forms an important component of education. Probably, holding attention of the learners in the classroom is the most difficult part of teaching. Because attending to a single stimulus continuously with the same intensity for a long duration is difficult. The role of attention is to select information from the text that the learner is exposed to. Therefore, the teacher should keep this in mind while designing his pedagogy. The ability to attend with focus, clarity, and purpose is a skill everyone needs. Students are particularly in need of good attention skills. They must be able to attend to instructions, focus on the details of assignments, and stay on task until an assignment is completed. The key point for the teachers to realize is that *maintaining attention is a skill.* It has to be trained and practiced. Catering to short attention spans by offering materials that can be managed with short attention spans will not develop the skill of maintaining attention.

## Cognitive Basis of Attention

Attention encompasses various cognitive activities that are carried out on representations. Attention is related to the way the cognitive system processes information. In 1958, Donald Broadbent proposed a two-stage processing view in which an initial parallel processing stage is followed by a second sequential one. In 1970s, some researchers such as Michael Posner, Richard Shiffrin and Walter Schneider gave another view based on the distinction between two types of processes—

(i) Automatic Processes—It involves rapid parallel processes that do not require attention. Target detention is said to be automatic when it is defined by a single elementary property, on a single dimension such as colour, brightness, size or shape that can be analysed by prewired, specialised detectors functioning in parallel.

(ii) Controlled Processes—These are slow, serial and strategically determined. When the target is defined by a combination of two elementary properties belonging to two different dimensions and for which there is no dedicated analyser, detection is controlled.

## Historical Development of Theories of Attention

In the early modern period a variety of explanatory roles were assigned to attention by a number of different writers.

Descartes' (1596-1650) account of attention describes about its important epistemic role: clarity and distinctness realise their epistemic potential only when attention is paid to the ideas that have them. Descartes' epistemology is a move from radical doubt to certainty about the truth of particular clear and distinct ideas. Attention mediates this transition from doubt to certainty.

Locke (1632-1704) gives a theory of the explanatory role that attention plays. According to him, "when the ideas that offer themselves are taken notice of, and, as it were, registered in the memory, it is attention" (*Essay Concerning Human Understanding*). He believes that attention does not need any new substantive theory. They are, in Locke's theory, simply 'modes of thinking'. Locke's modal view of attention implies that no substantive theory of attention is needed once our theory of thinking is in place, but it also entails that attention cannot figure in the explanation of how thinking itself is possible.

Berkeley's (1685-1753) account of attention can be found in the second edition of the *Principles of Human Knowledge.* According to him, it is attention and, in particular, the withholding of attention that is supposed to explain the possibility of thinking about abstraction without the need to postulate Abstract Ideas.

Over the course of the 18th century, the concept of attention was increasingly treated as a phenomenon with explanatory work to do, and so as a phenomenon for which a substantive independent theory is needed. During this period the explanations for theories of attention broadened in two directions. The first move was (i) away from the idea that attention acts on already-received ideas and (ii) towards the idea that attention is involved in the initial reception of those ideas. Locke had characterised attention as the registration of already-received ideas into memory. But by 1769, attention's role as a regulator of cognitive input was regarded as definitive of it. Attention was said to be that state of mind which prepares one to receive impressions. According to the degree of attention objects make a strong or weak impression.

The 18th century theories moved towards including a role for attention in the production of *behaviour and in the explanation of the reception of ideas*. Dugald Stewart (1792) retained Locke's view that attention has an essential role to play in determining which things get stored in memory. He added to that view the claim that attention also has a role in determining which particular memories get recalled and in the explanation of the development and deployment of at least some skilled behaviours.

The diversity among the phenomena that attention was expected to explain continued to grow. It continued to include phenomena from across the psychological spectrum from perception, to thought, to action. This diversity among the psychologists resulted into a chaotic situation. At the end of the 19th and the beginning of the 20th century, the theorists of attention wanted to get this chaos into order. William James in his *The Principles of Psychology (1890),* attempted to play down the more complex perceptual aspects of attention. However, he does assign attention to an important explanatory role in the production of behaviour. He claimed that volition is attention.

Bradley (1886) advocated a view according to which attention is not the sort of phenomenon for which an independent and substantive theory can either be given or is required. He claims that no particular attention-processes can be identified since any function whatever of the body or the mind will be active attention if it is prompted by an interest and brings about the result of our engrossment with its product. There is no primary act of attention, there is no specific act of attention, and there is no one kind of act of attention at all.

In the early 20th century, behaviourism dominated the psychological scenario and as such the explanation of attention as well. Behaviourists tended to neglect attention, but they did not ignore it entirely. In the middle of the 20th century, behaviourism's dominance waned, cognitive psychology established itself, and a new theoretical approach to the explanation of attention was developed.

Donald Broadbent, the author of *Perception and Communication (1958),* claimed that the human brain is subject to capacity limitations as well as that these limitations are clustered so that there is a single bottleneck in capacity that is especially critical to the brain's information handling. The bottleneck was said to occur at the junction of two systems operating in series. The first system has a large capacity for information processing and operates automatically on all of the stimuli to which the subject is exposed. The second system has a much smaller capacity and is, therefore, selective.

In the decades following Broadbent, a great many psychologists devoted themselves to the task of locating the attentional bottleneck that he had postulated and were guided to some degree by Broadbent's two-systems-and-a-bottleneck theory of information processing. The question of whether a given task is attention demanding was understood to depend on the question of whether the performance of that task requires the engagement of the small-capacity system that comes after the bottleneck of attention. Research into the attention demands of particular tasks, therefore, became another way to approach the issue of where the attentional bottleneck is located.

## Models or Theories of Attention

Psychologists use the concept of attention to explain how we are able to select some aspects of our environment while ignoring some others. A number of models/theories of attention have been developed by various scholars.

Various researches place attention as an inferred process that can be assessed only indirectly. As a paradigm amenable to the study of attentional phenomena, however, discrimination learning is especially important, for it points up two types of conceptualisations of attention (pre-reception and post-reception models), both of which stem logically from early formulations of the discrimination learning process.

The pre-reception models of attention focus on a process which operates prior to the associative learning of an instrumental response and the discriminative stimuli which signal reward, thus emphasising the manner in which these cues are selectively attended to.

The post-reception models of attention deal with a response process that is an integral part of associative learning. In particular these models are concerned with the manner in which the organism may perceptually organise, interpret, or code the discriminative stimuli into stimulus compounds to which the instrumental response leading to reward can be attached.

Though the models/theories of attention are vague and ambiguous, recently researchers have developed some computational models of attention which provide useful insights into how the brain selectively processes parts of its inputs on the basis of measures of saliency and task relevance.

### *Gating Models of Attention*

According to this model, attention acts as a 'gate' into short term memory. It regulates the flow of sensory information into conscious awareness. When the attentional cue is detected, the attention 'gate' is opened and the information is admitted into memory. To avoid overflow of memory capacity, the gate is automatically closed for a short while after opening. This prevents other stimulus items from entering memory. The strength of an item stored in the memory depends on the gating function G and the time at which the item occurred with respect to gate opening. The interaction is multiplicative: a stimulus S passes through the attention gate with output strength G × S.

Attention is directed to the selected location by a gating mechanism that allows the stimuli near the selected location to be conveyed to the higher processing centres and suppresses stimuli at other locations. The topographic representation of an input sensory field is called a saliency map. Each location in a saliency map contains a value that represents how different or salient that location is, compared with other locations in sensory field.

Shifter circuits were proposed as a computational model for how the brain may solve the problem of routing the selected information to higher centres in a position and size invariant way within the context of visual information processing. The primary components of shifter circuits are the control neurons. They set the size and position of the attentional window and modulate the strength of synaptic connections from the lower level to a higher level such that only the information from the attended region in the lower level is routed to higher level.

### *Filter Theory of Attention*

Donald Broadbent (1926-1993), an influential English experimental psychologist propounded the filter theory of attention. It is considered as one of the most famous theories within the human information processing framework. It is an abstract, functional account of attention. It describes component stages of processing that are assumed to intervene between a given stimulus and the corresponding response.

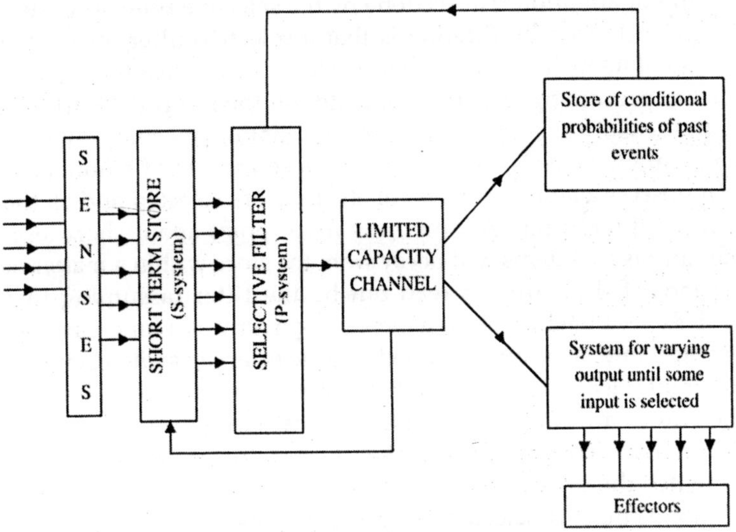


**Fig. 5.4:** Schematic representation of Broadbent's Filter Theory

In regard to information processing in humans, the outside world acts as the sender and the participant is the receiver. The limited capacity channel connects the sender with the receiver. Limited capacity means that there is an upper limit of the amount of information that can be transmitted down the channel at any given time. The central idea is that at an abstract level, the human central nervous system comprises a limited capacity information transmission channel. Sensory information is initially registered in parallel, but further processing operates in a serial mode. Moreover, because of the constraint of the limited capacity channel, only some of the information presented to the senses can be dealt with at once. Some of this information needs to be selected as being currently relevant—the rest is ignored. This notion of selection indicates to the notion of attention in the theory.

Broadbent schematically described the theory as—

Figure 5.3 shows that input to the senses is registered initially and is then forwarded to a short term store or sensory memory system (S system) in parallel. There is a large amount of sensory stimulation all of the time. It is assumed that, because of this, the S system handles various kinds of information in parallel. Now, the concern is to decide which aspects of this stimulation are worthy of attention. This is done by the selective filter. The basic idea of selection by filtering is that a selective filter affects the output of items from the short term store so as to pass them on for further processing. The filter operates on the information stored in the sensory memory, and such information specifies only the physical characteristics of stimuli. Those aspects of stimulation that possess a common physical attribute are selected and all the rest are filtered out. Another important point about short term memory is that items will decay from the store within a matter of seconds if they are not read out by the filter (assuming that probability of being selected increases directly as a function of its physical intensity). It is assumed that the filter can switch between different selection criteria but that such switches take time, because the filter can only follow one physical cue at once. So some information from the cue will likely be lost during the time it takes to switch the filter.

Items that are selected for read out by the filter are passed on to the limited capacity channel (P or perceptual system). If the system is in danger of information overload then any item selected for read out can be passed back from the P system and rehearsed, such that it is re-circulated into the short-term store. In this way, the limitations of the central channel are overcome to a certain extent.

Broadbent suggests that the P system affects perceptual-semantic categorisation, in that items in the P system are assigned to their corresponding mental categories. The output from the P system coded post categorical information. Sensory information is initially registered in the S system in some raw form that codes the physical nature of the stimulus, while outputs from the P system code the categorical nature of the stimulus—semantic information is made explicit.

The original filter theory suffers from various sorts of processing constraints. Moreover, the limited capacity channel (P system) provides a structural bottleneck. The upper limit of the capacity channel for a limited amount of information is its structural constraint. While the upper limit on how quickly any item can be cleared from the S system is the processing constraint.

**Late Filtering Accounts of Selection**

In the late filtering account of attention, selection takes place at a much later stage of processing and involves much more complex categories than physical stimulus properties. Deutsch and Deutsch (1963) discussed data that were taken to reveal semantic analysis of unattended material. Here, semantic analysis means the assignment of importance to the various stimuli. They took the evidence to show that 'all sensory messages which make impact on the organism are perceptually analysed at the highest level'.

Such a view has also been developed by Duncan (1984). According to him, each stimulus is fully identified before any selection takes place. This means that a representation of the stimulus is derived that codes its physical characteristics, its name if this is applicable, and its category assignment. According to Kahneman (1973), the late filtering model implies that 'the meanings of all concurrent stimuli are extracted in parallel and without interference'. Therefore any form of selection only takes place at a post categorical stage of processing prior to response execution. That means, everything is identified but that the critical constraints relate to responding.

Though the debate between early and late selection eventually led to fruitlessness, several capacity limitation based theories were developed. There are theories according to which attention corresponds to a capacity bottleneck (like Broadbent), but it is a bottleneck that moves, depending on the demands of the task at hand (Lavie and Tsal, 1994). Other theories retain Broadbent's idea that attentional selectivity is the result of capacity limitations, but rejects the early and late selection theories because they reject the idea that those capacity limitations are clustered into a single bottleneck.

**Feature Integration Theory**

This theory was developed by Anne Treisman (1935-), one of the most influential cognitive psychologists in the world. It is also known as the attenuated filter model of attention. She defined fundamental issues of how information is selected and integrated to form meaningful objects and memories that guide human thought and action. Some evidence were reported which indicate that unattended messages may be analysed at the semantic level. This led to a modification of the original filter theory. Experiments showed that occasionally the subjects followed the content of the message across the channels for one or two words after the messages switched but they then immediately reverted back to the attended channel. It led to the conclusion that some form of semantic analysis of the unattended message must have been taking place. This finding led Treisman to suggest that, in contrast to the original all-or-nothing filter in original filter theory; unattended messages were attenuated and were not completely blocked out from further analysis. The filter operates to dampen down the unattended message but it does not block it out completely.

This theory is based on 'the binding problem'. The binding problem is the problem of knowing how to put together the properties that are detected in separate specialised detection centres. Treisman's proposed solution to the binding problem is based on the fact that spatial representations are present everywhere simultaneously, and the idea that there is only one thing to be seen in any place at any time. She proposes that we achieve a correctly bound representation by moving a variously sized 'window' from one location in the perceptual scene to another. This window blocks out the information from all but a single location, and all the features found at that location can then be 'bound' as being features of the same object. The area covered by the window within which features are bound is taken to correspond to the region to which attention is being paid. As the features of the stimuli found at one location are integrated, it is known as Feature Integration Theory.

**Coherence Theories**

In 1970s, Ulreic Neisser and others showed through an experiment that when appropriately trained, a subject can perform two attention involving tasks concurrently without much interference between them. Neisser interpreted that, in so far as there is a bottleneck that attention is needed to manage, it must often be a bottleneck in behavioural co-ordination, rather than in simple information processing capacity.

In 1987, Odmar Neumann and Alan Allport also presented similar views. However, they emphasized that the constraints are placed on cognition by the need to maintain a coherent course of action. According to them, the function of attention is not the management of capacity limitations. Instead, it is the management of capacity excess. It is because we can process multiple stimuli that we get distracted by them, not because we can't process them, that we need mechanisms of attention to provide selectivity and focus. Thus, attention serves to lend coherence to, and to prevent competition and interference between, the activities of components in a system that has the capacity to handle far more stimuli than those pertaining to the subject's current task.

### Competition Theories

The coherence theories are natural accompaniments to views according to which the mechanisms of attentional selection are something other than the capacity bottlenecks. The clearest non-bottleneck mechanisms for achieving selectivity are competitions. Well organised competitions can always select one winner, however well, and however numerous, the competitors are.

Competition based mechanisms for achieving selectivity come in at least two varieties: in a simple race mechanism, each of the competitors independently completes a process that is comparable along some dimension of variation with the processes completed by the other competitors. The competitor that achieves the highest value on the relevant dimension of variation is selected as the winner. Another is struggle (race mechanism), in which the competitors also involve in active suppression of other competitors along with their own processing.

### Spotlight Theories

Bottleneck metaphors attempt to locate the cognitive resources that operate only on attended stimuli. Spotlight theories attempt to say which features of a stimulus determine whether attention is being paid to that stimulus at any given moment. The central idea suggested by the spotlight metaphor is that the determinant of whether or not a stimulus is attended is the stimulus's location. It resembles the idea that we have a small field of vision and it is hard to see things outside of this spotlight region, although attention can be shifted by moving this light.

### Pedagogical Implications of Attention

Attention constitutes an important concept in the pedagogical process. The importance of attention in a pedagogical situation can be inferred from the fact that the first event of instruction is gaining attention (Gagne, 1974). Good instructional design directs the learners' attention, helping them to avoid distractions and "information overload". It is claimed by some teachers that every form of education is an education of attention above all. The call of education is to introduce a degree of co-ordination, meaningfulness and direction into the chaotic and uncoordinated reactions of the child. The fundamental principle of education lies in the selection of those most essential and most important reactions that have to be preserved. Therefore, it is essential for the teachers (pedagogue) to understand the nuts and bolts of attention. If a teacher understands the philosophical, psychological and neural basis of attention, it becomes helpful for designing as well as practicing his pedagogy.

Jang, Schunn and Nokes (2011) suggest that simply manipulating the spatial format of instructions, leaving learning task materials alone, may suffice to significantly improve both task performance and learning. The study shows that the act of distributing instructions while holding task material format constant is enough to improve learning significantly. In terms of theoretical implications for the split-attention effect, the results suggest that the effect appears not to be binary in nature (as the integrated vs. separated framework would suggest); rather, there appear to be degrees of effects as access costs increase (e.g., integrated displays < distributed displays < stacked displays along a dimension of access cost).

The results of the study by Baijal, Jha, Kiyonaga, Singh, and Srinivasan (2011) are that conflict resolution, indexed by current trial performance, regardless of previous trial conditions, was significantly improved in the students attending the Concentrative Meditation Training (CMT) vs. other school, in all age groups. Concentrative attention is that which is restricted to a specific focus. While conflict adaptation was not improved in this group, relative to the Control group in terms of reaction time, there was an improvement in terms of accuracy. This CMT-related benefit during previous trial analysis, involved a convergence of age and trial conditions in which proactive control was least likely to have been engaged. That is, the CMT group's accuracy was significantly better than the Control group, when the current trial was incongruent and preceded by a congruent trial. This context may maximise the need to employ reactive control, and it was only under these circumstances that the CMT outperformed the control group.

Despite its importance to learning, focussed attention is rarely if ever systematically trained or cultivated in most educational settings.

Another aspect of attention related to pedagogy is that it can be developed as a skill among the learners. Shapira, Brown and Astin (2008) suggest that attention and the behavioural responses associated with it may be flexible skills that can be cultivated through concentration and mindfulness meditation practices.

Zylowska *et al.*, (2008) and Woolacott (2007) also suggest that meditative practice may help to improve the deficits associated with Attention Deficit Hyperactivity Disorder (ADHD), as assessed by computer-based tasks in controlled laboratory settings and parental report. For concentrative meditations, first the focus is set and attempt is made to retain it on a particular object (such as the sensation of breathing or a word), the loss of the intended focus is noticed, after this, unintended focus is discontinued (e.g., worrying about some impending task), and then the intended focus is restored. Research suggests that meditative practices can enhance specific aspects or subsystems of attention.

Commenting on attentional feedback and rewards, Watling, Mansvelder, Roelfsema and Ooyen (2010) suggest that the attentional feedback and reward signals are both necessary and sufficient to explain the formation of the category specific internal representations that have been observed to accompany learning.

During the early years of the child, attention is almost reflexively instinctive in nature. Gradually, it turns into voluntary orientation through gradual, lengthy and complex training guided by the most important needs of the organism and in turn, guiding the full course of its behaviour. This reflex and passive character of attention which makes the child seem to belong less to himself than to every object which happens to catch his notice, is the first thing which the teacher must overcome.

Therefore, the child's interest (involuntary attention) has great pedagogical importance. An important issue in pedagogy is to take the appropriate path in between the path followed by the child's natural interest and the path mapped out by the tasks required for the child. Education means neither simply following the child's natural inclinations nor a fruitless struggle against these inclinations. It is a path in between and requires combining the two extremes together into a unified whole. Education proceeds by taking these inclinations as the starting point. But it intervenes actively in these natural inclinations of the child, brings them together, grouping them, preserving some of them, stimulating some of them, and in this way, introduces the spontaneous process of the child's inclinations into the organising and shaping channel of the social environment in the school.

Teaching, in general, is possible only in as much as it relies on the child's own interests. Therefore, the teacher should work alongside the child's natural interest or attention. He should orient the subject matter according to the natural inclination of the child and from there he can gradually demand attention for the required tasks. The question is how far this interest may be directed along the path of the actual subject being studied. The teacher has to design his pedagogy in such a way as to utilise the natural interests of children in motivating the children towards the task in hand.

Thus, the analysis has helped in building a historical background of the field of cognitive science, both in western and Indian perspectives. The analysis of the components has brought out that the psychological aspects related to the mind or cognition constitute the field of cognitive science. Although many of these components are relevant in education, five components were further analysed to find out the pedagogical problems and the pedagogical implications. These are—learning, problem solving, creativity, intelligence and attention. The concepts, the cognitive theories and the pedagogical implications of these components have been analysed theoretically from the perspective of cognitive science. The cognitive theories of learning which have been discussed are Gestalt theory, Tolman's theory, Lewin's theory, Piaget's theory, Bruner's theory, Ausubel's theory, Vygotsky's theory, Information processing theory and the learning systems. The pedagogical problems related to learning and the pedagogical implications for each theory have been analysed. Likewise, the cognitive approaches to problem solving (Gestalt theory and Information Processing theory), the problems of teaching problem solving and the pedagogical implications have also been analysed. The cognitive theories of creativity included Taylor's Level theory, Freud's psychoanalytic theory, Arieti's theory, Creative Cognition theory, Amabile's theory, Wallas' model, Gruber's model and Greene's model. The pedagogical problems of creativity and the implications of the cognitive

**Table 5.3:** Pedagogical Problems and Implications of Cognitive Science

| *Components* | *Pedagogical Problems* | *Pedagogical Implications of Cognitive Science* |
|---|---|---|
| LEARNING | Concept of learning | Instructions in learning processes |
| | Perplexed goal of learning | Instructions in learning processes |
| | Relating new learning to previous learning | Insight based on past experience, so past and present should be presented together |
| | Mismatch of content and pedagogy | Problem-solving approach<br>More importance to values in the content than to content itself |
| | Differentiating learning from knowledge accumulation | Comparing-contrasting solutions procedures helps in gaining procedural knowledge<br>Instruction in learning processes |
| | Fragmented learning | Follow Gestalt principle (whole to part)<br>Insightful learning |
| | Less time for practice | Adequate time for practice for internalisation and meaningful learning |
| | Knowledge construction | Use of Socratic method among students as well as with teacher<br>Provide necessary resources (classroom full of interesting things) |
| | Social and individual nature of learning | Collaborative learning with small groups to respect individuality |
| CREATIVITY | Rigidity | Open and challenging environment<br>Creative problem solving |
| | Excess media consumption | Techniques like brainstorming, thumbnail sketches, synectics, matrixes, etc. |
| | Structured environment | Experimental and error-welcoming teaching |
| | Balancing between nature of creative students and others | Appreciation of learner's individuality<br>Self-confidence of learners |
| | Misconceptions about creativity | Teacher must believe and realize that creativity can be taught<br>Sensitive and imaginative pedagogic practice |
| INTELLIGENCE | Creating environment for fostering intelligence | Rich learning environment<br>Emotional safety<br>Challenges through experience |
| | Evaluating intelligence | Authentic methods of assessment<br>Diverse assessment of school achievement |
| | Handling intellectual relativism | Teaching all types of intelligence<br>Multimodal delivery (techniques, tools and strategies)<br>Avoid labeling intelligence<br>Consider individual differences |
| PROBLEMSOLVING | Haphazard problem solving | Consider all factors of problem solving<br>Promote meaningful learning rather than rote learning |
| | Lack of background knowledge | Using mental models to represent the structure of concepts<br>Using intuition and logic to develop problem solving skills |
| | Application of background knowledge | Guide metacognition<br>Variable problem context should be used<br>Facilitate analogy |
| | Not focussing on the problem | Recognising the essence of the problem<br>Giving sufficient time to ponder over the problem<br>Proper representation of problem |
| | Using only knowledge rather than reasoning | Focus on the process of problem solving rather than its product<br>Use of concrete thinking (examples) |
| | Decision-making process | Focus explicitly on decision-making process |
| ATTENTION | Handling numerous stimuli | Concentrative meditation training |
| | Catering to different natural interests | Intervene in natural interests, bring them together, group them, preserve some, stimulate some and channelise others. |
| | Spilt attention | Distributing instructions while holding task material format constant |
| | ADHD | Meditative practices |

theories and cognitive science research have been evaluated. Intelligence constitutes an important component of cognitive science. The theories of intelligence considered in cognitive science are Sternberg's Triarchic theory, Cattell and Horn's theory, Jensen's mental functioning theory, Gardner's Multiple Intelligence theory, Newell and Simon's theory, PASS theory and Perkin's theory. The analysis shows that pedagogically, Gardner's theory has more implications than the other theories. The Gating model of attention, the Filter theory, the Feature Integration theory, Coherence theories, Competition theories, Spotlight theories have been analysed to understand the cognitive perspective of attention. The pedagogical problems related to attention and the implications of cognitive science research on attention have been analysed.

So far the problems related to the components have already been discussed with the respective components. However, on the basis of the works and models referred by Ivie (1998), Whiteley (2006), Rittle-Johnson and Star (2007), Kumar and Gupta (2009), Limjap (2002), Ross (2007), Hamza and Griffith (2006), Lin (2011), Fogarty (1998), Jang, Schunn and Nokes (2011), etc. the researcher has developed a chart to make it convenient to follow the pedagogical problems and implications of cognitive science, which is presented below (Table 5.3).

It is evident that an integrated approach is needed to knowledge and information along with the integrated level of understanding of the learner or the child for effective pedagogy.

## References


Abeille, A. (2003). Creativity (Lingistics). In O. Houde (Ed.), *Dictionary of cognitive science,* 94. New York: Psychology Press.

Amabile, T. (2013). Componential theory of creativity. In E.H. Kessler (Ed.), *Encyclopedia of management theory.* Sage Publications.

Armstrong, T. (2000). *Multiple intelligences in the classroom* (2nd ed.). Alexandria, VA: Association for Supervision and Curriculum Development.

Ashman, A.F., and Conway, R.N.F. (1989). *Cognitive strategies for special education: Process-based instruction*. London: Routledge.

Ausubel, D.P., Novak, J.D. and Hanesian, H. (1978). *Educational psychology: A cognitive view.* New York: Holt, Rinehart and Winston.

Baijal, S., Jha, A.P., Kiyonaga, A., Singh, R., and Srinivasan, N. (2011). The influence of concentrative meditation training on the development of attention networks during early adolescence. *Frontiers in Psychology, 2*, p. 153.

Barb, C., and Quinn, A.L. (1997). Problem solving does not have to be a problem. *The Mathematics Teacher, 90* (7), pp. 536-541.

Bernardo, A.B.I. (1997). The psychology of mathematical learning and problem solving: Implications for mathematics education. Proceedings of *Mathted'97 Conference.* Manila: De La Salle University.

Bradley, F.H. (1886). Is there any special activity of attention? *Mind, 11* (43), pp. 305-323.

Bransford, J.D., Sherwood, R., Vye, N.J., and Rieser, J. (1986). Teaching thinking and problem solving. *American Psychologist, 41* (10), pp. 1078-1089.

Brower, R. (2003). Constructive repetition, time and the evolving systems approach. *Creativity Research Journal, 15, pp.* 61-72.

Brown, R.T. (1989). Creativity: What are we measure? In J.A. Glover, R.R. Ronning and C.R. Reynolds (Eds.). *Handbook of creativity,* pp. 3-32. New York: Plenum.

Camus, J-F. (2003). Attention (Psychology). In H. Oliver (Ed.), *Dictionary of Cognitive Science,* pp. 28-30. New York: Psychology Press.

Chavez- Eakle, R.A. (2010). The relevance of creativity in education. *New Horizons for Learning, Spring.* Retrieved from http://education.jhu.edu

Christensen, T. (2013). What neuroscience teaches us about creativity. Retrieved from http://creativesomething.net/post/57423335221/what-neuroscience-teaches-us-about-creativity

Cole, D.G., Sugioka, H.L. and Yamagata-Lynch, L.C. (1999). Supportive classroom environments for creativity in higher education. *Journal of Creative Behaviour, 33* (4), pp. 277-293.

Das, J.P., Kirby, J.R., and Jarman R.F. (1975). Simultaneous and successive syntheses: An alternative model for cognitive abilities. *Psychological Bulletin, 82* (8), p. 103.

Decety, J. and Koenig, O. (2003). Learning (Neuroscience). In O. Houde (Ed.), *Dictionary of cognitive science,* pp. 198-199. New York: Psychology Press.

Deutsch, J.A., and Deutsch, D. (1963). Attention: Some theoretical considerations. *Psychological Review, 70,* pp. 80-90.

Dixon, J., and McPhee, A.D. (2001). Howard Gardner and education: The theory of multiple intelligences. In M. Peters, P. Ghiraldelli, B. Zarnic, A. Gibbons (Eds.), *Encyclopedia of philosophy of education.* Retrieved from http://eepat.net/doku.php?id=howard_gardner_and_education

Duncan, J. (1984). Selective attention and the organisation of visual information. *Journal of Experimental Psychology: General, 113,* pp. 501-517.

Elshout, J. (1995). Creativity. In T. Husen and T.N. Postlethwaite (Eds.), *The International Encyclopedia of Education,* 2. New York: Pergamon Press.

Feldhusen, J.F. (1983). Eclecticism: A comprehensive approach to education of the gifted. In C.P. Benbow and J.C. Stanley (Eds.), *Academic precocity: Aspects of its development* (pp. 192-204). Baltimore: Johns Hopkins University Press.

Fogarty, R. (1998). Intelligence-friendly classroom: It just makes sense. *Phi Delta Kappan, 79* (9).

Ford, D.Y. and Harris, J.J. (1992). The elusive definition of creativity. *The Journal of Creative Behaviour, 26* (3), pp. 186-198.

Fredericksen, N. (1984). The Real Test Bias: Influences of Testing on Teaching and Learning. *American Psychologist, 39*, pp. 193-202.

Gagne, R.M. (1974). *Essentials of learning instruction*. Hinsdale, IL: The Dryden Press.

Gagne, R.M. (1980). Learnable aspects of problem solving. *Educational Psychologist, 15* (2), pp. 84-92.

Ganascia, J-G. (2003). Learning (Artificial Intelligence). In O. Houde (Ed.), *Dictionary of cognitive science,* pp. 198-199. New York: Psychology Press.

Gardner, H. (1993). *Multiple intelligences: The theory in practice.* New York: Basic Books.

Gardner, H. (1999). *Intelligence reframed: Multiple intelligences for the 21st century*. New York: Basic Books.

Ghallab, M. (2003). Problem solving (Artificial Intelligence). In Olivier Houde (Ed.), *Dictionary of cognitive science, pp* 288-290. New York: Psychology Press.

Goldstein, E.B. (2005). *Cognitive psychology: Connecting mind, research, and everyday experience*. California: Thomson Wadsworth.

Gruber, H.E. and Davis, S.N. (1988). Inching our way up Mount Olympus: The evolving systems approach to creative thinking. In R.J. Sternberg (Ed.), *The nature of creativity: Contemporary psychological perspectives,* pp. 243-270. Cambridge, UK: Cambridge University Press.

Haier, R.J. and Jung, R.E. (2008). Brain imaging studies on intelligence and creativity: What is the picture for education? *Roeper Review, 30,* pp. 171-180. doi: 10.1080/02783190802199347

Hamza, M.K. and Griffith, K.G. (2006). Fostering problem solving and creative thinking in the classroom: cultivating a creative mind. *National Forum of Applied Educational Research Journal-Electronic, 19* (3), pp. 1-30. Retrieved from http://www.nationalforum.com/Electronic%20Journal%20Volumes/Hamza,%20Mohammed%20Fostering %20Problem%20Solving%20%26% 20Creative%20Thinking%20in%20the%20Classroom.pdf

Hayes, J.R. (1989). *The complete problem solver* (2nd ed.). Hillsdale, NJ: Erlbaum.

Hayes, J.R. and Simon, H.A. (1974). Understanding written problem instructions. In L.W. Gregg (Ed.), *Knowledge and cognition*. Potomac, MD: Erlbaum.

Houde O. (2003). Learning (Psychology). In O. Houde (Ed.), *Dictionary of cognitive science*, pp. 196-198. New York: Psychology Press.

Isaken, S.G., and Treffinger, D.J. (1985). *Creative problem solving: The basic course*. Buffalo, NY: Bearly Limited.

Ivie, S.D. (1998). Ausubel's learning theory: An approach to teaching higher order thinking skills. (Educational psychologist David Paul Ausubel). *High School Journal, 82* (1), p. 35.

James, W. (1890). *The principles of psychology*. New York: Holt.

Jang, J., Schunn, C.D., and Nokes, T.J. (2011). Spatially distributed instructions improve learning outcomes and efficiency. *Journal of Educational Psychology, 103* (1), pp. 60-72. doi: 10.1037/a0021994

Kahneman, D. (1973). *Attention and effort*. Englewood Cliffs, NJ: Prentice-Hall.

Kumar, R. and Gupta, V.K. (2009). An introduction to cognitive constructivism in education. *Journal of Indian Education, 35* (3), pp. 39-45.

Lautrey, J., and Lubart, T. (2003). Creativity (Psychology). In O. Houde (Ed.), *Dictionary of cognitive science*, pp. 93-94. New York: Psychology Press.

Lavie, N., and Tsal, Y. (1994). Perceptual load as a major determinant of the locus of selection in visual attention. *Perception and Psychophysics, 56*, pp. 183-197.

Limjap, A.A. (2002). Issues on problem solving: drawing implications for a techno-mathematics curriculum at the collegiate level. *TanglaW, 8*, 55-85. *Retrieved from archives.math.utk.edu/ICTCM/VOL12/C030/paper.pdf*

Lin, Y. (2011). Fostering creativity through education—A conceptual framework of creative pedagogy, *Creative Education*, 2 (3), pp. 149-155. doi: 10.4236/ce.2011.23021.

Lovett, M.C. (2003). Problem solving. In L. Nadel (Ed.), *Encyclopedia of cognitive science*, 3, pp. 728-733. New York: Macmillan Publisher Ltd.

Luger, G.F. (1994). *Cognitive science: The science of intelligent systems*. San Diego: Academic Press.

Mayer, R.E. and Wittrock, R.C. (2006). Problem solving. In P.A. Alexander and P.H. Winne (Eds.), *Handbook of educational psychology* (2nd ed.). Mahwah, NJ: Erlbaum.

McLeod, S. (2007). *Vygotsky*. Retrieved from http://www.simplypsychology.org/ vygotsky.html

McWilliam, E.L. (2007). Is creativity teachable? Conceptualising the creativity/pedagogy relationship in higher education. Proceedings of *30th HERDSA Annual Conference: Enhancing Higher Education, Theory and Scholarship*, Adelaide. Retrieved from http://eprints.qut.edu.au/

Mitchell, T.M. (1997). *Machine learning*. McGraw Hill.

Novick, L.R. (2003). Psychology of problem solving. In L. Nadel (Ed.), *Encyclopedia of cognitive science*, 3, pp. 734-740. New York: Macmillan Publisher Ltd.

Parnes, S.J. (1975). CPSI—A programme for balanced growth. *The Journal of Creative Behaviour*, 9 (1), pp. 23-29.

Reif, F. (2008). *Applying cognitive science to education: Thinking and learning in scientific and other complex domains*. Cambridge: The MIT Press.

Rittle-Johnson, B. and Star, J.R. (2007). Does comparing solution methods facilitate conceptual and procedural knowledge? An experimental study on learning to solve equations. *Journal of Educational Psychology, 99*, pp. 561-574.

Ross, B.H. (2007). Cognitive science: Problem solving and learning for physics education. *AIP Conference Proceedings of the Physics Education Research Conference*, 11-14, p. *951*. doi: 10.1063/1.2820910

Roy, R. (2001). *Status of tribal teachers in Assam and West Bengal: A comparative study* (Unpublished doctoral dissertation). Assam University, Silchar.

Schank, R. (2011). *Teaching minds: How cognitive science can save our schools*. New York and London: Teachers College Press.

Schoenfeld, A.H. (1983). Beyond the purely cognitive: Belief systems, social cognitions, and metacognitions as driving forces in intellectual performance. *Cognitive Science*, *7* (4), pp. 329-363.

Shapira, S.L., Brown, K.W., and Astin, J.A. (2008). Towards the integration of meditation into higher education: A review of research. Unpublished manuscript.

Simone, C.D. (2008). Problem-based learning: A framework for prospective teachers' pedagogical problem solving. *Teacher Development*, *12* (3), pp. 179-191.

Skinner, B.F. (1968). *The technology of teaching*. New York: Appleton-Century-Crofts

Sobe, N.W. (2004). Challenging the gaze: The subject of attention and a 1915 Montessori demonstration classroom. *Educational Theory*, *54* (3), *pp.* 281-297.

Sternberg, R. (2003*). Intelligence. In* L. Nadel (Ed.), *Encyclopedia of cognitive science*, 2, pp. 587-589. New York: Macmillan Publisher Ltd.

Sternberg, R.J. (1985). *Beyond IQ: A triarchic theory of human intelligence*. London: Cambridge University Press.

Sternberg, R.J. (1999). *Successful intelligence: finding a balance. Trends in Cognitive Sciences,* 3 (11), pp. 436-442.

Stewart, D. (1972). *Elements of the philosophy of the human mind.* London: Strahan & Cadell.

Ward, T.B., Smith, S.M. and Finke, R.A. (1999). Creative cognition. In T.B. Ward (Ed.), *Handbook of Creativity,* pp. 189-212. New York: Cambridge University Press.

Watling, L.A., Mansvelder, H.D., Roelfsema, P.R., and Ooyen, A. (2010). The attention-gated reinforcement learning model can explain experimentally observed changes in tuning curves that follow category learning. *7th FENS Forum of European Neuroscience.* Amsterdam, The Netherlands.

Wechsler, D. (1958). *The measurement and appraisal of adult intelligence* (4th ed.). Baltimore: Williams & Wilkins.

Wertheimer, M. (1959). *Productive thinking.* New York: Harper & Row.

Whiteley, T.R. (2006). Using the Socratic method and Bloom's taxonomy of cognitive domain to enhance online discussion, critical thinking, and student learning, *Developments in Business Simulation and Experiential Learning, 33,* pp. 65-70.

Woolacott, M. (2007). The effects of meditation on the efficiency of attentional processing: Physiological and behavioural measures. Paper presented at the *5th Annual International Scientific Conference Integrating Mindfulness-Based Interventions into Medicine,* Worcester, MA: Health Care and Society.

Zylowska, L., Ackerman, D.L., Yang, M.H., Futrell, J.L., Horton, N.L., Hale, T.S.,... Smalley, S.L. (2008). Mindfulness meditation training in adults and adolescents with ADHD. *Journal of Attention Disorders, 11* (6), pp. 737-746.

# 6

# Emerging Issues in Cognitive Science and Classroom

Cognitive science is a vast field and constitutes a large number of components. As discussed in earlier chapters, most of the components are relevant in the field of education. But the teachers have to face different problems while practicing these components in the pedagogical context. These are the issues to be addressed in the field of cognitive science in relation to pedagogy.

## Issues Related to Learning

The classroom is a place where the teacher teaches the learners. The essence of teaching is in learning. But the teacher faces various problems regarding learning in the classroom setting.

- *Understanding the inherent meaning of learning*: One major problem concerning learning is to understand the term 'learning' itself. While coping with the content and the technology to deliver it, the teacher's focus is sidetracked from the actual meaning of learning. If the teacher is able to understand the inherent meaning of learning and adopts the appropriate approach towards it, it becomes easier for both the learners to learn and the teacher to teach.
- *Perplexed goal of Learning*: Learning is a purposeful activity. If the goal of learning is disoriented, learning cannot take place. Cognitive science regards learning as 'change in cognitive abilities'. Most of the time, the teacher misinterpret this very purpose of learning as mere 'accumulation of information'.
- *Cannot relate new knowledge with the existing ones*: The teacher has to base the new learning upon some existing

conceptual knowledge. It has to be anchored on the existing knowledge base. If the conceptual base of the learner is not strong or if the teacher cannot relate the new learning with the existing one, it cannot be said that proper learning has taken place and even if it takes place, it is not enduring.

- *Mismatch of content and pedagogy*: The content is always designed with some goals and learning objectives in view. It is not the content that our education system wants us to learn but the values inherent in those contents. If the pedagogy to deliver the content is not appropriate for that particular content, the very purpose of the curriculum may be diminished.
- *Knowledge versus learning*: There is a difference between acquiring knowledge and learning. Learning is a broader term than mere acquiring knowledge. However, acquiring knowledge may be a part of learning. It is difficult for an average teacher to understand this difference and most teachers treat them equally. Everything can neither be taught nor learnt. So, being capable of using the knowledge acquired through learning to tackle situations in one's life is actual learning.
- *Fragmented learning*: In a hurry to deliver more information within a short period, the teacher often presents fragmented knowledge to the learners which become difficult for them to understand. They know the contents but they cannot relate them.
- *Lack of practice time*: Whatever the learners learns, they need some time to internalise it through some practice. But most of the times the learners are not given adequate time for practicing, for which the learners cannot internalize the concepts.
- *Providing appropriate environment for knowledge construction*: It is said that children are natural knowledge constructor. They construct knowledge form their surroundings. But it is difficult for the teacher to control all the components of the environment all the time.
- *Individual difference*: Learning is both an individualised and a social process. Every individual has his own characteristics according to which pedagogy is to be

designed and the individuals also have to support each other in knowledge construction.

## Issues Related to Problem Solving

There are some common obstacles to solving problems like—

- *Functional fixedness*: It refers to the tendency to regard the functions, objects and ideas as fixed. Functional fixedness is also sometimes called response set. It is the tendency for a person to frame or think about each problem in a series in the same way as the problem, even when doing so is not appropriate to later problems.
- *Negative transfer*: When the experience of solving an earlier problem impedes the solution of a later one, it is known as negative transfer.
- *Improper problem representation*: Inability to represent and interpret the problem in a way that the nature of the problem and the initial state and the goal state are clear to the problem solver impedes successful problem solving.

The teacher has the challenges of dealing with the following limitations that the students pose while teaching problem solving. Some problems that the students face in solving problems are—

(1) Students approach problems haphazardly. They lack a systematic approach towards problem solving. In the hurry to search the solution, they overlook understanding of the problem.
(2) They lack the background knowledge that would solve the problem solving procedure. They try to construct the solution of a problem while they are ill-prepared and not aware of some knowledge useful for the problem solving task.
(3) They lack knowledge of how to apply the background knowledge appropriately. Though they have the background knowledge, they are not sure of which knowledge to apply when, where and how (Ross, 2007).
(4) They get stuck not knowing how to arrive at a solution. They focus most of their attention on the actual

construction of a problem solution, but spend little prior time on carefully describing and analysing a problem.

(5) They rely predominantly on their accumulated knowledge of their previously encountered similar problems, rather than on reasoning based on a few general concepts and principles.

(6) Teachers most commonly teach problem solving by means of examples and practice. The reasoning part of the problem solving procedure is mostly ignored.

Teachers rarely emphasise the important decision processes needed for problem solving. Decision processes include how to search for potentially useful options and how to make sensible choices among these.

**Issues Related to Creativity**

Our educational system, though gives importance to creativity in policies and papers, but do not foster creativity in the actual classroom. Its rigid routine and definite time frame stifles the creativity of the students.

Some common misconceptions about creativity also hinder development of creativity in the classroom. For instance, misconceptions about creativity as mysterious (undefined), magical (only certain people have the "gift"), madness (to be creative you have to be strange or abnormal), and the 'eureka' concept (Cole, Sugioka and Yamagata-Lynch, 1999). These beliefs on the part of the teacher or even in students hinder the teaching of creativity.

It is a fundamental fact that most children spend the majority of their day in a highly structured, perhaps overly rigid learning environment. The teachers have to tackle the problem of preserving the child's inherent and natural curiosity and creativity. This highly structured environment may result due to excess media consumption, because students are spending much time interacting with smart phones, video games and television, standardised testing or other root causes.

The nature of the creative person poses as a problem for the teacher in the classroom like—non-conformity to the contemporary trends, hyper-activity, high verbality, not following the routines, etc. It becomes difficult for the teacher to balance between the nature of such creative children and the academic routine that they have to follow. However, there is evidence that creativity and divergent thinking are not totally contrasted with academic achievement and convergent thinking. The major difference between the two types of thinking is that in academic achievement, the tendency is to reproduce already established conclusions and in creative thinking, the tendency is to go beyond it.

The main problem in regard to creativity in classroom is the debate between providing a structured or unstructured learning environment for the students. Though the highly structured classroom also has excellent provisions for fostering creativity, it is questionable whether it can be limited within these structures.

**Issues Related to Intelligence**

The most critical problem with intelligence in the classroom is its broad and relative concept. It is easy to deal with a concept which is definite and can be easily described. But the complexity of the concept of intelligence creates various problems for the teachers to deal with the intelligence of the students. Though the theories proposed by various psychologists come for the rescue of the teacher, but the variations in their opinions again create problem for them.

Sternberg's theory is criticised in regard to practical applications. He has repeatedly implied that he has evidence for a general factor of practical intelligence that is largely independent of g and that predicts life success at least as well as g, if not better. However, sufficient evidence cannot be found in support of this. The major points of criticism focus on the difficulties of reliably measuring "unconventional" (e.g., creative and practical) abilities and differentiating them psychometrically from abilities measured by more conventional tests of intelligence and achievement.

Applying Gardener's multiple intelligence theory in the classroom has some problems. The theory may be misinterpreted regarding intellectual relativism. Students' failures may be explained away as being an example of a different kind of intelligence, and not accounted as failure. This theory suggests that 'someone may be good in one intelligence but not in another'. But this assertion is not supported by correlation studies. On the basis of such studies, it is argued that persons who excel in one type of intelligence usually excel in several others; and many times in all. The third major criticism of multiple intelligences as an application in schools is that there is a risk of teachers excusing students from doing well in an area in which they are weak. The goal of the students is to succeed in all areas defined as intelligence by Gardner, and not default to their strengths. Another criticism is that the distinction between developmental stage and "intelligence" is not sufficiently well accounted for.

### Issues Related to Attention

Attention comprises one of the most important components or say factors in a teacher's agenda while teaching in a classroom. It is one of the main challenges for the teacher to hold the attention of students in the classroom.

- *Numerous stimuli:* The learners are exposed to a number of and a variety of stimuli in and outside the classroom. Directing their interest towards the desired task or bringing the focus of their mind to the task at hand is a problem.
- *Identify natural interest:* The challenge for the teacher is to identify the natural interest (natural distractions) of the learners and direct their attention towards the task without forcing them.
- *Exposure:* How much of exposure will be good to hold the attention of the students is another question to be answered. The teacher has to decide on the amount of exposure. It has to be enough to attract the attention of the learner as well as limited to the degree that they are not distracted by exposure to a large number of stimuli.
- *Catering to different natural interests:* It is also difficult to cater to different natural interests of the learners. Presenting the learning materials to the learners so as to attract their natural attention is also a problem.
- *Split attention effect:* Instructional split attention occurs when learners are required to split their attention between and mentally integrate several sources of physically or temporally disparate information, where each source of

information is essential for understanding the material. It increases the cognitive load of the learners. Handling the split attention effect of the students is another issue to be addressed in pedagogy.

- *ADHD:* Another problem faced by the teacher is to deal with the Attention Deficit Hyperactivity Disorder children. They are characterised by deficits in response inhibition, error monitoring, attentional disengagement, attentional networks, and motivational style (delay aversion).
- *Feedback:* Whether paying attention by the learners need feedback is another question. If yes, then when and how this feedback should be given is also a question.

## Brief Analysis of the Issues in Cognitive Science

It may be concluded that different kinds of problems emerges while using the components of cognitive science in the field of education. These problems are mostly related to cognitive processes of the learners. For example, problems like lack of background knowledge, relying on accumulated knowledge, ADHD, etc. Not only learners, some problems also arise due to lack of understanding of the concepts and the underlying cognitive processes by the teachers. For example, teaching problem solving through examples, providing feedback for attention, providing fragmented knowledge, misconceptions about creativity, etc. Some problems are also environmental in nature, which have indirect implications to cognitive processes of the learners. For example, Providing appropriate environment for knowledge construction, Lack of practice time, Numerous stimuli. However, these problems can be solved by using the principles of cognitive science.

## References

Cole, D.G., Sugioka, H.L. and Yamagata-Lynch, L.C. (1999). Supportive classroom environments for creativity in higher education. *Journal of Creative Behaviour, 33* (4), pp. 277-293.

Ross, B.H. (2007). Cognitive science: Problem solving and learning for physics education. *AIP Conference Proceedings of the Physics Education Research Conference,* 11-14, p. 951. doi: 10.1063/1.2820910

# 7

# Research Trends in Cognitive Science

## The Educational Aspects

Various researches have been carried out in the field of cognitive science. Some of the studies are related to education and its various aspects. This chapter has been designed to get acquainted with and to expound the relevant researches in this field which are directly or indirectly related to the field of education.

Glaser (1988) in his paper "Cognitive science and education" agrees that cognitive science offers a re-conceptualisation of the nature of the learning process and new approaches to the investigation of learning. He believes that detailed methods exist for inferring mental processes from empirical data. Growth of information-processing theory also offers an important tool for theory building in the domain of complex intellectual processes. The relevance of cognitive science for education has grown as it has tackled more of the complex activities of everyday cognition and of formal areas of human competence.

Leong (1993) argues in the paper "Towards an applied cognitive science perspective in education" for the role of an applied cognitive science perspective in education. It states that the concept of parallel distributed processing, bolstered by the social construction of knowledge, provides powerful frameworks for the teaching and learning of basic school subjects.

Cobb's (1997) "Cognitive science, instructional design, and teaching" is a review of the article of Griffin and Case. It provides a comprehensive overview of their research programme. He frames their work as a definitive illustration of the potential contributions of cognitive science to educational reform. According to the researcher, they succeed in demonstrating "that educational programmes and practices that are grounded in cognitive science theory and research can be highly effective in improving children's mathematics learning and achievement".

Kruse (1998) reports on the implications of brain research on education in the article "Cognitive science and its implications for education." The researcher gives details on how the brain works; information on the structure of the brain; and an in-depth look at human learning in relation to the brain.

Crane and Richardson (1999) provide an overview of the "cognitive revolution" and recent work on the brain, and then discuss the dominant strains within cognitive linguistics, arguing for wider applicability to literary theory and criticism in their article "Literary studies and cognitive science: Toward a new interdisciplinary". They argue that cognitive science offers new paradigms for rethinking the relations among culture, linguistic activity, and agency.

Kala and Ramadas (2001) carried out a study on "History and philosophy of science, cognitive science and science education" in which they reviewed some research relating philosophy of science and cognitive science with science education. They discussed research trends under two categories: domain-specific issues related to the conceptual content of science (conceptual structure, conceptual change, constraints to learning, cross cultural studies, language) and domain-general related to conceptualisation of science-epistemological studies (nature of science, studies in reasoning and scientific thinking, coordination of theory and evidence). They pointed out that developments in cognitive science were found to contribute towards research paradigms and methods, including expert novice studies, problem solving and linguistic analysis.

Halpern (2002) shows that educational reform efforts should keep in focus the knowledge about how people think, learn and remember in the paper "Cognitive Science and the Work of Reform". It suggests against lectures, "canned" laboratory work, and frequent testing. Knowledge about human cognition can enhance how much and how well students can learn, which can be used to redesign higher education. The paper talks about the gap between empirically validated theories and pedagogical practice. It has been found that cognitive psychology and learning theory have much to offer in guiding how higher education is designed and reformed.

Croy (2002) explores pedagogical innovations that may be necessitated by the recent changes in the aims and methods of the philosophy of mind in "Philosophy of Mind, Cognitive Science, and Pedagogical Technique". He describes computer simulations in particular which have emerged as a means of constructing empirically and conceptually defensible theories of mind. One question raised is whether hands-on teaching of simulation methods should be a standard part of philosophy of mind courses. These courses, because of an increasing empirical orientation, are becoming more interdisciplinary, and certain consequences of this development are elaborated in the paper.

Siegler (2003) in his study "Implication of cognitive science research for mathematics education" draws conclusions about a number of aspects of mathematics learning. It examines conclusions based on cognitive science research on some aspects of mathematics learning. The work informs us regarding how children typically learn particular skills and concepts, the stumbling blocks that many of them encounter, and instructional practices that can produce greater learning. It advocates that successful teaching and learning depends on careful, detailed, analysis of the particulars of individual children learning particular skills and concepts as well as the particular procedures and concepts to be learned. Some of the pedagogical implications which can be drawn from the study are—understanding what children already know when they enter school, providing students with instruction and examples that help them learn the component skills, anticipating types of misunderstandings that most often arise in the learning process, helping students move beyond these misunderstandings, retaining cognitive variability (spontaneous feature of children's thinking), providing flexibility of choosing the strategy, attending to children's non-verbal gestures as well as their verbal statements as indicators of their understanding and readiness to learn, attending to both cognitive and social variables (for co-operative learning), asking children to explain both why correct answers are right and why incorrect answers are wrong, etc.

Klahr and Li (2005) conducted a study on "Cognitive Research and Elementary Science Instruction: From the Laboratory, to the Classroom, and Back". They stated that cognitive research can generate usable knowledge for elementary science instruction and that issues raised by classroom practice can drive the agenda of laboratory cognitive research. They discussed five studies of the teaching, learning, and transfer of the "control of variables strategy" in elementary school science. The study begins from basic theoretical questions to subsequent inquiries within authentic educational debates—contrasting hands-on manipulation of physical and virtual materials, evaluating direct instruction and discovery learning, replicating training methods in classroom, and narrowing science achievement gaps. They suggest that those engaged in discussions about implications and applications of educational research focus on clearly defined instructional methods and procedures, rather than vague labels and outmoded "-isms."

Ansari and Coch (2006) presents the recent growing interest in and debate about the relation between cognitive neuroscience and education in "Bridges over troubled waters: education and cognitive neuroscience". The authors aim at advancing the debate beyond both recitation of potentially education-related cognitive neuroscience findings and the claim that a bridge between fields is a wild fantasy. In an attempt to begin a dialogue about mechanisms among students, educators, researchers and practitioner-scientists, they propose that multiple bridges can be built to make connections between education and cognitive neuroscience, including teacher training, researcher training and collaboration. They argue that these bridges—concrete mechanisms that can advance the study of mind, brain and education—will benefit both educators and cognitive neuroscientists, who will gain new perspectives for posing and answering crucial questions about the learning brain.

In their paper, "Principles of cognitive science in education: The effects of generation, errors, and feedback", Metcalfe and Kornell (2007) found that principles of cognitive science hold the promise of helping children to study more effectively, yet they do not always make successful transitions from the laboratory to applied settings and have rarely been tested in such settings. The studies reviewed here address three interlocking questions in an effort to better implement a computer-based study programme to help children learn: (1) Does generation help? (2) Do errors hurt if they are corrected? And (3) What is the effect of feedback? The findings reveal that generation helps; errors that are corrected do not hurt; and feedback is beneficial in verbal learning. These answers may help put cognitive scientists in a better position to put their well-established principles in the service of children's learning.

Schunn (2009) in the paper "How kids learn engineering: The cognitive science perspective" argues that age is not a bar to learn engineering. What is necessary is proper environmental support. He stated four principles which support engineering learning. These are—engaging children in solving significant design problems from the beginning, making visible models to support design task, iterative design and redesign are better than single design cycles and providing sufficient time for exposure to engineering material.

Akyol, Sungur and Tekkaya (2010) examine the differences in the level of 7th-grade Turkish students' cognitive and metacognitive strategy use in science in the paper "The contribution of cognitive and metacognitive strategy use to students' science achievement". It also explores the relationships between students' background characteristics (gender, prior knowledge, socioeconomic status) and their cognitive and meta-cognitive strategy use and science achievement. The statistical analyses revealed significant differences in the level of students' cognitive and meta-cognitive strategy use scores. Besides, elaboration, organisation, and meta-cognitive self-regulation strategy use were found to make a significant contribution to students' science achievement. Moreover, prior knowledge, parents' educational level, number of reading materials at home, frequency of buying a daily newspaper, presence of a separate study room, and presence of a computer with internet connection at home were significantly associated with cognitive and meta-cognitive strategy use and science achievement.

Roebers, Schmid and Roderer (2010) in their study "Metacognitive monitoring and control processes involved in primary school children's test performance" examine metacognitive monitoring and control processes in elementary school children's test taking behaviour and explore the impacts of these meta-cognitive skills for the accuracy and the quantity of test performance. Results reveal well-developed monitoring skills indicating that by the age of 9, children can reliably distinguish between correct and incorrect answers. As for control skills, 11- and 12-year-olds proved to be better able to improve their test performance by selectively withdrawing answers that would have been incorrect than the 9- to 10-year-olds. The study offers evidence for the impact of meta-cognitive processes in students' learning outcomes and documents strategic behaviour during test taking, as well as developmental progression in the involved skills.

Tytler and Prain (2010) in their paper "A Framework for Re-thinking Learning in Science from Recent Cognitive Science Perspectives" states that recent accounts by cognitive scientists of factors affecting cognition imply the need to reconsider current dominant conceptual theories about science learning. These new accounts emphasise the role of context, embodied practices, and narrative-based representation rather than learners' cognitive constructs. In this paper they analyse data from a longitudinal study of primary school children's learning to outline a framework based on these contemporary accounts and to delineate key points of difference from conceptual change perspectives. The findings suggest this framework provides strong theoretical and practical insights into how children learn and the key role of representational negotiation in this learning. They argue that the nature and process of conceptual change can be re-interpreted in terms of the development of students' representational resources.

King (1994) carried out the study on "Guiding knowledge construction in the classroom: Effects of teaching children how to question and how to explain". Following teacher-presented science lessons, pairs of fourth and fifth-graders studied the material by asking and answering each other's self-generated questions. In one condition, students' discussion was guided by questions designed to promote connections among ideas within a lesson. In a second condition, discussion was guided by similar lesson-based questions as well as the ones intended to access prior knowledge/experience and promote connections between the lesson and that knowledge. All students were trained to generate explanations (one manifestation of complex knowledge construction). Analysis of post-lesson knowledge maps and verbal interaction during study showed that students trained to ask both kinds of questions engaged in more complex knowledge construction than those trained in lesson-based questioning only and controls. These findings, together with performance on comprehension tests for material studied, support the conclusion that, although both kinds of questions induce complex knowledge construction, questions designed to access prior knowledge/experience are more effective in enhancing learning.

Ivie (1998) advocated in the study "Ausubel's learning theory: An approach to teaching higher order thinking skills" that developing thinking skills in students requires specific instruction and practice rather than application. Teachers should address analysis, evaluation and synthesis using advance organisers that encourage students to operate at higher levels of abstraction. Strengthening cognitive structures helps students retain information longer, and subsumptions provide students with basic structures on which to build new concepts.

Penuel's (1999) paper "Designing learning: Principles and Technologies" is based on the premise that workplace learning can be designed and that innovative organisations can take principles from the cognitive science of learning and use them to organise their own company's training and development projects. The paper reviews some of the key principles of cognitive science of learning as they can be observed in the way people think and act in different workplace activities. The Principles involved are—learning takes place within communities of practice; novices learn to become experts through practice in solving a variety of problems in a domain; becoming an expert means applying learning to new contexts; prior knowledge mediates learning; learning is advanced when thinking is made visible by collaboration; and reflection among learners.

Clump (2005) in his study "Changes to students' learning processes following instruction on the topic" investigated the effect of teaching students about effective learning processes in general to determine if this would alter their learning processes. 26 Cognitive Psychology students completed the Inventory of Learning Processes one week before and one week following instruction on the topic of effective learning processes. The students' scores on the Deep Processing and Elaborative Processing subscales significantly increased from before instruction to after instruction, which is substantial given the significant relations between scores on these subscales and academic achievement.

Whiteley (2006) in the study "Using the Socratic method and Bloom's taxonomy of cognitive domain to enhance online discussion, critical thinking, and student learning" addresses the issue of implementing Socratic Method and Bloom's taxonomy of cognitive domain in Virtual Classroom Setting (VCS). The application of the Socratic Method can help the students in a step-by-step fashion, to acquire a higher-level learning (analysis, synthesis and evaluation). In this method, the role of the instructor is to assess the situation, direct the student in the right direction, but without providing the answers. This approach reflects scaffolding, providing a certain degree of assistance to guide the student. The teacher has to empathise with the students by understanding the problems faced by them during the learning process and to gradually guide the students to a proper understanding of the subject area. This method develops critical thinking and reflective thinking in the students. Throughout the application of the Socratic Method, the course facilitator needs to be aware of the level of learning that is relevant. Since the Socratic approach focusses on the area of critical thinking, it is, thus, an approach that can effectively be used to help students to achieve the higher-order learning level of Bloom's Taxonomy of cognitive domain. It has been found in the study that incorporating the Socratic Method in VCS as a means to develop critical thinking skills of students would provide a sound pedagogical foundation or model in VCS. The author has also suggested VCS can serve in a support role in a TCS to increase the effectiveness of TCS.

Rittle-Johnson and Star (2007) conducted the study entitled "Does comparing solution methods facilitate conceptual and procedural knowledge? An experimental study on learning to solve equations". According to them, encouraging students to share and compare solution methods is a key component of reform efforts in mathematics, and comparison is emerging as a fundamental learning mechanism. To experimentally evaluate the effects of comparison for mathematics learning, the authors randomly assigned 70 seventh grade students to learn about algebra equation solving either by (a) comparing and contrasting alternative solution methods or (b) reflecting on the same solution methods one at a time. At post-test, students in the compare group had made greater gains in procedural knowledge and flexibility and comparable gains in conceptual knowledge. These findings suggest potential mechanisms behind the benefits of comparing contrasting solutions and ways to support effective comparison in the classroom.

The purpose of Brown Leonard (2008) in the study "Integrative learning as a developmental process: A grounded theory of college students' experiences in Integrative studies" was to learn how students in an explicitly integrative learning environment make meaning of and understand integrative learning. Keeping consistency with the constructivist grounded theory methodology, the researcher developed an emerging theory about students' experiences with integrative learning that is grounded in the data. 10 students enrolled in an Integrative Studies Programme were interviewed. The students defined integrative learning very broadly. To capture the range of learning described by students, a continuum of different forms of integration that vary by complexity, application, comparison, understanding, context and synthesis was created. Students engaged in the least complex form of integration, application, by finding their coursework personally relevant and applying what they learn to their own lives. Through class discussion and reading students identified multiple perspectives, which led to integration as comparison. When different perspectives are in conflict, students began to engage in integration as understanding context. By reconciling conflict, students may reach the most complex form of integration synthesis.

Belenky, D.M. and Nokes, T.J. (2009) in their paper "Examining the Role of Manipulatives and Metacognition on Engagement, Learning, and Transfer" investigates the nature of students' learning of math concepts when using manipulatives. We examined how the type of manipulative (concrete, abstract, none) and problem-solving prompt (metacognitive or problem-focussed) affect student learning, engagement, and knowledge transfer. Students who were given concrete manipulatives with metacognitive prompts showed better transfer of a procedural skill than students given abstract manipulatives or those given concrete manipulatives with problem-focussed prompts. Overall, students who reported low levels of engagement showed better learning and transfer when getting metacognitive prompts, whereas students who reported high levels of engagement showed better learning and transfer when getting the problem-focussed prompts. The results are discussed in regards to their implications for education and instruction.

Jacobs and Shams (2010) in their paper "Visual Learning in Multisensory Environments" claimed that multi-sensory environments are useful for visual learning because non-visual percepts can be processed to produce error signals that people can use to adapt their visual systems. This hypothesis is motivated by a Bayesian network framework. The framework is useful because it ties together three observations that have appeared in the literature: (a) signals from non-visual modalities can "teach" the visual system; (b) signals from non-visual modalities can facilitate learning in the visual system; and (c) visual signals can become associated with signals from non-visual modalities.

Gadgil and Nokes-Malach (2011) hypothesise that some classroom activities may afford benefits for collaborative learning over individual learning in their paper "Overcoming collaborative inhibition through error correction: a classroom experiment". They created a classroom writing activity that incorporated features such as shared prior knowledge and error-correction processes, which have been hypothesised to eliminate collaborative inhibition and to support constructive collaboration. Students participated in this activity either individually or in dyads. Results showed that the individuals who worked collaboratively performed equally well as those who worked individually and also showed better learning as measured by performance on a future writing assignment. They investigated whether it was possible to overcome the collaborative inhibition effect. They also examined whether collaboration can have facilitative effects on performance and learning, and whether these effects would depend on whether the task was a simple task or a complex task. We created a task to facilitate constructive collaborative interaction by adding the features of shared knowledge and error correction, which were hypothesised to reduce the cognitive costs of collaboration. The error correction task consisted of error detection and revision, and for each component there were surface and structural errors that students could find or correct. Most importantly, they found that those students who had participated in dyads were significantly more likely to get correct the summary elements corresponding to their revisions of structural errors compared with those who participated as individuals.

Richland, Bjork, Finley and Linn (2005) in their paper "Linking cognitive science to Education: Generation and Interleaving Effects" Performance during a learning event is frequently used as a measure of learning; however, basic cognitive research suggests that this may be an unreliable predictor of long-term learning and transfer. Rather, in some training paradigms, higher error rates during training may predict greater retention and generalisation of learning. One such paradigm is training in which learners generate, rather than read, during study opportunities. A second is training in which study for two sets of information is interleaved rather than grouped into separate blocks. Educationally relevant learning requires retention and the capacity to generalise information across contexts, leading to the hypothesis that these paradigms may have important implications for educational practice. An experiment is described in which the effects of generation and interleaving are examined using complex, educationally-relevant materials. Findings indicate that these effects are relevant for instructional design, but that there is not a straightforward relationship between laboratory research with simple materials and educational practice. Rather, the educational goal must be considered when determining the utility of generation and interleaving principles in designing instructional technology.

Yao (2004) in the study "Concept Formation and Learning: A Cognitive Informatics Perspective". Cognitive informatics aims at building machines and systems that simulate human ways of knowing and thinking. The study of concept formation and learning is central to cognitive informatics. The objective of this paper is to investigate basic issues of concept formation and learning from cognitive informatics perspectives. From the perspective of cognitive informatics, a layered framework is suggested for concept formation and learning. It combines cognitive science and machine learning approaches. The philosophical issues and various views of concepts are reviewed. Concept learning methods are presented based on the classical view of concepts. The philosophical level addresses questions about knowledge, the algorithm level concentrates on knowledge discovery methods, and the application level deals with the utility of the discovered knowledge.

Saxena (1980) carried out "A study of children's problem solving and decision making strategies" to investigate the possible strategies adopted by children in a sample problem solving and decision making situation. The findings revealed that in a problem solving situation, the dead ends were overcome by the creation of sub-goals related to the final goal sates, the subjects in a decision making situation abandoned the goal itself. In a decision making situation, the interpersonal character of the situation where no strategy could be worked out without the co-operation of the partner, did not provide scope for the manifestation of total strategy or plans as made by the subjects. If the constraints of the interpersonal situation were made more relaxed, interspersed with no contingent gains and losses, the strategic manoeuvres were better understood.

Schoenfeld (1983) in the study "Beyond the Purely Cognitive: Belief Systems, Social Cognitions, and Metacognitions as Driving Forces in Intellectual Performance" explores the way that belief systems, interactions with social or experimental environments, and skills at the "control" level in decision-making shape people's behaviour in problem solving. It is argued that problem solvers' beliefs about what is useful in mathematics may determine the set of "cognitive resources" at their disposal as they do mathematics. In other cases, individuals' reactions to an experimental setting may induce behaviour that is almost pathological and at the same time, so consistent that it can be modeled. In general, such "environmental" factors establish the context within which individuals' access and utilise the information potentially at their disposal. The paper presents and discusses the protocols illustrating these points. He outlined a model based on an axiomatisation of students' beliefs about plane geometry, and is shown to correspond closely to their problem-solving performance. He offered a framework for analysing problem-solving performance at three qualitatively different levels: access to cognitive resources stored in Long Term Memory, executive or control decision-making, and belief systems.

Ross (2007) in his study "Cognitive Science: Problem Solving and Learning for Physics Education" presents three issues relevant to difficulty in problem solving: specialised systems of memory and reasoning; importance of content in thinking; and characterisation of memory retrieval in problem solving. He states that because of the different memory and reasoning systems, the processing may differ enough from prior learning to lead to lack of transfer. Students need to develop their ability to generate their own solution. Specific (content based) thinking influences the learning of abstract thinking. The paper also argues that the type of problem solving can often be understood in terms of the memory and cues. The representation of the problem with cues is critical and has huge influences on problem solving at least partly due to what knowledge is retrieved. Moreover, novices might be able to improve their problem solving by learning to do some more structural analysis and storing the results in memory.

Simone (2008) in the paper "Problem-Based Learning: a framework for prospective teachers' pedagogical problem solving" discussed that current educational reform movements emphasise preparing teachers for pedagogical problem solving in the classroom. This study examines the impact of problem-based learning on prospective teachers' problem-solving abilities. Two classes of prospective teachers were included in this study. The experimental class used problem-based learning while the control group used a more traditional approach. The dependent measure was the participants' analyses of a problem. The participants in problem-based learning were significantly better than the controls in constructing the central problem, elaborating the problem, relating their solutions to the problem, and using multiple resources. The results are promising because they give prospective teachers a powerful approach that fosters certain aspects of pedagogical problem solving. The implications of these results for prospective teachers are discussed.

Salden, Aleven, Renkl and Schwonke (2009) investigated a combination of two instructional approaches, tutored problem solving and worked examples in "Worked Examples and Tutored Problem Solving: Redundant or Synergistic Forms of Support?" Worked-out examples have been shown to be an effective complement to untutored problem solving, but it is largely unknown whether they are an effective complement to tutored problem solving. Further, while computer-based learning environments offer the possibility of adaptively transitioning from examples to problems while tailoring to an individual learner, the effectiveness of such machine-adapted example fading is largely unstudied. To address these research questions, one lab and one classroom experiment were conducted. Both studies compared a standard Cognitive Tutor with two example-enhanced Cognitive Tutors, in which the fading of worked-out examples occurred either in a fixed way or adaptively. Results indicate that the adaptive fading of worked-out examples leads to higher transfer performance on delayed post-tests than the other two methods.

Booth and Koedinger (2011) "Are diagrams always helpful tools? Developmental and individual differences in the effect of presentation format on student problem solving." This study was carried out to identify developmental and individual differences in the use of diagrams, story, and equation representations in problem solving. When do diagrams begin to aid problem-solving performance? Does the verbal advantage replicate for younger students? Two experiments were carried out for the study. In both experiments, students solved algebra problems in three matched presentation formats (equation, story, story + diagram). The textual advantage was replicated for all groups. The study yielded the result that while diagrams enhance performance of older and higher ability students, younger and lower-ability students do not benefit, and may even be hindered by a diagram's presence. The textual advantage is in place by sixth grade. Diagrams are not inherently helpful aids to student understanding and should be used cautiously in the middle school years, as students are developing competency for diagram comprehension during this time.

Mead, Nokes and Morrow (2012) in their paper "The effect of expertise on collaborative problem solving" found that collaborative success is a complex interaction of the prior knowledge and experience of the individuals working together, and the relation of their combined knowledge to the task (complexity level and task structure). This paper brings together multiple perspectives on what factors contribute to collaborative success by examining both learner factors (prior knowledge and experience in the domain) and contextual factors (task complexity). They aim to link this contextual perspective to a cognitive view by examining participants' prior knowledge and how that knowledge changes with experience in the domain. To understand collaborative problem solving, social theories must be anchored to cognitive approaches to get grip on the underlying knowledge representations and problem-solving mechanisms, and cognitive theories must move beyond individual cognitive analyses and consider interaction patterns as critical, irreducible, and fundamental to learning and performance of dyads and groups.

Limjap, A.A. (2002) in her paper, "Issues on problem solving: drawing implications for a techno-mathematics curriculum at the collegiate level" presented various issues about pedagogical and cognitive aspects of problem solving and explored ways to lessen the heavy cognitive load of a problem solving task. It established a problem type schema for students at different levels. It recognised the role of modern technology as a cognitive tool that promotes learning mathematics with understanding. It designed the framework of a techno-mathematics curriculum for algebra at the collegiate level.

Prasad (1979) has reported the application of discovery method for teaching physics to high school pupils for promotion of creativity in the paper "Promotion of Creativity and Achievement by Discovery Method". It was found that one of the basic abilities that should be taught in the schools is the ability to discover, to search answers instead of passively waiting answers and directions from the teacher. The results of the experimental study showed that the students taught by the discovery method showed significant improvement in achievement and creativity. For awakening the faculties of creative thinking in pupils, learning by discovery method should be encouraged. Therefore, pedagogy should emphasise the discovery of both problems and their solutions by the students themselves. If it is impressed upon pupils that there are many ways of reaching a solution to a given problem, they will then try to respond in a variety of ways to the same situation, thus preparing them for future creative action.

Sharma (1982) carried out a study on "Factors Related to Creativity" to explore the relationship of creativity with certain background, psychological and organisational factors of students of higher secondary schools of Delhi. It was found in the study that boys were more creative as compared to girls, scholastic achievement was positively related to the measures of creativity, creativity was significantly higher in the high I.Q. group in comparison to the middle and low I.Q. groups, and perception of teacher behaviour by students was related to creativity in students.

Nandan Pawar (1986) carried out an experimental study on "Development of Linguistic Creativity among the Students". It was hypothesised that teaching through a creative method improves Marathi language proficiency of students, develops linguistic creativity among students and develops such abilities as are involved in linguistic creativity as vocabulary, sentence construction, poem composition, story writing and imagination among the students. It was found that the experimental group scored significantly higher than the control group in (i) language proficiency, (ii) overall creativity, and (iii) all the abilities involved in linguistic creativity.

Torrance (1987) in his study "Teaching for creativity" summarised the results of 142 studies designed to test approaches to teach children to think creatively. It was found that the most frequently reported types of experiments are those that emphasise teacher-classroom variables, complex programmes involving packages of materials, and modifications of the Osborn-Parnes training programme in creative problem solving. Those having the highest percentages of success in teaching children to think creatively are those that emphasize the Osborn-Parnes training programme, other disciplined approaches, the creative arts and media-oriented programmes. It was concluded that the most successful approaches perhaps are those that involve both cognitive and emotional functioning, provide adequate structure and motivation, and give opportunities for involvement, practice and interaction with teachers and other children. Deliberate teaching is a significant factor in creative functioning.

Trimurthy (1987) carried out "A Study of Creative Thinking Ability of Secondary School Students in the Context of Some Psycho-socio Factors". The objectives of the study were to design and construct reliable and valid verbal and non-verbal tests of Creative Thinking Ability (CTA); to determine the extent to which sex, urban-rural location and grade influenced creative thinking ability; to study the trends of creative thinking ability in relation to age and I.Q.; to study the relation of test anxiety, self-sufficiency vs. dependency, socioeconomic status, leadership and emotional stability with CTA. The tests for measuring creative thinking ability were constructed and standardised. It was found that the variables like sex, area and I.Q. had their influence on CTA whereas other variables like test anxiety, self-sufficiency, dependency, leadership, emotional stability and SES did not exert significant influence on CTA.

Amin, M.J. (1988) conducted the research "To Study the Effectiveness of Creative Thinking Programmes on the Creativity

Level of the School Children in relation to the Programme Correlates". The objective of the study was to develop a Creative Thinking Programme (CTP) for enhancing the level of creativity in children with special reference to time duration for implementing the programme, teacher variability, discussion pattern in a group and programme correlates. It was found that there was significant effect of the creative thinking programme on creativity and its component measures: fluency and originality. The main effects of the two factors, time duration and group discussion, were found significant on creativity and fluency thinking ability. After the completion of every creative thinking programme, group discussion seemed to be worthwhile in terms of ideas produced.

Cole, Sugioka and Yamagata-Lynch (1999) conducted a qualitative study on "Supportive classroom environments for creativity in higher education". They identified four areas as important characteristics of the supportive environment for fostering creativity—teacher-student relationship, assessment, degree of freedom, and classroom activities. It was found that personal teacher-student relationship, de-emphasising standardised assessment, an open environment with freedom of choice and encouraging multiple perspectives was significant for developing creativity in the classroom.

Hamza and Griffith (2006) in the article "Fostering problem solving and creative thinking in the classroom: Cultivating a creative mind" put forth a discussion of the complex nature of creativity and shares the results of a one-year study conducted at a college in the state of Texas. In this study, the researchers explored teaching methods and instructional approaches, styles and methodologies that contributed into building creative learning environments in which creative thinking and problem solving skills were promoted.

Mc William (2007) in the paper "Is creativity teachable? Conceptualising the creativity/pedagogy relationship in higher education" explored reasons for the growing interest in creativity as a learning outcome and elaborated key imperatives in the post-millennial ideational and policy context. The paper then moves to consider questions of the teach ability of creativity and the pedagogical implications of this. Teachers and students act as co-creators of information products, drawing on a network of people and ideas that is fluid and organic. The pedagogical work, then, consists of mutual involvement of teacher and student in assembling and dissembling cultural products designed to inform, entertain, subvert, problem-solve and investigate. The students need the capacity to edit reality—to organise it and re-organise it by mixing form and content, to juxtapose through display, to compare texts to understand their difference. It is the capacity to engage in value adding assembling and dissembling processes—not the ability to regurgitate content knowledge—that needs to be prioritised in any authentic regime of assessment for creative capacity building.

Basantia and Panda (2010) examined the effect of multi-dimensional activity-based integrated approach over traditional method of teaching in developing creative abilities among elementary school children through the subject in the study "Development of creative abilities among elementary schools students through multi-dimensional activity-based integrated approach".

Lin (2011) in the paper "Fostering Creativity through Education—A Conceptual Framework of Creative Pedagogy" identify capacities and qualities of creativity and proposed strategies in fostering children's creative thinking skills to create supportive environments in an educational setting. There is little consistent rhetoric, however, among these insights and strategies concerning different aspects of fostering creativity. In light of this, a three-element framework of creative pedagogy is proposed to offer a more holistic view of enhancing creativity through teaching, to cover the aspect of creative learning which was overlooked in the past, and to provide a different explanation to some arguments about teaching creativity. This framework is also a starting point for studies which intend to understand the teachers and pupils' responses to creative pedagogy, and to provide implications for applying creative pedagogy in a classroom and in Asian context as well. In the end, several possible routes are suggested for future research in creative pedagogy.

Fogarty (1998) in her paper "The Intelligence-friendly classroom: It just makes sense" provides guidelines that serve as a bridge between theory and practice in the intelligence-friendly classroom. She assumes intelligence to be emotional, nurturable, constructed, experiential, multiple, modifiable and elusive. Accordingly, it makes sense to provide emotional safety, create rich environments, provide tools for the mind, challenge through doing, target many dimensions, mediate learning and vary the ways to measure it. The article investigates the theoretical underpinnings of intelligence-friendly classrooms briefly and their practical implications in more depth. Some guidelines have been developed which are derived from various theories of intelligence and have compelling classroom implications. These are—emotional safety and care for all learners; rich learning environment in which science equipment, art supplies, tools and workbenches, toys and building blocks, optical illusion posters, etc. are present; teaching of mind-tools and skills of life which include critical thinking skills, creative thinking skills, social skills, technological skills, visual skills, skills in the performing arts, and skills of the elite athlete; develop skillfulness of the learners through formal teaching-learning structures, independent readings, research, dialogue, discussion, articulations of peer coaching, mentoring, or internships and with experiences; provide challenges through experience of doing, i.e. inviting the learner to become an integral part of the teaching learning process; target multiple dimensions of intelligence, i.e. learning is structured in naturally integrated ways that call upon various intelligences; transfer learning through reflection; assessment measures should be balanced and integral to all other interactions.

Sternberg (1999) in the paper "Successful intelligence: finding a balance" argued that two extremes have prevailed in the study of intelligence. At one extreme are general-ability (*g*) theorists, who have collected large amounts of data to test the theory of general intelligence, but often using restricted ranges of participants, materials or situational contexts. They also show a tendency to limit their methods of data analysis (e.g. to exploratory factor analysis). At another extreme are theorists arguing for new, multiple intelligences, whose theories have been subjected to few or no empirical tests. He argues that a middle ground is needed that recognises the multifarious nature of intelligence and of people's conceptions of it, but subject to rigorous empirical tests. The author talks about having firm footing with respect to the scientific basis of intelligence. This article places more emphasis on creative and practical abilities than others in the field.

Haier and Jung (2008) conducted "Brain Imaging Studies on Intelligence and Creativity: What is the picture for education?" The goal of the study is to summarise current brain research on intelligence and creativity that may be relevant to education in the near future. The paper addresses five issues: (a) Why is there a neuroscience interest in intelligence? (b) Can intelligence be located in the brain? (c) Why are some brains smarter than others? (d) What do we know about creativity and the brain? And (e) Can information about an individual's brain structure and function be useful to benefit his or her education? Integrating neuroscience findings into education practices is a challenge that will require educators to re-examine old ideas and acquire fundamental backgrounds in new areas.

Watve (2010) studies the inter-relationship between the eight intelligences assumed by Howard Gardner in the paper "Multiple intelligences: Nature and interrelations". Almost all the correlations were found to be significantly high, except that between Linguistic and Interpersonal intelligences. Significant high correlations between Linguistic and Intrapersonal, but insignificant correlation between Linguistic and Interpersonal were revealed. Logico-mathematical appeared to be least correlated with others. Some probing into various such relationships is also discussed.

Tsai (2011) in the paper "The meta-epistemology of knowing-how" offers a meta-epistemology of knowing-how, including considerations of the subject matter, task, and nature of the epistemology of knowing-how. This aim is achieved by distinguishing varieties of knowing-how and by introducing and elaborating the concept of hybrid knowing-how, which entails a combination of ground-level ability and a meta-level perspective on that ability. He advocates that the epistemology of knowing-how is a normative discipline whose main task is to study the nature and value of human practical intelligence required to do things in a particular manner.

Tomlin and Villa (1994) examined in "Attention in Cognitive Science and Second Language Acquisition" how the cognitive notion of attention has been employed in Second Language Acquisition (SLA) and how it is understood in cognitive science. It summarises recent research on attention from cognitive and neuroscience approaches. Current research offers detailed ideas about attention and its component processes. These ideas, elaborated theoretically and empirically in cognitive neuroscience, may help untangle some important but difficult issues in SLA. Early, coarse-grained conceptions of attention, such as the limited-capacity metaphor or the automatic versus controlled processing dichotomy, are recast into an integrated human attention system with three separate yet inter-related networks: alertness, orientation, and detection. This finer grained analysis of attention is employed in a model of the role of attention in SLA.

Hanauer (1999) carried out the study "Attention and literary education: A model of literary knowledge development" The aim of this paper is to describe the workings of one cognitive model for the development of literary knowledge. The central aspect of this model is the role of the systems of awareness and attention in developing the individual's ability to detect and internalise specific information from literary texts. The paper starts by defining literary education within the theoretical framework of the cognitive processes of control and analysis. This is followed by a model of the development of literary knowledge based on the central role of awareness and attention. Empirical evidence which is relevant to the assumptions and predictions of the model is then discussed. Finally, the implications of this model on literary education and recommendations for future research are presented.

Feil (2009) in his thesis "Attention and encoding in physics learning and problem-solving" presents several studies designed to probe the mental representations that physics experts and novices form when interacting with typical instructional materials, such as diagrams and problem statements. By using recognition tasks and a change detection task, the mental representations of experts and novices are studied in a more direct way than with tasks such as problem sorting or interviews. Results show that the experience and knowledge of physics experts influence the features of visual stimuli that they encode. The final study revealed that animating multimedia learning content can help to focus learner's attention towards relevant items on the screen and in some cases reduce cognitive load as well.

Srivastava (2009) carried out an experimental study on attentional blink in her study "Time Course of Visual Attention". The objectives of the study are to understand the time course of shift of visual attention when attention is allocated to objects differently and to understand the explanations for attentional blink such as limited attentional resource or temporary loss of control. The study investigates the time course of shifts of visual attention modulated by different aspects of objects or object based information by manipulating emotion (happy and sad) and perceptual levels.

Baijal (2010) carried on the study "Relationship between Attention and Consciousness" with the aim to explore how information gets accessed when type of attention is varied. The goals were specifically stated as—to investigate the limitations in the amount of information that can be consciously accessed by different types of attention, to investigate the rate of encoding (a consolidation) of information in working memory by focussed and distributed attention and the nature of interferences when the central processing resources have to be shared between them, to examine the effect of attentional state on perceptual awareness.

Jang, Schunn and Nokes (2011) in their paper "Spatially distributed instructions improve learning outcomes and efficiency" have stated that learning requires applying attentional resources along with limited working memory to intrinsic, germane, and extraneous aspects of the learning task. To reduce the split-attention effect, spatially integrated learning materials are suggested instead of spatially separated materials. Recent work, however, has suggested a new distinction between two common formats of spatially separated displays: spatially distributed (multiple sources of information are placed side by side) versus spatially stacked (only one at the top is visible). With materials more typical of practice, the distributed-display instructions led learners to more efficient and fast learning and scored higher in the overall learning test. With materials more tightly controlled for spatial format per se, it was found that the benefit of the distributed instructions appeared to be associated with changes in cognitive load. It states that simply manipulating the spatial format of instructions, leaving learning task materials alone, may suffice to significantly improve both task performance and learning.

Aran-Fillippetti and Krumm (2013) in their paper "Executive function and attention in school age children according to the behavioural profile rated by their teachers" have concluded that individual variations in the attentional dimension would be associated with individual differences of cognitive performance and though data indicate that children with higher levels of inattention obtain a lower performance in attention and executive function tasks, it is important to clarify that, according to the present study, this fact does not imply the presence of cognitive deficit.

**Future Implications of the Researches**

It is revealed that there are very limited studies on cognitive science. This may be attributed to its young age. It was found that most of the studies are relevant to neuroscience or conducted from the perspective of neuroscience. This fact is also supported by Gupta (2001), who says that three dominant trends in cognitive science research can be discerned—neurobiology of cognition, human neurocognitive architecture and cognitive technology. This conclusion has been drawn on the basis of research reports in the journals, commentaries, review articles and discussion trends in several conferences, seminars and meeting of Cognitive Science Society. Some research articles have established the implication of cognitive science on different aspects of education like curriculum, instructional methods for specific subjects, etc. But there is dearth of doctoral (intensive) work on it. It was found that very less number of works have been conducted on the implications of cognitive science on pedagogy for attention (7 studies) and intelligence (5 studies). Feil (2009) studied the mental representations of experts and novices in a direct way by using recognition tasks and a change detection task and found that animating multimedia learning content can help to focus learner's attention towards relevant items on the screen and in some cases reduce cognitive load as well. Jang, Schunn and Nokes (2011) found that simply manipulating the spatial format of instructions, leaving learning task materials alone, may suffice to significantly improve both task performance and learning. Fogarty (1998) developed some guidelines which are derived from various theories of intelligence and have compelling classroom implications. Studies on cognitive science which are relevant to creativity (11 studies) and learning (12 studies) are more in number. For e.g., Hamza and Griffith (2006) explored teaching methods and instructional approaches, styles and methodologies that contributed into building creative learning environments in which creative thinking and problem solving skills were promoted. Penuel (1999) reviews the principles of cognitive science which can be used in organisation. Whitely (2006) showed the use of Socratic Method and Bloom's taxonomy of cognitive domain in Virtual Classroom teaching for higher level learning. Yao (2004) investigates basic issues of concept formation and learning from cognitive information perspectives. Eight studies have been found on problem solving. Ross (2007) established that content-based thinking and representation of the problem with cues helps problem solving and Limjap (2002) explored ways to lessen the cognitive load of a problem solving task and recognised the role of technology for it. There are 16 studies which draw implications of cognitive science on education as a whole. For e.g., Glaser (1988), Leong (1993) and Kala and Ramadas (2001) advocated for the application of cognitive science principles in education. All these studies will pave the way to the researchers who are interested to take up the project in the field of cognitive science, pedagogy and education.

## References


Amin, M.J. (1988). To Study the Effectiveness of Creative Thinking Programmes on the Creativity Level of the School Children in relation to the Programme Correlates. Ph.D. Edu., SPU. In M.B. Buch (Ed.). *Fourth Survey of Research in Education, 1983-1988* (Vol. I). New Delhi: NCERT.

Ansari, D., and Coch, D. (2006). Bridges over troubled waters: education and cognitive neuroscience. *Trends in Cognitive Sciences, 10* (4), pp. 146-151. Retrieved from http://search.ebscohost.com/login.aspx?direct=true&db=aph&AN=20403281&site=ehost-live

Aran-Fillippetti, V., and Krumm, G.L. (2013). Executive function and attention in school age children according to the behavioural profile rated by their teachers. *International Journal of Psychological Research, 6* (2), pp. 89-97.

Aykol, G., Sungur, S., and Tekkaya, C. (2010). The contribution of cognitive and metacognitive strategy use to students' science achievement. *Educational Research and Evaluation, 16* (1), pp. 1-21. Retrieved from http://search.ebscohost.com/login.aspx?direct=true&db=aph&AN=49141892&site=ehost-live

Baijal, S. (2010). *Relationship between Attention and Consciousness* (Unpublished doctoral dissertation). University of Allahabad, Allahabad.

Basantia, T.K., and Panda, B.N. (2010). Development of creative abilities among elementary schools students through multi-dimensional activity-based integrated approach. *Indian Educational Review, 46* (1), pp. 31-49.

Belenky, D.M., and Nokes, T.J. (2009). Examining the Role of Manipulatives and Metacognition on Engagement, Learning, and Transfer. *The Journal of Problem Solving,* 2 (2), pp. 102-129.

Booth, J.L., and Koedinger, K.R. (2011). Are diagrams always helpful tools? Developmental and individual differences in the effect of presentation format on student problem solving. *British Journal of Educational Psychology, 82* (3). doi: 10.1111/j.2044-8279.2011.02041.x

Brown Leonard, J.B. (2008). Integrative learning as a developmental process: A grounded theory of college students' experiences in Integrative studies (Unpublished doctoral dissertation). University of Maryland, College Park.

Clump, M.A. (2005). Changes to students' learning processes following instruction on the topic. *Journal of Instructional Psychology, 32* (4), pp. 293-297.

Cobb, P. (1997). Cognitive science, instructional design, and teaching. *Issues in Education, 3* (1), pp. 51-59. Retrieved from http:// search.ebscohost.com/ login.aspx?direct=true&db=f5h&AN= 731048&site=ehost-live

Cole, D.G., Sugioka, H.L., and Yamagata-Lynch, L.C. (1999). Supportive classroom environment for creative in higher education. *Journal of Creative Behaviour, 33* (4), pp. 227-298. doi: 10.1002/j.2162-6057.1999.tb01407.x

Crane, M.T., & Richardson, A. (1999). Literary studies and cognitive science: Toward a new interdisciplinary. *Mosaic: A Journal for the Interdisciplinary Study of Literature,* 32 (2), pp. 123-140. Retrieved from http://proquest.umi.com/pqdweb?did=43340652&sid=1&Fmt=3& clientId= 23791&RQT=309&VName=PQD

Croy, M. (2002). Philosophy of Mind, Cognitive Science, and Pedagogical Technique. *Metaphilosophy, 33* (1-2), pp. 49-69. doi: 10.1111/1467-9973.00216

Feil, A.J. (2009). Attention and encoding in physics learning and problem-solving. Ph.D., University of Illinois at Urbana-Champaign. In *Dissertation abstract international, 71* (1).

Fogarty, R. (1998). Intelligence-friendly classroom: It just makes sense. *Phi Delta Kappan, 79* (9).

Gadgil, S. and Nokes, T. (2011). Overcoming collaborative inhibition through error correction: a classroom experiment. *Applied Cognitive Psychology, 26* (3), pp. 410-420. doi: 10.1002/acp.1843

Glaser, R. (1988). Cognitive science and education. *International Social Science Journal, 40* (1), pp. 21-44. Retrieved from http://search.ebscohost.com/ login.aspx?direct=true&db=aph&AN=5709484&site=ehost-live

Gupta, G.C. (2001). Trends in cognitive science research. In G.C. Gupta (Ed.), *Cognitive science: Issues and perspectives*, pp. 520-543. New Delhi: Icon Publications Pvt. Ltd.

Haier, R.J., and Jung, R.E. (2008). Brain imaging studies on intelligence and creativity: What is the picture for education? *Roeper Review, 30*, pp. 171-180. doi: 10.1080/02783190802199347

Halpern, D.F. (2002). Cognitive science and the work of reform. *New Directions for Higher Education, 119*, pp. 41-44. Retrieved from http://dx.doi.org/ 10.1002/he.68

Hamza, M.K., and Griffith, K.G. (2006). Fostering problem solving and creative thinking in the classroom: cultivating a creative mind. *National Forum of Applied Educational Research Journal-Electronic, 19* (3). Retrieved from http://www.nationalforum.com/Electronic%20Journal%20Volumes/Hamza,%20Mohammed%20Fostering%20Problem% 20Solving%20%26%20Creative %20Thinking%20in%20the%20Classroom.pdf

Hanauer, D. (1999). Attention and literary education: A model of literary knowledge development. *Language Awareness, 8* (1), *pp*. 15-29.

Ivie, S.D. (1998). Ausubel's learning theory: An approach to teaching higher order thinking skills (Educational psychologist david paul ausubel). *High School Journal, 82* (1), p. 35. Retrieved from http://find.galegroup.com/ itx/infomark.do? &contentSet=IACDocuments&type=retrieve&tabID= T002&prodId=EAIM&docId=A54023245&source=gale&srcprod=EAIM&userGroupName=csus_main&version=1.0

Jacobs, R.A., and Shams, L. (2010). Visual Learning in Multisensory Environments. *Topics in Cognitive Science, 2* (2), pp. 217-225. doi: 10.1111/j.1756-8765.2009.01056.x

Jang, J., Schunn, C.D., and Nokes, T.J. (2011). Spatially distributed instructions improve learning outcomes and efficiency. *Journal of Educational Psychology, 103* (1), pp. 60-72. doi: 10.1037/a0021994

Kala, L., and Ramadas, J. (2001). History and philosophy of science, cognitive science and science education. In *Sixth Survey of Educational Research, 1993-2000* (Vol. II). New Delhi: NCERT.

King, A. (1994). Guiding knowledge construction in the classroom: Effects of teaching children how to question and how to explain. *American Educational Research Journal, 31*(2), pp. 338-368. doi: 10.2307/1163313.

Klahr, D., and Li, J. (2005). Cognitive research and elementary science instruction: from the laboratory, to the classroom, and back. *Journal of Science Education and Technology, 14* (2), pp. 217-238. Retrieved from http://search.ebscohost.com/login.aspx?direct=true&db=aph&AN=17434265&site=ehost-live

Kruse, G.D. (1998). Cognitive science and its implications for education. *NASSP Bulletin, 82* (598), pp. 73-79. Retrieved from http://search.ebscohost.com/login.aspx?direct=true&db=f5h&AN=528819&site=ehost-live

Leong, C.K. (1993). Towards an applied cognitive science perspective in education. *International Journal of Disability, Development and Education, 40* (1), pp. 63-73. doi: 10.1080/0156655930400105

Limjap, A.A. (2002). Issues on problem solving: drawing implications for a techno-mathematics curriculum at the collegiate level. *TangldW, 8*, pp. 55-85. *Retrieved from archives.math.utk.edu/ICTCM/VOL12/C030/paper.pdf?*

Lin, Y. (2011). Fostering creativity through education—A conceptual framework of creative pedagogy, *Creative Education*, 2 (3), pp. 149-155. doi: 10.4236/ce.2011.23021.

McWilliam, E.L. (2007). Is creativity teachable? Conceptualising the creativity/pedagogy relationship in higher education. In *Proceedings of 30th HERDSA Annual Conference: Enhancing Higher Education, Theory and Scholarship*, Adelaide. Retrieved from http://eprints.qut.edu.au/

Mead, M.L., Nokes, T.J., and Morrow, D.G. (2012). The effect of expertise on collaborative problem solving. *Thinking and Reasoning, 18* (1), pp. 32-58. Retrieved from http://dx.doi.org/10.1080/13546783.2011.642206

Metcalfe, J., and Kornell, N. (2007). Principles of cognitive science in education: The effects of generation, errors, and feedback. *Psychonomic Bulletin and Review, 14* (2), pp. 225-229. Retrieved from http://search.ebscohost.com/ login.aspx?direct=true&db=aph&AN=26269833&site=ehost-live

Nandanpawar, B.S. (1986). Development of linguistic creativity among the students. Ph.D. Edu., Nagpur University. In M.B. Buch (Ed.). *Fourth Survey of Research in Education, 1983-1988* (Vol. I). New Delhi: NCERT.

Penuel, B. (1999). Designing learning: Principles and technologies. *SRI Project*. 10099, sponsored by Centre for Technology in Learning, SRI International.

Prasad, V. (1979). Promotion of creativity and achievement by discovery method. *Indian Educational Review, 14* (4), pp. 86-94.

Richland, L.E., Bjork, R.A., Finley, J.R., and Linn, M.C. (2005). Linking cognitive science to education: Generation and interleaving effects. In *Proceedings of the twenty-seventh annual conference of the cognitive science society*. Mahwah, NJ: Erlbaum. Retrieved from http://learninglab.uchicago.edu/Publications_files/5-CogsciIddeas2005.pdf

Rittle-Johnson, B., and Star, J.R. (2007). Does comparing solution methods facilitate conceptual and procedural knowledge? An experimental study on learning to solve equations. *Journal of Educational Psychology, 99*, pp. 561-574.

Roebers, C.M., Schmid, C., and Roderer, T. (2009). Metacognitive monitoring and control processes involved in primary school children's test performance, *British Journal of Educational Psychology, 79*, pp. 749-767.

Ross, B.H. (2007). Cognitive science: Problem solving and learning for physics education. *AIP Conference Proceedings of the Physics Education Research Conference, 951*, pp. 11-14. doi: 10.1063/1.2820910

Salden, R.J.C.M., Aleven, V.A.W.M.M., Renkl, A., and Schwonke, R. (2009). Worked Examples and Tutored Problem Solving: Redundant or Synergistic Forms of Support? *Topics in Cognitive Science, 1* (1), pp. 203-213. doi: 10.1111/j.1756-8765.2008.01011.x

Saxena, M.A. (1980). A study of children's problem solving and decision making strategies. In M.B. Buch (Ed.). *Third Survey of Research in Education, 1978-1983*. New Delhi: NCERT.

Schoenfeld, A.H. (1983). Beyond the purely cognitive: Belief systems, social cognitions, and metacognitions as driving forces in intellectual performance. *Cognitive Science, 7* (4), pp. 329-363.

Schunn, C.D. (2009). How kids learn engineering: The cognitive science perspective. *The Bridge, The Fall Issue of the Bridge—On K-12 Engineering Education, 39* (3), pp. 32-37.

Sharma, K. (1982). Factors Related to Creativity. Ph.D. Soc. Sc., IIT, Delhi. In M.B. Buch (Ed.). *Fourth Survey of Research in Education, 1983-1988* (Vol. I). New Delhi: NCERT.

Siegler, R.S. (2003). Implications of cognitive science research for mathematics education. In J. Kilpatrick, W.B. Martin, and D.E. Schifter (Eds.), *a research companion to principles and standards for school Mathematics*, pp. 219-233. Reston, VA: National council of teachers of Mathematics

Simone, C.D. (2008). Problem-based learning: A framework for prospective teachers' pedagogical problem solving. *Teacher Development, 12* (3), pp. 179-191.

Srivastava, P. (2009). *Time Course of Visual Attention* (Unpublished doctoral dissertation), University of Allahabad, Allahabad.

Sternberg, R.J. (1999). Successful intelligence: finding a balance. *Trends in Cognitive Sciences, 3* (11), pp. 436-442.

Tomlin, R.S., and Villa, V. (1994). Attention in cognitive science and second language acquisition. *Studies in Second Language Acquisition, 16* (2), pp. 183-203. doi: 10.1017/S0272263100012870

Torrance, E.P. (1987). Teaching for creativity. In S.G. Isaken (Ed.), *Frontiers of Creativity Research: Beyond the Basics*, Buffalo, New York: Bearly Limited.

Trimurthy, S.P. (1987). A Study of Creative Thinking Ability of Secondary School Students in the Context of Some Psycho-socio Factors. Ph.D.

Edu., SPU. In M.B. Buch (Ed.), *Fourth Survey of Research in Education, 1983-1988* (Vol. I). New Delhi: NCERT.

Tsai, C-h. (2002). The meta-epistemology of knowing-how. *Phenomenology and the Cognitive Sciences, 10* (4), pp. 541-556. doi: 10.1007/s11097-011-9208-0

Tytler, R., and Prain, V. (2010). A framework for re-thinking learning in science from recent cognitive science perspectives. *International Journal of Science Education, 32* (15), pp. 2055-2078. Retrieved from http://search.ebscohost.com/login.aspx?direct=true&db=aph&AN=53787840&site=ehost-live

Watve, S. (2010). Multiple intelligences: Nature and interrelations. *Indian Educational Review, 46* (1), pp. 20-30.

Whiteley, T.R. (2006) Using the Socratic method and Bloom's taxonomy of cognitive domain to enhance online discussion, critical thinking, and student learning, *Developments in Business Simulation and Experiential Learning, 33*, pp. 65-70.

Yao, Y.Y. (2004). Concept formation and learning: a cognitive informatics perspective. In C. Chan, W. Kinsner, Y. Wang, and D.M. Miller (Eds.), *Proceedings of the third IEEE International Conference on Cognitive Informatics*, August 16-17, 2004, Victoria, British Columbia, Canada: IEEE Computer Society, University of Victoria. Retrieved from http://www.cs.uregina/yyao.

# Bibliography

Anderson, J.M. (1996). Historical linguistics. In K. Malmkjoer (Ed.), *The Linguistic Encyclopedia*. London and New York: Routledge.

Anderson, J.R. (2004). *Cognitive Psychology and its Implications* (6th ed.). New York: Worth Publishers.

Andler, D. (2009). Philosophy of cognitive science. In A. Brenner and J. Gayon, (Eds.), *French Studies in the Philosophy of Science: Contemporary Research in France* (pp. 255-300), Springer.

Antonietti, A., and Colombo, B. (2007). Computer-supported learning tools: A bi-curricular bi-directional framework. *New Ideas in Psychology, 26* (1), pp. 120-142.

Arieti, S. (1976). *Creativity: The Magic Synthesis.* New York: Basic Books.

Ashman, A.F., and Conway, R.N. F. (1997). *An Introduction to Cognitive Education: Theory and Applications*. London and New York: Routledge.

Ausubel, D.P. (1968). *Educational Psychology: A Cognitive View*. New York and Toronto: Holt, Rinehart and Winston.

Ayres, P., and Sweller, J. (2005). The split attention principle in multimedia learning. In R.E. Mayer (Ed.), *The Cambridge Handbook of Multimedia Learning* (pp. 135-146). New York: Cambridge University Press.

Banister, P., Burman, E. Parker, I., Taylor, M., and Tindalle, C. (1994). *Qualitative Research Methods in Psychology: A Research Guide*. Buckingham, Philadelphia: Open University Press.

Barlett, F.C. (1958). *Thinking: An Experimental and Social Study*. London: Allen & Unwin.

Baron, R.A. (2001). *Psychology*. New Delhi: Prentice-Hall of India Pvt. Ltd.

Berk, A.A. (1985). *LISP: The Language of Artificial Intelligence*. New York: Van Nostrand Reinhold Company.

Bernard, H.W. (1965). *Psychology of Learning and Teaching* (2nd ed.). U.S.A.: McGraw Hill Book Company.

Bernard, H.W. (1972). *Psychology of Learning and Teaching*. US: McGraw-Hill.

Berry, D.C., and Broadbent, D.E. (1995). Implicit learning in the control of complex systems. In P.A. Frensch and J. Funke (Eds.), *Complex Problem Solving: The European Perspective* (pp. 131-150). Hillsdale, NJ: Erlbaum.

Bruner, J.S. (1983). *In Search of Mind: Essays in Autobiography*. New York: Harper & Row.

Burr, J.E., and Hofer, B.K. (2002). Personal epistemology and theory of mind: Deciphering young children's beliefs about knowledge and knowing. *New Ideas in Psychology, 20* (1), pp. 199-224.

Chaube, S.P. (1999). *Educational Psychology* (4th ed.). Agra: Lakshmi Narain Agarwal.

Comeau, D. (2005). *Multiple Intelligences: Theory and Pedagogy. EGallaery—A Peer Reviewed Journal,* 8 (3). Retrieved from *http://www.ucalgary.ca/~egallery*

Cooper, D.E. (1999). *Epistemology—the Classic Reading*. Wiley-Blackwell Publishers.

Covington, M.V., Crutchfield, R.S., and Davies, L.B. (1966). *The Productive Thinking Programme*. Columbus, OH: Merrill.

Curren, R. (Ed.) (2003). *A Companion to Philosophy of Education*. Malden, USA: Blackwell Publishing.

Danielson, J.A., Mills, E.M., Vermeer, P.J., Preast, V.A., Young, K.M., Christopher, M.M., Bender, H.S. (2007). Characteristics of a cognitive tool that helps students learn diagnostic problem solving. *Educational Technology Research and Development, 55* (5), pp. 499-520. Retrieved from http://www.jstor.org/stable/30220505

Davis, S.F., and Buskist, W. (Ed.) (2008). *Twenty-first Century Psychology: A Reference Handbook*. Sage Publication.

Davids, R. (1978). *The Birth of Indian Psychology and its Development in Buddhism* (1st Indian ed.). New Delhi: Oriental Books Reprint Corporation.

Farnham-Diggory, S. (1972). *Cognitive Processes in Education: A Psychological Preparation for Teaching and Curriculum Development*. New York: Harper & Row.

Feuerstein, R. (1980). *Instrumental Enrichment*. Baltimore: University Park Press.

Finke, R.A., Ward, T.B., and Smith, S.M. (1992). *Creative Cognition: Theory, Research and Application*. Cambridge, MA: MIT Press.

Fischer, K.W. (2009). Mind, brain and education: Building a scientific groundwork for learning and teaching. *International Mind, Brain and Education Society and Wiley Periodicals, 3* (1).

Fulop, S., and Charter, N. (2013). Why formal learning theory matters for cognitive science. *Topics in Cognitive Science,* 5 (1), pp. 3-12.

Gagne, R.M. (1980). Learnable aspects of problem solving. *Educational Psychologist, 15* (2), pp. 84-92.

Gallaghar, S., and Zahavi, D. (2008). *The Phenomenological Mind: An Introduction to Philosophy of Mind and Cognitive Science.* London and New York: Routledge.

Girash, J. (2010-11). Talking with faculty about cognitive science and learning. *Essays on Teaching Excellence,* 22 (3).

Greene, R.T. (n.d.). *A Model of 42 Models of Creativity*. Retrieved from http://papers.ssrn.com/sol3/papers.cfm?abstract_id=2242840

Gregory, R.L. (Ed.). (1998). *The Oxford companion to the mind*. New York: Oxford University Press.

Gross, C.G. (2007). The discovery of motor cortex and its background. *Journal of the History of the Neuroscience, 16* (3), pp. 320-331. doi: 10.1080/09647040600630160

Hart, T. (2004). Opening the contemplative mind in the classroom. *Journal of Transformative Education,* 2 (1). doi: 10.1177/1541344603259311

Heihden, A.H.C.V.D. (1999). Attention. In W. Betchel and G. Graham (Eds.) *A Companion to Cognitive Science* (pp. 121-128). Oxford: Blackwell Publishing Ltd.

James, W. (1890). *Principles of Psychology*. New York: H Holt & Company.

James, W. (2009) Attention. In R.W. Proctor and L.E. Read (Eds.) *Attention,* 1, *Theories of Attention,* (pp. 3-37). London: Sage Publication.

Kellog, R.T. (2002). *Cognitive Psychology*. USA: Sage Publications.

Kimble, G.A. (1961). In Hilgard and Marquis (Ed.) *Conditioning and Learning* (2nd ed.), Englewood Cliffs, N.J.: Prentice Hall.

Kirschner, P.A. (2009). Epistemology or pedagogy that is the question. In S. Tobias and T.M. Duffy (Eds.), *Constructivist*

*Instruction: Success or Failure?* (pp. 144-157). New York: Routledge.

Kolak, D., Hirstein, W., Mandik, P., and Waskan, J. (2006). *Cognitive Science: An Introduction to Mind and Brain.* New York and London: Routledge.

Koul, L. (1997). *Methodology of Educational Research* (10th ed.). Noida: Vikas Publishing House Pvt. Ltd.

Kulshrestha, S.P. (2004). *Educational Psychology.* Meerut: Surya Publication.

Lambert, K. (1995). Theories of cognition: Conceptual knowledge and problem solving. In C. Hollin (Ed.), *Contemporary Psychology: An Introduction* (pp 49-61). Taylor & Francis.

Lamberts, K. (2008). *Cognitive Science, 2, (Attention-Learning).* London: Sage Publications.

Langley, P., and Rogers, S. (2005). An Extended Theory of Human Problem Solving. Proceedings of the *Twenty-seventh Annual Meeting of the Cognitive Science Society,* Stresa, Italy. Retrieved from ccl.stanford.edu/~langley/papers /icarus.cs05.pdf

Languis, M.L., Martin, D.J., Naour, P.J., and Buffer, J.J. (Eds.) (1991). *Cognitive Science: Contributions to Educational Practice.* Philadelphia, Pennsylvania: Gordon & Breach Science Publication.

Lavery, D. (1993). Creative work: On the method of Howard Gruber. *The Journal of Humanistic Psychology,* 33 (2), pp. 101-121.

Lindsay, R.K., Buchanan, B.G., Feigenbaum, E.A., and Lederberg, J. (1980). *Applications of Artificial Intelligence for Organic Chemistry: The Dendral Project.* McGraw-Hill Book Company.

Livingston, P. (2005). Creativity. In D.M. Borchert (Ed.), *Encyclopedia of Philosophy,* 2, (2nd ed.) USA: Macmillan Reference.

Livingston, P. (2006). Creativity. In D.M. Borchert (Ed.), *Encyclopedia of Philosophy,* 2, pp. 589-591. USA: Macmillan Reference.

Look, B.C. (2014). Gottfried Wilhelm Leibniz. In E.N. Zalta (Ed.), *The Stanford Encyclopedia of Philosophy* (Spring 2014 Edition). Retrieved from http://plato.stanford.edu/archives/spr2014/entries/leibniz/>.

Mangal, S.K. (2013). *Research Methodology in Behavioural Sciences.* Delhi: PHI Learning Private Limited.

Misra, G. (2007). Psychological dimension of educational research in India. In NCERT (Ed.), *Sixth Survey of Educational Research,* 2, (1993-2000).

Murphy, G. (1968). *An Introduction to Psychology*. New Delhi: Oxford and IBH.

Newell, A., and Simon, H.A. (1972). *Human Problem Solving*. Englewood Cliffs, NJ: Prentice Hall.

Nickerson, R.S. (1994). Project intelligence. In R.J. Sternberg (Ed.), *Encyclopedia of Human Intelligence,* (pp. 392-430). New York: Cambridge University Press.

Nokes, T.J., Schunn, C.D. and Chi, M.T. H. (2010). Problem solving and human expertise. In P. Peterson, E. Baker and B. McGaw (Eds.), *International Encyclopedia of Education,* 5, pp. 265-272.

Norton, P.B., and Esposito, J.J. (Eds.), (1994). *New Encyclopedia of Britannica,* 18, (15th ed.). Chicago: Encyclopedia Britannica, Inc.

Osherson, D.N., Stob, M., and Weinstein, S. (1982). Ideal learning machines. *Cognitive Science,* 6, pp. 277-290.

Pillsbury, W.B. (1908). *Attention*. New York: MacMillan.

Posner, M.I. (1999). *Foundations of Cogntive Science.* Cambridge: MIT Press.

Riley, B.T. (Ed.) (2000). *Introduction to Psycholinguistics*. New Delhi: Cosmo Publication.

Sajadi, S.S. (2013). *The 7Ms Pedagogy Model: Instructional Design for Learners with Attention Deficit Hyperactivity Disorder* (Unpublished doctoral dissertation). Brunel University, London.

Sankhala, D.P. (2007). *Research Methodology in Education*. New Delhi: Adhyayan Publishers.

Seifert, K., and Sutton, R. (2009). *Educational Psychology.* Switzerland: Jacobs Foundation.

Shi-xu (2006). Mind, self and consciousness as discourse. *New Ideas in Psychology,* 24 (1), pp. 63-81.

Sinha, J. (1992). *Elementary Psychology*. Kolkata: New Central Book Agency (P) Ltd.

Sinha, J. (2008). *Indian Psychology: Cognition,* I. Delhi: Motilal Banarasi Das.

Slavin, R.E. (2011). *Educational Psychology: Theory and Practice,* Pearson.

Smith, E.E. (2007). How the brain gives rise to the mind. In E.E. Smith and S.M. Kosslyn (Eds.), *Cognitive Psychology: Mind and Brain*. Delhi: PHI Learning Pvt. Ltd.

Spearman, C. (1931). *Creative Mind*. New York: D. Appleton & Co.

Stanley, R.M. (1984). Creativity and play materials: The origins and development of creativity in preschool children. Ph.D., A

& M University, Texas. In *Dissertation Abstract International,* 45 (12), p. 310.

The Principles of Learning and Teaching P-12 were developed as part of the Blueprint for Government School's Flagship Strategy 1.

Torrance, E.P. (1965). *Rewarding Creative Behaviour*. Englewood Cliffs, New Jersey: Prentice Hall.

Vygotsky, L.S. (1999). *Educational Psychology*. (R. Silverman, Trans.). Florida: St. Lucie Press. (Original work published 1926)

Wadikar, S., and Gudipudi, A.B. (2011). Towards ICT driven pedagogy in teacher education. *Educational Quest—International Journal of Education and Applied Social Science,* 2 (1), pp. 105-109.

Ward, T.B., and Saunders, K.N. (2003) Creativity. In L. Nadel (Ed.), *Encyclopedia of Cognitive Science,* 1, pp. 862-869. New York: MacMillan Publisher Ltd.

Watkins, M. (2009). Pedagogic affect/effect: Embodying a desire to learn. *Pedagogies: An Introductional Journal, 1* (4), pp. 269-282. Retrieved from http://dx.doi.org/10.1080/15544800701341533

Wilson, K.G., O'Donohue, W.T., and Hayes, S.C. (2001). Hume's psychology, contemporary learning theory, and the problem of knowledge amplification. *New Ideas in Psychology, 19* (1), pp. 1-25.

### *Websites*

*www.catalogue.pearsoned.co.uk/assets/hip/gb/hip_gb.../Chapter%2008.pdf?* retrieved on 5th March, 2013.

www.compapp.dcu.ie/~mfarren/cognitive.pdf

www.education.com

www.uir.unisa.ac.za/bitstream/handle/10500/1522/06Chapter3.pdf

www.wisegeek.org/what-is-linguistic-intelligence.htm

www.EzineArticles.com/?expert=Martin_S.

# Index